D1287406

Between Heaven and Earth

Between Heaven and Earth

Christian Perspectives on Environmental Protection

FRED VAN DYKE

 PRAEGER

AN IMPRINT OF ABC-CLIO, LLC
Santa Barbara, California • Denver, Colorado • Oxford, England

Library of Congress Cataloging-in-Publication Data

Van Dyke, Fred, 1954-
  Between Heaven and Earth : Christian perspectives on environmental protection / Fred Van Dyke.
    p. cm.
  Includes bibliographical references and index.
  ISBN 978–0–313–37536–1 (hard copy : alk. paper) — ISBN 978–0–313–37537–8 (ebook)
1. Human ecology—Religious aspects—Christianity. I. Title.
BT695.5.V35   2010
261.8′8—dc22   2010016026

ISBN: 978–0–313–37536–1
EISBN: 978–0–313–37537–8

14 13 12 11 10   1 2 3 4 5

This book is also available on the World Wide Web as an eBook.
Visit www.abc-clio.com for details.

Praeger
An Imprint of ABC-CLIO, LLC

ABC-CLIO, LLC
130 Cremona Drive, P.O. Box 1911
Santa Barbara, California 93116-1911

This book is printed on acid-free paper ∞

Manufactured in the United States of America

Contents

Preface

It is not hard to find a book about Christianity and the environment today. There are books on this subject by pastors, books by theologians, books by scientists, books by environmental activists, and books by people who make their living writing books. Many of these books tell people what the Bible "says" about the environment, or how to do "practical" things that will save the Earth. Some, like *Green Revolution*, appeal to the current generation now learning and living on our college campuses, while others, like *Serve God, Save the Planet*, are highly individualist journeys of self-discovery into the "relevance" of environmental stewardship for the "average" Christian.

I understand something of this literary genre. In 1996, I wrote, with David Mahan, Joe Sheldon, and Ray Brand, *Redeeming Creation: The Biblical Basis of Environmental Ethics*. We, too, wanted to tell our audience what the Bible had to say about the care of the Earth. This is not a bad goal, and it fills a real need. However, in the years that have passed, and the reading, experience, and reflection that has filled them, I have come to the conclusion that the question, "What does the Bible say about the care of creation?" is the wrong question if Christians want to reach an audience beyond themselves. It is the wrong question for those who have never read the Bible, because it is not a successful conversation starter. I want to ask some questions in this book that are important to this latter audience, and in doing so attempt to broaden the conversation.

For those who do not read the Bible, but are nevertheless fully engaged in the work of conservation, I think there are other questions more interesting to them. Why should we treat nature as something of value, even when the values are not things from which we directly benefit? What makes human beings think they have some sort of responsibility toward nature anyway, and who gave us the right to "manage" it? And is there any meaningful outcome to this effort? If endangered species are, in the long run, doomed relics of environments and conditions past, why make the effort today if you can't change their fate tomorrow?

People, including people who are conservationists, would, I think, like some answers to these questions, but they will be suspicious of answers they perceive to have been recently, and disingenuously, "invented" from traditions they view as indifferent, or even hostile, to their work. That is how many conservationists view Christianity. And, if they read the current run of popular works by Christians on "the environment," their suspicions will be aroused even further. Most of these books, consciously or subconsciously, give the impression that the author has "discovered" something in the scriptures that lies where no one has gone before, or at least where no Christian has gone before, and what they offer is something "new." The "new" idea in this book is that these ideas are really quite old. That we are unfamiliar with them is a result of a selective loss of our collective cultural memory. And this is a memory we must recover.

The questions of value, responsibility, and outcome are good questions for conservationists to ask. But there is also a deeper question, one that people are not always raising, but one for which the world has an even more fundamental, unspoken yearning. Is there a tradition that practices conservation? This is often a question conservationists do not overtly ask, but nevertheless they long for an answer.

Many of the newer works on Christianity and the environment are written by Protestants, and one of the most important historical traditions of Protestantism is the Protestant suspicion of the authority of historical tradition. There are reasons for this. The authority of historical tradition can be abused, as well as inflated, and so diminish other authorities that should supersede it, like the Scripture itself. Nevertheless, if you do not have a history you do not really have a future, at least not one that will make sense. Without a history you do not know where you are, and therefore you cannot know where you are going. This is the very definition of what it means to be "lost."

In the course of developing this book, I have made a new discovery too, at least it was new for me. I discovered that the Christian tradition is a tradition that has historically practiced conservation. The practices differed in place and time. They were individualized by real people, who had real differences from other people. They sometimes took the form of what was done, and sometimes took the form of what was taught, for teaching is part of tradition too, and action inevitably flows from it into the river of human experience we call "life." But in all its variety of form (and one should expect some variety from a religion that is almost 2000 years old and, today, over 2 billion people strong), it taught and practiced the goodness of creation, the responsibility of people to serve and protect what God has created, and the future hope of a redemption of the entire created order, which gave significance and meaning to even the smallest acts, rightly directed, in the present moment.

I was myself hopeful that I might find such a tradition, but by no means assured. But the strength of the conservation tradition within the Christian tradition was waiting for me. Not that I am the first to find it or to know it, but I am glad that I have found it and that I know it now. For any who long for an answer to this question, "Is there a tradition that practices conservation?" I encourage you to read this book. I offer that encouragement to everyone, but particularly to my fellow conservationists. We who are actually engaged in this work are all aware that today the world conservation effort faces serious challenges. Some would go further, and say that it is in serious trouble. Conservation in our present world is still seen as an interesting, albeit noble, distraction for those who are not troubled by the more pressing issues of life, like paying the mortgage, holding a job, and getting the kids through college. And the conservation community must take the blame for much of this problem of perception on itself. It has consistently framed conservation as a tactical problem to be solved by better science (applied by better professionals), rather than a moral endeavor that every person can and should engage. Everyone can learn much from the engagement, but only when we begin to see nature as a subject of common and universal responsibility, as well as a source of revelation from which every one can learn. In the pages that follow I will explain how. I hope you will take up and read. But this is an invitation for the Christian too, for, in this present age, we have lost touch with our historic traditions and beat the air till we are breathless trying to invent new ones. We need not do so in this case. The Christian tradition of conservation needs to be re-discovered. It does not need to be reinvented. We can learn a new language in this tradition altogether, and in that language learn to throw off our current bondage to a worldly, and destructive, way of thinking about nature. In this tradition, we can learn a new way of speaking. And when we have, we will discover that we have something to say. Take up the book. Let's begin.

CHAPTER 1

Ethics, Environment, and Christian Faith: Framing a Complex Interaction

> Believing, as I do, that matters of morality admit of truth, I am reluctant to conclude that we can devise or invent a new ethic; and, even if we could invent one, I do not see how it could establish its credibility unless it were not a new departure but an extension, analogical or otherwise, of existing patterns of moral thought.
>
> Robin Attfield, 1983[1]

WHY AREN'T WE HONEST ABOUT WHAT WE VALUE?

In one of the main concourses of a major U.S. airport, there was once displayed, along several feet of one of the concourse walls, a large, full-color photograph of a giant tropical toad. The toad looked out from the poster face first, eye to eye with thousands of travelers hurrying by each day. Below the picture, a caption read, as if the toad were speaking, "My skin could save your life. Please save mine."

In smaller print below the toad's picture, the poster's authors explained that many wonder-working pharmaceuticals, all a great boon to human health and well-being, had been, were, or could be developed from chemical compounds secreted from the toad's skin—but that there could be no such benefit if there were no toads. Therefore, the toad should be protected.

What was interesting about this poster, even more than the toad itself or the argument to save it, was the organization that sponsored it.

Certainly a global pharmaceutical company such as Merck, Eli Lily, or Pfizer would have had reason to advance an argument in favor of the toad's pharmaceutical value. They might have made millions in revenue from compounds developed from the toad's skin secretions, employed thousands of people in doing so, and treated, even cured, a multitude of human diseases. But no drug company paid for this poster. The sponsor was, in fact, not a company at all, in the business sense of the word. It was an international conservation organization. What does this poster, and its sponsor, tell us about the state of environmental ethics?

Wildlife ecologist Aldo Leopold told a story of a bird dog he once owned whose name was Gus. Gus wasn't the best of hunting partners because, as Leopold put it, "When Gus couldn't find pheasants he worked up an enthusiasm for sora rails and meadowlarks. This whipped-up zeal for unsatisfactory substitutes masked his failure to find the real thing. It assuaged his inner frustration. We conservationists are like that."[2]

The conservation organization in the poster example behaved a lot like Gus. They postured a "whipped-up zeal" for finding new pharmaceuticals, an objective that had nothing to do with their own conservation mission, as a substitute for their real purpose. They told the poster's readers that the toad should be saved for its instrumental value when their real passion was the toad's *intrinsic* value, the value of the toad itself, a unique and beautiful creature that was in growing danger of extinction because of habitat destruction and climate change associated with human activity. But they were unwilling to admit this publicly or at least to admit it in the poster. Environmental ethicist Mark Sagoff explains why: "We environmentalists often appeal to instrumental arguments for instrumental reasons, i.e., not because we believe them, but because we think that they work. I submit, however, that advances in technology will continue to undermine these arguments."[3] Sagoff is right. Pharmaceutical companies might use the skin secretions of a toad to develop drugs to treat human diseases. But, with practice and study, they might be able to create the same compounds in the lab with the right combinations and reactions of appropriately proportioned chemicals. When they succeed, what value will the toad have then? If his skin can no longer save your life, will you save his?

The endangered toad illustrates one dimension of the need for a primary environmental ethic, one that recognizes and could defend the intrinsic value of nature and non-human species, even when technology makes their former utilitarian values obsolete. But this is not the only problem. Environmental economist Herman Daly once called conservation "a policy in pursuit of a purpose,"[4] and his assessment was correct. But conservation as *purpose* is often practiced in the guise of conservation as *science*, and therein lies the problem. As conservation biologist and environmental ethicist Kyle Van Houtan puts it, "Is nature conservation a virtue or is it just good science? ... If conservation is a virtue then scientific arguments alone are insufficient and the battle visibly involves social traditions, as well as science. ... Then ..., asking why we should care about conservation is not the right question ... 'Does the tradition regard conservation?' is a better question."[5] What ethical tradition regards conservation as an ethical practice?

THE FUNDAMENTAL FRAMEWORK: WHAT DO WE MEAN BY "ENVIRONMENT"?

Environment is a big word—not just because it has four syllables, but because it can encompass such a large entity that if we are not careful, we shall have no real idea what we are talking about. Generally, people use the word to mean one of two things: At its broadest level, we speak of an environment in the sense of physical surroundings, and operating within those surroundings, a system of causes and effects. We might refer to the first as a "forest environment" and then say, of a particular kind of plant, "It wouldn't grow well here." In both cases, we are not only making a reference to the physical surroundings but also to the system of causes and effects that operate within them.

If that were all we meant by the term "environment" then a book like this would not need to be written. If an environment were *only* a physical space and its surroundings and the causes and effects that operate within them—affecting matter and energy transfer, population sizes, and species composition of a community—then it would make no more sense to speak of an *ethic* of the environment than to speak of having an *ethic* for my living room. The reason is obvious: A *place*, as a physical location, cannot be treated rightly or wrongly in a moral sense. It is, as some would say, "just there." Similarly, even if we add all sorts of physical, chemical, and biological interactions to the place, it is still "just there." Our understanding of the place is now at once more accurate and more complex, but such understanding still fails to transform physical space, however complex in its interactions, into moral object.

But there is a second way in which people use the term environment that does begin to lead to moral consideration. People also use the word to indicate what some philosophers call a field of significance— that is, an arena in which things not only happen (through cause and effect), but the things that happen really *matter* in some ethical sense because of the way in which we interact with them. Thus, it makes sense to speak of an *ethic* of human relations, or an *ethic* of medical practice, or an *ethic* of corporate management. It makes sense because each of these examples, and many others like them, suggests arenas in which we care deeply about the outcome of events within the specified system of cause and effect. Is it possible, then, to have an ethic of the environment?

Well, as a wise person once said, that depends. And what it depends on is what we perceive the environment to be. If we see our physical surroundings as a collection of physical resources, essential for meeting our own needs and those of other human beings, then, although such an environment is in one sense significant, what makes it so is not the environment itself but the way humans use it, what they get from it, and who gets what and how much. In this view, the environment is a stage upon which ethical decisions are made, but the environment itself is not the object of ethical consideration. People are the object, and environmental uses and practices are measured against human welfare. In this view, the environment has no value until humans use or develop it. This approach is what environmental ethicist Holmes Rolston III referred to as a secondary environmental ethic,[6] which is really no environmental ethic at all. We simply extend some form of traditional ethics, such as utilitarianism, into the realm of environmental decision-making, and we have the ready-made criteria of aggregate human welfare as our guide to what is ethically right.

A primary environmental ethic is different. Suppose that the environment itself, or at least some components of it, were to be treated as a moral subject, and that there might exist non-human things or entities in the environment which could be treated rightly or wrongly in a moral sense. If there were reasonable grounds for thinking of at least some environmental entities this way, then a more genuine or primary environmental ethic would be needed. But what would have to change in our thinking?

The most fundamental alteration would be our judgment of what kind of value environmental entities should receive and whether the non-human environment is itself a field of significance, an area of legitimate ethical and moral concern. If we valued environmental entities as resources that have no value until used or developed for use by humans, then, as they say in Maine, you can't get there from here. We would have no basis for saying that any action of ours was "good for" a resource. We can only say it is good for us. For example, we cannot say that a particular environmental action is good for subterranean deposits of oil, only that they might be good for the human economy. And that would be the end of the argument. But suppose we were talking about something that was not inert, like oil, but alive, such as, for example, a grizzly bear.

When speaking of the bear, it is rational, if we know something about the needs of bears, to say that some human management actions or forest management policies, like protecting stands of white bark pine trees (which produce large crops of nuts, which bears can eat) could be "good for" bears. That is, there could be actions that help grizzly bears as individuals, and there could be actions that are good for grizzly bears as a species, actions that help populations grow, increase in range, and persist through time. If there are human actions or policies that could be said to be good for bears, it follows that there also could be actions or policies that could be bad for bears. Now we begin to see why a primary environmental ethic might be needed, because if some things are good for bears and some things are good for humans, these might be different things, or even conflicting things.

If one takes the view that the needs of people are always more important than the needs of bears, or fish, or trees, or wildflowers, then the battle is over without much of a fight. There are certainly circumstances in which we might say so. But would this always be the case?

I have, so far, been making an introduction to one of the great questions of environmental ethics—namely, what is the basis of valuing nature, or the environment and the things we find in it? That is a very big question that will receive its fair share of attention in a later chapter. My immediate goal is not to answer that question, but to show that it is a question worth answering; in other words, to show the need for a primary environmental ethic that could provide warrant for the moral consideration of non-human entities. One might think that this is a settled question in modern times. With the plethora of conservation organizations that surround us, surely we could expect to see individual organizations particularly, and the conservation community generally, provide the public with a reasonable, primary environmental ethic. Unfortunately, this is not the case.

MANAGEMENT DECISIONS AND
ETHICAL ACTIONS

Ever since the Enlightenment, science has sought to understand and present itself as an objective, value-free enterprise in which there is a clear distinction between the investigated object and the investigating scientist. Things the scientist learns about the object can then be regarded as facts, and whatever decisions are made about the object based on such facts must be objective, value-free decisions. Unfortunately, this view of reality is little more than an Enlightenment fairy tale. The real nature of science is far more complex, and particularly so in the world of conservation and environmental management. We must move from fairy tales to reality. Let us look at a real story from Tanzania.

Tanzania's Lake Manyara National Park has been a traditional home to a large population of elephants, at one time numbering more than 500. But the park is, at a scale relative to elephants, small, only 127 square miles, and more than 70 of those miles are usually under water in the lake that gives the park its name. Elephants are nomadic creatures, frequently traveling long distances in search of food and water, which change seasonally, or even daily, in sub-Saharan Africa. In a national park like Manyara, elephants are protected, but they are also functionally confined, since leaving the park can mean death at the hands of poachers, hunters, or villagers defending their crops and homes from the destruction an elephant can cause. Elephants are not stupid. They learn these lessons quickly, and so learn to stay within the park's protective boundaries. But in such a state of relative confinement, elephants will begin to destroy native vegetation, especially small trees.

In the late 1960s and early 1970s, that is what began to happen at Manyara. The trees that suffered most were the acacias, an important species in African grassland savannahs that support large numbers of wildlife. In Manyara, Iain and Oria Douglas-Hamilton began one of the first and eventually most famous studies of African elephants ever completed and, in their effort, found themselves in the midst of a raging controversy. To stop the destruction of the acacias, elephant numbers would have to be reduced, and that meant that some elephants would have to be killed. But the scientists who worked at Manyara did not want to exercise that option. They felt a strong emotional attachment to the elephants and saw them as creatures of value in their own right, but they did not know how to express these sentiments within the objective framework of science they had been taught or how to make their sentiments part of the management decision that had to be made. In their book *Among the Elephants*, the Douglas-Hamilton's describe the dilemma: "The very desire to preserve the animals was a subjective statement of faith in the animal's intrinsic worth. It was a feeling possessed by most of the scientists there . . . , but they would not admit this sentiment into their arguments because it could not be backed up by facts; the right and wrong of aesthetics being imponderables not open to scientific analysis."[7]

Dilemmas like this one in Manyara are not rare in conservation. They happen all the time, and they will always and inevitably happen when people fail to understand that values, as well as facts, are a form of *knowledge* and a way of *knowing*. These scientists had values, and they also had preferences, in this case *preferring* the elephants to the acacia trees. The problem was, they had no scientific basis for defending either. Under the burden of an Enlightenment view of objectivity, they never would. What is needed is a different way of looking at the world.

Environmental and conservation science have been slow, to the point of embarrassment, of recognizing that a different perspective is needed. One cannot keep telling the public that elephants, manatees, polar bears, furbish louseworts, or rare orchids are valuable in and of themselves and worth preserving over other things that might take their place, and at the same time pretend that values don't matter in making a decision about what to preserve. This is what the novelist George Orwell correctly called *doublethink*, which he defined as "the power of holding two contradictory beliefs in one's mind simultaneously, and accepting both of them."[8] This kind of approach simply won't do.

Of course, we have to admit that some conservation biologists, even very prominent ones, think it will do just fine. For example, conservation biologists Gary Meffe and Steven Viederman have told their fellow conservation scientists that, "In an ideal world, biologists would experiment, observe, tell policy makers what to do, and it would be done."[9] This is a view that environmental conservation should be seen as a form of regulatory science, whose purpose, in the word's of environmental legal scholar A. Dan Tarlock, is, "to develop scientific standards that can be applied to regulatory criteria and then to develop management strategies to meet those standards."[10] If we look at conservation this way, science defines both the standards and the strategies for conservation, and all will be well.

This view of conservation profoundly affects how scientists communicate with the public. It is an approach called *professional advocacy* or, more colorfully, the trickle down theory of information access. From the perspective of professional advocacy, publication in books and journals is the only appropriate way for scientists to transfer information and influence value judgments. No further ingredients are needed. Unfortunately, the kinds of outlets that are appropriate for this sort of information transfer suffer under the same limitations and delusions as the scientists at Manyara. They *refuse* to acknowledge or include a discussion of values as part of management recommendations and strategies. If all discussions of values are absent, then exactly what are scientists informing policy makers and the public about?

Thankfully, we see signs that even the most vigorous proponents of this view of science and advocacy are probably better than their words. For example, noted conservation biologists Peter Brussard and John Tull have publically advocated a narrow sense of professional advocacy for science, where the advocacy should be limited to "informing policy makers, managers, and the public about issues that arise in one's area of expertise."[11] But, in their own studies, even Brussard and Tull reveal that this approach doesn't work very well, especially because it is invariably too slow to do much good. For example, Brussard and his students study, among other things, pikas, a small mammal that lives on talus slopes in mountainous regions of western North America. Winters in these environments are long and harsh, but pikas survive by spending their summers cutting (nipping) down more vegetation than they can eat, then spreading and drying the excess vegetation they cut on the rocks around them, eventually storing the "hay" they have made (while the sun shines) in preparation for the hard times ahead. Living in an environment that is more often cold than hot, it is not surprising that pikas have low thresholds of heat stress, and when over-heated, they stop cutting and drying vegetation. In recent decades, Brussard has documented that populations of pikas living at lower (and warmer) elevations have become more prone to extinction than those at higher elevations, an outcome of ongoing global climate change.[12]

In the state of Nevada, where Brussard and Tull live and work, it was clear that swift action was needed to protect pikas. Faced with this situation, Brussard and Tull admit that, "Because of the importance of these findings, we distributed reprints of this article [on the risk of lower elevation pika populations to climate-induced extinction] to agency heads at a Nevada Biodiversity Initiative meeting. By speeding up information transfer in this way in this way the Nevada Department of Wildlife incorporated the findings from this paper into their Comprehensive Wildlife Conservation plan for the state in 2005."[13] But doesn't calling this information "important" and not just "interesting" suggest that Brussard and Toll think *pikas* are important, that they *ought* to be spared extinction, if humans have anything to say about it? And doesn't the act of handing out reprints of their pika study directly to decision makers at the decision-making meeting look like a very direct effort to save pikas, not the "professional advocacy" that only moves information through books and journals? In the final analysis, doesn't the behavior of Brussard and Tull look more like an advocacy in which action and recommendation are based on value, not the dispassionate, and ethically anemic, regulatory science described by Tarlock?

This problem isn't limited to pikas in Nevada. Drawing upon his experiences in working for The Nature Conservancy in Indonesia, Erik Meijaard and his colleague Douglas Sheil, a scientist with Indonesia's Center for International Forestry Research, addressed the problem even more directly in the international journal *Biodiversity and Conservation*. Being commendably forthright and direct, they started by expressing the title of their assessment in the form of a rather rude question, "Is Wildlife Research Useful for Wildlife Conservation in the Tropics?" After an examination of 284 publications on tropical wildlife studies, including 153 from peer-reviewed journals, Meijaard and Sheil felt compelled to state that few of these studies "address threats to species and fewer still provide input for or guidance to effective management. . . . Research is seldom judged on its relevance to pragmatic problem solving. . . . We consulted conservation leaders about our conclusions and all responses suggest that our concerns are not unique to Borneo but reflect wider problems. We conclude that conservation research across most of the tropics is failing to address conservation needs."[14]

What if Meijaard and Sheil are right? Does environmental conservation today require something made of sterner stuff than professional advocacy as described by Brussard and Tull? Does it require a much more aggressive advocacy that is armed with an ethical and moral clarity about what is the *right* action to take, a clarity that many modern conservation efforts typically lack?

Conservation is, in fact, a strategy of management decisions designed to achieve "right" outcomes such as protecting species, designing nature preserves, restoring ecosystems, or promoting sustainable use. When Stuart Pimm, one of the world's most eminent conservation scientists, declares he has "a moral responsibility as a citizen to make people aware of what the science means,"[15] he is, in the words of environmental ethicist Kyle Van Houtan, "demonstrating his conviction that conservation takes a moral stance and weighs value judgments to specific decisions."[16]

Assertions of the moral "rightness" of conservation aims might be accepted without question within the community of conservation scientists but become less credible when other audiences question their credentials. What legitimates such ethical judgments beyond the personal preference of scientists about the way things ought to be? Scientists can, and often do, resort to various lines of defense. We must save rare bird species because people take pleasure in watching them, or, perhaps more pragmatically, we must save tropical rainforests because their plant species might someday provide a cure for cancer, or, focusing on "just-the-facts," we must save species because they are the "facts" of nature; their existence is their own justification for being. But such defenses are naïve at best, disingenuous at worst. In any case, such appeals are in no way scientific grounds for ethical judgments. That is, these judgments do not use scientific facts and methods as a way of knowing the right thing to do. They are rather the kind of Orwellian doublethink we have already described in which one tries to hold two or more contradictory views simultaneously and believe them both. The manifestation of such confusion in the professional community is that conservationists hold strong positions about the intrinsic value of every species but then pretend that such values are not involved in determining the technical solution to the problem of their decline or potential extinction. Ethical appeals grounded in this state of confusion sometimes succeed where values are not needed as conceptual categories for conflict resolution, but they are useless in solving conservation problems that require explanation of a basis for intrinsic value of species, biodiversity, or ecosystems.

The founder of modern conservation biology, Michael Soulé, defined the discipline as one that is *value laden* and *mission driven*, a mission organized around what Soulé called four normative postulates that direct its intentions. These are (1) *diversity of organisms is good*, (2) *ecological complexity is good*, (3) *evolution is good*, and (4) *biotic diversity has intrinsic value, regardless of its utilitarian value*.[17] These normative postulates assume, and require, normative outcomes. As the environmental philosophers Dwight Barry and Max Oelschlaeger wrote,

"To deserve its title, conservation biology must be ethically overt— that is, it must affirm its mission to be the protection of habitat and the preservation of biodiversity. Otherwise its name is as linguistically dishonest as the (Orwellian) claim that 'war is peace.' ... conservation biology is not applied biology but rather hinges on an explicit evaluative judgment: Biodiversity is good and should be preserved. Apart from such a value judgment, one must wonder why there would be any reason to invest effort in conservation biology."[18]

THE ETHICAL SEQUENCE OF INTELLIGENT ENVIRONMENTAL MANAGEMENT

Management can be defined in the field of environmental conservation as human action taken to remedy a deficiency in a system as determined by scientific assessment.[19] The action is informed by scientific assessment, but such assessment does not dictate which action to take. Ethics intrudes into management decisions on two fronts, one with understanding what is meant by deficiency. To judge a system as being deficient, one must have a comparative standard of what is normative or best for the system to achieve. But what standard is that? If using historical norms, one must choose a particular point in a system's history as the target condition. That choice reflects not scientific research but value judgment. Again to quote Tarlock, "Ecosystems are patches or collections of conditions that exist for finite periods of time ... At best, ecosystems can be managed, but not restored or preserved"[20] because each system represents a time-specific state. Present conditions are retained by dynamic inputs of matter and energy, and these inputs can be altered through management actions. The system's management, then, will not be determined by the manager's science but by the manager's values.

The problem gets worse if we try to pretend it isn't there. If managers and policy makers don't recognize that value judgments are needed to make management and policy decisions and don't know how to defend these judgments, they will attempt to make the scientific assessment itself, such as the results of a management model, appear to be *offering* judgments, diagnoses, and prescriptions about the system which they then must follow because "science says so." If this confusion goes unchecked, managers and policy makers will present their value judgments to the public as if they were judgments dictated by models and experiments, not by their own values. This is a particularly serious problem in the use of environmental models, in which the manager changes the model's prediction of "what would happen if. . . . " to "what the model says we must do to save the system." As environmental modeler J. B. Robinson put it, "By cloaking a policy decision in the ostensibly neutral aura of scientific forecasting, policy makers can deflect attention from the normative nature of that decision."[21]

Two conservation biologists who come clean on this issue, and with commendable candor, are William Porter and Brian Underwood, who, without apology, admit that ethical norms play a role in every management decision in environmental conservation. They note, "Whether we define ecological integrity in terms of species or processes, we must inevitably make a decision as to where in the . . . sequence we choose to intervene. That choice represents a value judgment. Although the connotation often associated with value judgments is negative, such decisions are the essence of management and cannot be avoided."[22]

To put some flesh on these ideas, take an example of an "ordinary" conservation management decision on one unit of one district in a U.S. national forest in the western United States. A range manager, informed by site-specific, scientific studies, decides to burn 100 acres of sagebrush in an area used by elk as winter range. His goal is to increase forage production for elk during a period of the year when their food supply is limited. His own studies on this very site show that winter forage production is poor, and the population of elk using this area is suffering some winter mortality. The manager's plan meets all the criteria of our previous definition of management. The site of the burn is located in a management unit designated as elk habitat (i.e., an area with priority to the needs and welfare of elk). Thus, the manager's plan to burn the sagebrush is a specific outcome of a "rule" established by a policy: in this unit, increase the production of resources that benefit elk.

At first glance, this action doesn't appear to be an "ethical" decision at all. To paraphrase Nike, "Just burn the sagebrush." But a first glance is not enough. The action being considered is filled with ethical implications. To start with, we must ask, what is the purpose of the management action? Put another way, what *value* will be produced or enhanced by completing the action? The planned burn will generate more forage for elk, but other species that depend on sagebrush, like Brewer's sparrow and sage grouse, will have less habitat when the fire is out than they did before it was started. Second, what is the deficiency of the system that the action is supposed to remedy?

The manager would say that the deficiency is low forage production for elk. But is that deficiency important, and how reliable is the scientific assessment of it? Third, who are the stakeholders with defined and legitimate interests in this system? Will these stakeholders be affected positively or negatively by this management action? Finally, when the burn is over, can the manager offer the public a reasonable explanation and defense as to why he chose one action over another, to burn or not to burn?

If we break down the decision-making process into a series of steps, it is easier to see the ethical implications.

What action does a manager propose to take?   (Identify the management *action*)

↓

What value does the action produce or enhance?   (Identify the action's *purpose*)

↓

What is it about the system that we are trying to fix?   (Identify the system's *deficiency*)

↓

How well do we understand the system we are trying to fix?   (Identify the *reliability* of the scientific assessment)

↓

Who are the stakeholders in this system and how will the action affect them?   (Identify *vested interests* and *legitimate obligations*)

↓

Can the manager explain the warrant for the action to the public?   (Identify the *defense* of the management action)

Without exception, every management decision in environmental conservation has to answer these questions. And, understood in this light, every such decision is a value judgment. If values fail to clearly and explicitly inform the management decision, it is a poor management decision, and the manager who makes it will not have a strong defense for the decision to offer to the public. In these fundamental problems lies the tale, the trouble, and the tragedy of the modern conservation movement.

Despite the appropriateness, indeed, the necessity, of such questions in environmental conservation, the scientific tradition of Enlightenment-derived objectivism upon which most environmental and conservation science is based excludes their admittance. As a result, the very elements needed to actually render a decision, namely a carefully informed ethical analysis of the values and preferences in play in a given environmental management context, have been tossed out of the toolbox. We are then left with the confusion that previous examples have revealed: disingenuous, even deliberate, misrepresentation of conservation motives (the tropical toad), inability to engage real values and preferences in the management decision (elephants and acacia trees), frustration with traditional "professional advocacy" methodologies (scientific books and journals) of informing decision makers (extinct pika populations), and fundamental disjunctions between conservation research and conservation effectiveness (Meijaard and Sheil's review of "useless" wildlife research). In such a state of ethical chaos, it is necessary, even if impolite, to ask the question, "Should environmental conservation rethink and re-examine its current intellectual tradition?" Is there a better tradition, a tradition that could provide more productive engagement between scientific facts and ethical analysis, and lead to better, more fully informed decisions that admit and reflect ethical norms? And is there a tradition that can do these things while at the same time speaking to an audience beyond science, even to elements of a global culture that unites people of diverse origins and backgrounds, whether they are scientifically educated or not?

A TRADITION REGARDING CONSERVATION

The purpose of this book is to describe one such cultural framework: the Judeo-Christian tradition and its thinking and practice of environmental conservation, or in terms more commonly employed, environmental (creation) stewardship. This admission might move some readers to drop the book without any further reading. In the mid-twentieth century, the Judeo-Christian tradition was repeatedly named as the *cause* of the environmental crisis, so suggesting that it is in fact the solution to it as a tradition that possesses and practices an environmental ethic might sound to some like a proposal for entrusting the foxes to guard the henhouse. The practice of naming Judeo-Christian teaching as the root cause of the environmental crisis needs examination before we can go forward.

In 1966, the American Association for the Advancement of Science (AAAS) chose eminent historian Lynn White, Jr. to offer the keynote address at their annual meeting. He entitled his speech "The Historical Roots of Our Ecologic Crisis." In it, White offered an analysis of how Western societies perceived their environment and of the worldview that gave them this perception. White began by noting that all human societies shape and change their environment, but Western society, beginning in the fourteenth century, began to advance in its power to do so through increasingly sophisticated technologies.

With this increasing technological sophistication and application, Western societies began to use the Earth and its resources not based on the needs of individuals or families, but on the capacity of machines to do work. White noted evidence of this change in illustrated Frankish calendars: "They show men coercing the world around them—plowing, harvesting, chopping trees, butchering pigs. Man and nature are two things, and man is master."[23]

White asserted that the dominant worldview of this society was a Christian one. "What," he asked, "did Christianity tell people about their relations with the environment?"[24] White spent the remainder of his speech answering that question, explaining that Christian faith told them a great deal, all of it extremely destructive from an environmental point of view. Its first fault was its human-centered perspective. "Especially in its western form, Christianity is the most anthropocentric religion the world has seen," said White.[25] Out of this perspective arose the view that everything in the world existed for the use of man, and without such use there was no value in natural objects. Use came through exploitation, and the power of exploitation increased through technology. To those who saw the environmental crisis as primarily a technological problem, and therefore amenable to technological solution, White asserted that the problem was not a problem of technology but a problem of worldview: "More science and more technology are not going to get us out of the present ecologic crisis until we find a new religion, or rethink our old one."[26] White's conclusions were unequivocal. "We shall continue to have a worsening ecologic crisis until we reject the Christian axiom that nature has no reason for existence save to serve man. . . . Both our present science and our present technology are so tinctured with orthodox Christian arrogance toward nature that no solution for our ecologic crisis can be expected from them alone."[27]

Published the following year in *Science*, the premier journal of the AAAS, *The Historical Roots of Our Ecologic Crisis* became one of the most widely reprinted and repeatedly quoted (with and without acknowledgment) essays of its generation. The Ecological Society of America awarded White their prestigious George Mercer Prize, given annually for "outstanding ecological research," although White had done none. The views of *Historical Roots* became a staple in any discussions of ecological ethics. The Judeo-Christian tradition was vilified in all things environmental, from discussions of landscape architecture[28] to pollution and species extinctions[29] to literary criticism.[30] White's essay was part of an overall trend in the late 1960s and early 1970s to discover single root causes for the environmental crisis, with other such efforts variously blaming common property institutions,[31] capitalism, or colonialism.[32] None of these explanations were able to stick when placed under serious intellectual scrutiny, but White's ideas proved the most popular and enjoyed a vigorous and extended life in environmental circles long after they had been discredited in academic ones.

Today much has changed in the perception of what the Judeo-Christian tradition teaches about the stewardship of the environment and whether or not it was in fact the cause of the ecologic crisis. By the 1990s, noted environmental ethicist J. Baird Callicott was telling his readers in a textbook on conservation biology that, "The Judeo-Christian Stewardship Environmental Ethic is especially elegant and powerful. It also exquisitely matches the requirements of conservation biology."[33] Where did Callicott get this idea? And how was the Judeo-Christian tradition transformed from being the *cause* of the environmental crisis into being a *solution* to it?

This remarkable transformation has been grounded in the re-examination and re-application of the historic teachings of the Scripture and the Church. In 1970, the American Baptist Church had adopted its *Resolution on Environmental Concerns*, and similar statements by numerous other denominations began to appear, especially in the 1980s and 1990s. On January 1, 1990, on the World Day of Peace, Pope John Paul II added his voice in his official message which he entitled "The Ecological Crisis: A Common Responsibility.[34] The World Council of Churches issued similar and repeated statements on environmental stewardship. Christian declarations, along with the subsequent activism they inspired, became so frequent during this period that by 1998 Carl Pope, executive director of the Sierra Club, issued a public apology to Bartholomew I, patriarch of the Orthodox Church. Speaking at a symposium on religion and the environment sponsored by the church and the patriarch, Pope acknowledged that, "We [environmentalists] sought to transform society, but ignored the fact that when Americans want to express something wiser and better than they are as individuals, by and large they gather to pray. We acted as if we could save life on Earth without the same institutions through which we save ourselves."[35] Speaking of the effect of Lynn White, Jr.'s essay on the perceptions of environmentalists about Christianity's role in the environmental crisis, Pope confessed, "Too many environmentalists considered the case closed. We became as narrow-minded as any religious zealot, and proceeded to glorify creation and smite those who would sin against it on our own, without regard for the faith community."[36]

THE HISTORY AND PRACTICE OF ENVIRONMENTAL STEWARDSHIP IN THE JUDEO-CHRISTIAN TRADITION

The history, teaching, and tradition of the Christian faith in regard to environmental stewardship is a web of complex relationships, and so are the rules of engagement required for any attempt to derive an environmental ethic from them. Some ethicists would throw the whole project overboard from the start. One group might begin by stating the obvious, that not everyone concerned with environmental ethics is a Christian and not everyone will treat the Bible, theology, or church tradition as normative, or even reliable, sources of information. The way forward, therefore, is to construct ethics from more universal or self-evident principles that every thinking person can agree on.

This approach sounds, to use Holmes Rolston's memorable phrase, "vaguely reasonable as long as it is kept reasonably vague,"[37] but it never works in practice because it is always doomed by ethical particulars. The universal principles that some philosophers consider self-evident usually end up being more self-evident to some people than to others and far from universal in any case. What most such approaches do have in common is their aversion to *religious traditions* as grounds for ethical action, and that is a different objection entirely. As Callicott has pointed out, the modern version of moral pluralism in environmental ethics is not really as pluralistic as advertised.[38] In fact, most modern efforts in ethical pluralism, including ethics of the environment, show a strong affinity for more democratic ethical systems such as utilitarianism (the greatest good for the greatest number), or for systems which elevate reason to that of an independent arbiter of "the good," as in Kant's deontological ethics (the "categorical imperative" of defined duty), or those based in ecological relationships, like Leopold's land ethic ("A thing is right when it tends to preserve the integrity, stability and beauty of the biotic community. It is wrong when it tends otherwise."). The same pluralistic approaches to environmental ethics show a distinct aversion, indeed, contempt, for ethics that invoke theories of divine command, the independent existence of the Good (with a capital "G"), or the idea that reason must be aided by revelation to achieve well-formed ethical understanding. The pluralist ethical party, on closer inspection, turns out to be one that can be attended by invitation only.

A second group of objectors might say that the effort to articulate a Christian environmental ethic will only snatch defeat from the jaws of impending environmental victory or, more precisely, discord from the jaws of unity. After all, don't most people of good will and reasonable intelligence agree about *what* ought to be done to preserve the environment? Why waste time confusing the issue with debates about *why* something ought to be done? This objection presumes that different worldviews never lead to different actions, but this is not true of ethical decisions in general or of environmental ethics in particular. For example, the difference between whether we consider the act of saving a species an expression of the public's *preference* for a species or the recognition of the actual *value* possessed by the species makes an enormous difference in the way we craft environmental policy. And the difference between environmentalists who value *individual creatures* as opposed to those who value *species and biodiversity* will also lead to distinctly different responses when faced with identical ecological problems.

Finally, yet another group of ethicists would object to the underlying foundations. They would charge that what I am attempting reveals a hegemonic approach to ethics or, to use Callicott's words, an attempt to create "a single sovereign superpower to 'overawe' them all." In an essay entitled "Multicultural Environmental Ethics" that is both scathing and sarcastic in its assessment of this perspective, Callicott declares, "This [hegemonic method] is the untempered top-down approach, in which one culture dominates all others."[39]

Callicott does not condemn Christianity as the only form that a hegemonic method could take, but he clearly intends to include it in his critique of the method. In truth, any attempt to provide a meaningful explanation of a Christian environmental ethic, which combines elements of that tradition's teaching, tradition, and practices, does possess at least some of the qualities that Callicott identifies with hegemony. But of all world religions, Christianity is the most global and, as a consequence, the most multicultural. The fact that 2.1 billion people on Earth self-identify as Christians does not make it less so.

Before enumerating the "vices" of hegemony that might be legitimately ascribed to a Christian environmental ethic, let me first state what a Christian environmental ethic does *not* require. Christian environmental ethics, like Christian faith itself, do not require a Christian to believe that all other ethical positions are rot, that no worldview but Christianity contributes anything to an understanding of reality or truth, or that everyone who holds a different position is a fool. A Christian environmental ethic, like Christian faith asserts, rather, that there is common knowledge (or, in more theologically correct terms, general revelation) about truth that is available to all people everywhere who will seek and study it, in ethics as well as in anything else. Within this field of common truth, people of different ethical viewpoints can find common ground of thought, motive, and action. Indeed, we would expect so. What Christian environmental ethics, and Christian faith, require is not the kind of ethical or intellectual hegemony that Callicott describes in such pejorative language, but rather an insistence that the ideas that are *distinct* to a Christian worldview, be they ever so (apparently) small, are precisely those ideas that make the biggest difference in our ethical perspective. And therein lies a tale.

This book is that tale. It is not an attempt at intellectual oppression but a response to a question being repeatedly asked of the Christian community today. What does Christianity teach about the relationship of human beings to their environment, and what past traditions and current practices are associated with that teaching? Lynn White, Jr. considered this an important question, but his answer was not only false but inadequate. My answer will be different from White's, and I will give it in the pages that follow.

Some of Callicott's concerns and charges about a hegemonic approach *do* apply to a Christian environmental ethic. Christian faith is what it is. Christians believe that, indeed, there is such a thing as Truth, with a capital *T*, and Good, with a capital *G*. Christians also would confess that such Truth is not always congenial to human perception and prejudice, and that an ethic that is accepted simply because it is friendly to a particular theory or group has in no way proved that it is a correct way of looking at things. Rather, an ethic merits consideration if it accurately expresses the reality of how things are, in this case the reality of how things are between humans and nature, as well as the reality of how they "ought to be."

In good ethics, as in good journalism, good reporting is not the same as good news. Often it is quite the opposite. The person who wants a congenial environmental ethic, one compatible with and sympathetic to all current cultural prejudices and uncritical assumptions about humans and nature, should do their moral window-shopping elsewhere. Christianity has a definable body of source data from which it derives its teaching. Although Christians disagree regarding some aspects of interpretation and application of some teachings, the source data itself is a real entity with a real existence. It is rooted in real history, real events, and real people. Specifically, Christian belief and behavior arise from four normative sources: the Bible, theology, historical Christian tradition, and the church. The divisions between these compartments are not airtight. The boundaries can be leaky, but I will use all of them in examining the relationship between Christian belief and environmental stewardship.

I would be disingenuous to imply that this book is "only" a polite answer to an increasingly common question, as if there were no other purpose than to satisfy intellectual curiosity. The book is also written to address a growing need, a need driven by a growing mood of hopelessness in conservation, a sense that the world, and most of its species, are going to hell in a handbasket and there is nothing that can be done to prevent the trip. If the ultimate evolutionary end of every species is extinction, why not live and let die? And if humans have proven, by the rules of natural selection and Darwinian fitness, that they are the most fit and adaptive species, why not celebrate? We are the big winners! Some do, and say so. Norman Levine, professor emeritus in the College of Veterinary Medicine as the University of Illinois, did. Writing in the journal *BioScience* Levine stated, "Some nature lovers weep at this passing [of non-human species which have become extinct] and collect money to save species. They make lists of animals and plants that are in danger of extinction and sponsor legislation to save them. I don't. What the species preservers are trying to do is stop the clock. It cannot and should not be done. Extinction is an inevitable fact of evolution, and it is needed for progress. New species continually arise, and they are better adapted to their environment than those who have died out. Extinction comes from a failure to adapt to a changing environment."[40]

If we believe as Levine does, the matter is pretty well settled. Most conservationists don't believe this, but they have difficulty responding to those who do, especially since their adversaries seem to have Darwin on their side. Again, it is Van Houtan who defines the problem clearly: "There is no robust hope in the dominant versions of ethics as practiced in the conservation sciences. To succeed as a social cause, conservation needs a hope that academic science itself cannot provide. Conservation needs a cultural legitimacy that inspires enthusiasm, allegiance, and personal sacrifice—in other words, actual changes in human behavior. Such a vision does not provide a straight line path to easy answers, it offers a description of ethics currently estranged from conservation science."[41]

Not every scientist in conservation is so estranged. Many conservation biologists identify themselves as Christians and are ready and willing to explain the basis of their hope to their colleagues. Writing in *Conservation Biology*, the official journal of the Society for Conservation Biology, Simon Stuart of the World Conservation Union and 29 other conservation biologists from five continents explained their hope this way: "Every time we celebrate a conservation success story such as the recovery of the white rhinoceros in southern Africa, we are strengthened in this present hope that God is working with us to redeem his creation; furthermore, these present successes are a very real foretaste of even greater things to come on that day when God will fully restore all that He has made."[42]

This is forceful and theologically astute language. It is clear that Stuart and his colleagues possess a fairly sophisticated and biblically informed vision that provides them with a foundation for hope—hope in the significance of present efforts grounded in the hope of a coming day of redemption for the Earth and its creatures. They have a very different vision of the future than Norman Levine. But to understand this hope fully requires an examination of concepts we have yet to address, and to say more of that now would be to get ahead of ourselves.

For the moment, our subject is ethics, and, for now, we will let that subject reside in the present. Ethics, in a present context, represent an organized system of values that prescribe what one must do to attain a desired end that is morally right. The end that we choose is based on the values we assign. If an ethic is going to "work" in defining the human relationship to nature, it must successfully address five fundamental questions, the answers to which will frame all aspects of the human relationship to nature:

1. Does the non-human environment possess intrinsic value, a "good of its own," or does it possess value only in relation to human need and use?

2. Is there a rational basis for human obligation toward the welfare of the non-human environment?

3. What value is being affirmed (that is, what purpose is being advanced) by the work of conservation?

4. Is there a normative basis and pattern for "environmental virtues" or "behaviors of excellence" that should guide human behavior toward the environment and, in the process, contribute to the formation of "better" people who can continually grow in their capacities to do good toward nature?

5. What is the fate of the Earth, and does present conservation activity align with this ultimate fate? In other words, does the Earth have a future that makes sense in the light of conservation effort?

This book is an examination of a community and a tradition that can answer these questions.

In describing the book's purpose, it would be misleading if I failed to admit that there is yet one further goal. Yes, this work will attempt to answer the question, "What does Christian faith tell us about the human relationship to nature?" And, yes, it is an attempt to speak to a real need, indeed, a growing problem in the conservation community, the inability to articulate a coherent environmental ethic that makes sense in terms of values greater than enlightened human self-interest. But it is also an attempt to speak to the Christian community itself. I make no assumption that all 2.1 billion Christians in the global community of the modern world, or the collective Christian traditions of the past twenty centuries, speak with a single, unequivocal voice about the ethical treatment of the environment. Would that it was so, but it is not. As Kyle Van Houtan and Stuart Pimm have recently documented, there are, even if we limit our view to contemporary settings, at least four major worldviews about the environment within the U.S. Christian community alone. These Van Houtan and Pimm have described as the Earthkeeping, Skeptic, Priority, and Indifferent worldviews. Speaking of them, the authors note, "The Earthkeeping worldview engages biodiversity conservation and embraces it as an ethical issue with a biblical origin. The Skeptic worldview recognizes biodiversity issues, but disagrees with the scientific community that there is a biodiversity crisis. . . . The Priority worldview focuses not on scientific credibility but on a sort of practical urgency. Simply put, other moral issues trump conservation. The Indifferent worldview does not address biodiversity, endangered species, or extinction whatsoever. Either consciously or unconsciously, the topic is unattended."[43]

As one who is both a Christian and a conservation biologist, I am an Earthkeeper. In the first role, I speak in this book to brothers and sisters in Christ, people with whom I share common sources of knowledge, revelation, tradition, and mission. My effort is one of persuasion. I aim to explain the biblical ethic of environmental stewardship and its expression in the history, theology, traditions, and practices of Christian faith in a way that will be both compelling and appealing to other Christians. I would, if I could, persuade every Christian to become an Earthkeeper.

Christians have been blamed for environmental problems before Lynn White, Jr. The early church patriarch Tertullian noted, in the first century Roman Empire, "If the Tiber floods or the Nile fails to flood, if the skies darken, if the earth trembles, if famine, war or plague occurs, then immediately one shout goes up: 'The Christians to the lion.' "[44] That sentiment is still here and is often expressed in the modern conservation community. In the chapters that follow, I shall endeavor to speak directly to it.

NOTES

1. Robin Attfield, *The Ethics of Environmental Concern* (New York: Columbia University Press, 1983), p. 4.

2. Aldo Leopold, *A Sand County Almanac with Essays on Conservation from Round River* (New York: Ballantine, 1966), p. 200.

3. Mark Sagoff, "Zuckerman's Dilemma: A Plea for Environmental Ethics," *Hastings Center Report*, September–October (1991): 32–40, p. 34.

4. Herman Daly, "The Lurking Inconsistency," *Conservation Biology* 13 (1999): 693–694, p. 694.

5. Kyle Van Houtan, "Conservation as Virtue: A Scientific and Social Process for Conservation Ethics," *Conservation Biology* 20 (2006): 1367–1372, p. 1371.

6. Holmes Rolston III, *Philosophy Gone Wild: Essays in Environmental Ethics* (Buffalo, NY: Prometheus Books, 1986).

7. Iain and Oria Douglas-Hamilton, *Among the Elephants* (New York: Viking, 1975), pp. 75–76.

8. George Orwell, *1984* (New York: New American Library of World Literature, 1962), p. 176.

9. Gary Meffe and Steven Viedeman, "Combining Science and Policy in Conservation Biology," *Wildlife Society Bulletin* 23 (1995): 327–332, p. 327.

10. A. Dan Tarlock, "The Nonequilibrium Paradigm in Ecology and the Partial Unraveling of Environmental Law," *Loyola of Los Angeles Law Review* 27 (1994): 1121–1144, p. 1130.

11. Peter F. Brussard and John C. Tull, "Conservation Biology and Four Types of Advocacy," *Conservation Biology* 21 (2007): 689–691.

12. Erik A. Beever, Peter F. Brussard, and Joel Berger, "Patterns of Apparent Extirpation Among Isolated Populations of Pikas (*Ochotoma princeps*) in the Great Basin," *Journal of Mammalogy* 84 (2003): 37–54.

13. Brussard and Tull, p. 21.

14. Erik Meijaard and Douglas Sheil, "Is Wildlife Research Useful for Wildlife Conservation in the Tropics? A Review for Borneo with Global Implications," *Biodiversity and Conservation* 16 (2007): 3053–3065.

15. Jocelyn Kaiser, "Taking a Stand: Ecologists on a Mission to Save the World," *Science* 287: 1188–1192, p. 1188.

16. Van Houtan, p. 1368.

17. Michael Soulé, "What Is Conservation Biology?" *BioScience* 35 (1985): 727–734.

18. Dwight Barry and Max Oelschlaeger, "A Science for Survival: Values and Conservation Biology," *Conservation Biology* 10 (1996): 905–911, 906, p. 909.

19. I thank my colleague, William F. Porter, College of Environmental Science and Forestry, State University of New York—Syracuse, for sharing this definition with me, one that both he and I have found very helpful in introducing and teaching the key elements of environmental management to our students.

20. Tarlock, p. 1129.

21. J. B. Robinson, "Of Maps and Territories: The Use and Abuse of Socio-economic Modeling in Support of Decision-making," *Technological Forecasting and Social Change* 42 (1992): 147–164.

22. William F. Porter and H. Brian Underwood, "Of Elephants and Blind Men: Deer Management in the U.S. National Parks," *Ecological Applications* 9 (1999): 3–9, p. 6.

23. Lynn White, Jr., "The Historical Roots of Our Ecologic Crisis," *Science* 155 (1967): 1203–1207, p. 1205.

24. Ibid.

25. Ibid.

26. Ibid., p. 1206.

27. Ibid., p. 1207.

28. Ian McHarg, *Design With Nature* (Garden City, NJ: Natural History Press, 1969).

29. Paul Ehrlich and Richard L. Harriman, *How to be a Survivor* (New York: Ballantine, 1971).

30. Leo Marx, "American Institutions and Ecological Ideals," *Science* 170 (1970): 945–952.

31. Bonnie J. McCay and Svein Jentoft, "Market or Community Failure? Critical Perspectives on Common Property Research," *Human Organization* 57 (1998): 21–29.

32. J. O'Connor, "Capitalism, Nature, Socialism: A Theoretical Introduction," *Capitalism, Nature, Socialism* 1 (1988): 11–38.

33. J. Baird Callicott, "Conservation Values and Ethics," In *Principles of Conservation Biology*, ed. Gary K. Meffe and C. Ronald Carroll (Sunderland, MA: Sinauer Associates, 1994), 24–49, p. 36.

34. Available at http://www.ncrlc.com/ecological_crisis.html. Accessed 9 January 2009.

35. Carl Pope, "Reaching Beyond Ourselves: It's Time to Recognize Our Allies in the Faith Community," *Sierra Magazine* 83 (1998): 14–15 (November/December), p. 14.

36. Ibid.

37. Holmes Rolston III, "Winning and Losing in Environmental Ethics," In *Ethics and Environmental Policy: Theory Meets Practice*, ed. Frederick Ferré and Peter Hartel (Athens: University of Georgia Press, 1994), 217–234, p. 230.

38. Callicott, "The Case Against Moral Pluralism," in *Beyond the Land Ethic: More Essays in Environmental Philosophy* (Albany: State University of New York Press, 1999), 143–169.

39. Callicott, "Multicultural Environmental Ethics," *Daedalus* 130 (2001): 77–97, p. 82.

40. Norman Levine, "Evolution and Extinction," *BioScience* 39 (1989): 38.

41. Van Houtan, p. 1371.

42. Simon Stuart and others, "Conservation Theology for Conservation Biologists—An Open Letter to David Orr," *Conservation Biology* 19 (2005): 1689–1692, pp. 1690–1691.

43. Kyle S. Van Houtan and Stuart L. Pimm, "The Various Christian Ethics of Species Conservation," in *Religion and the New Ecology: Environmental Prudence in a World in Flux*, ed. David M. Lodge and Christopher Hamlin (Notre Dame: University of Notre Dame Press, 2006), 116–147, p. 124.

44. Quoted in R. H. Bainton, *The Horizon History of Christianity* (New York: American Heritage, 1964), p. 89.

CHAPTER 2

The Great Questions
of Environmental Ethics

Visible nature is all plasticity and indifference—a moral multi-verse . . . and not a moral universe. To such a harlot we owe no allegiance; with her as a whole we can establish no moral communion . . .

William James[1]

FUNDAMENTAL QUESTIONS AND PROBLEMS

Modern environmental ethics come in many forms, but all attempt, in a variety of ways, to answer five fundamental questions about the human relationship to nature:

1. Does the non-human world possess intrinsic value, a "good of its own," that exists independently of uses humans might find for it, and, if it does, what is the source of that value?

2. Is there a rational basis for human responsibility toward the non-human environment that goes beyond enlightened (human) self-interest?

3. What is the purpose of environmental stewardship? That is, what value or values are being affirmed or advanced by the actions we collectively call conservation?

4. Is there a normative basis and pattern for environmental virtues (behaviors of "excellence") that should direct human action toward the environment and, in the process, contribute to the

formation of human beings as "better" people, people who are able to grow in their capacities and skills to do good to nature?

5. What is the fate of the Earth, and does present conservation activity make sense in light of that future fate?

Not every system of environmental ethics attempts to answer all of these questions explicitly. Some concentrate only on the question or questions they think most important. But all attempts at environmental ethics must eventually face these questions, whether they admit it or not, because no ethic of the environment can be complete unless all five are addressed. Some of the most influential paradigms of environmental ethics today organize their thinking around just one of these questions, the one they consider foundational to all others. Unfortunately, different ethical systems do not agree on which question that is. So influential are these questions, and so pervasive is the attempt to answer them, that the major "strategies" of environmental ethics can be organized according to which question they attempt to answer.

Traditionally, ethicists have agreed with William James, that nature is ethically "all plasticity and indifference," that it is an ethical "harlot" that provides no moral norms. Not surprisingly, then, James concluded that we owe no obligations to nature, and we can learn nothing from her; that between nature and humans there can be "no moral communion."[2] The philosopher John Stuart Mill said the same. "Conformity to nature," said Mill, "has no connection whatever with right and wrong."[3] If this is so, then even the term *environmental ethics* would seem to be an oxymoron, as well as a doomed enterprise. But is there any alternative view? Is it possible that natural objects possess values or states of worth that belong uniquely to themselves, but that can be discovered and assessed by human beings?

THE STRATEGY OF NATURE'S MORAL STANDING

One of the most pervasive and influential efforts in modern environmental ethics is a strategy that gives pride of place to establishing the intrinsic value of nature, an approach that ethicist Willis Jenkins has called "the strategy of moral standing."[4] In this approach, the problem to be solved is that of making a convincing argument for nature's intrinsic, nonutilitarian value. The aim of this approach, as noted in Chapter One, is to make nature a moral "field of significance" in which decisions about nature matter on the basis of "what is good for nature" as opposed to what is the best use of nature for humanity.

Perhaps the most common, and increasingly influential, basis for the intrinsic value of nature is derived from the concept of the *connation* of natural entities, notably living things, and their pursuit and defense of their own ends and purposes. Rolston expresses the idea elegantly in speaking of a beautiful woodland wildflower, the trillium. "[T]here is some ought-to-be beyond the is, and so the plant grows, repairs itself, reproduces, and defends its kind. If, after enjoying the Trillium in a remote woods, I step around it to let it live on, I agree with this defense, and judge here is an objective intrinsic value, valued by me, but for what it is itself."[5]

In this view, the fact that non-human species pursue their own ends, their own purposes, and their own goods is taken as sufficient warrant for imputing their intrinsic value. They possess a "good of their own" that humans ought to perceive, admire, and respect. Recognition of such intrinsic value is assumed to be the first and foremost defense of nature against economic utilitarianism. It rejects the idea that humans must somehow develop or transform nature before it can be the bearer of any value. Rolston articulates the concept by tracing the intrinsic value of an organism down to its very genetic constituency.

> We pass to value when we recognize that the genetic set is a *normative set*; it distinguishes between what *is* and what *ought to be*. So the tree grows, reproduces, repairs its wounds, and resists death. The physical state that the organism defends is a valued state. A life is defended for what it is in itself, without necessary further contributory reference. Every organism has a *good-of-its-kind*; it defends its own kind as a *good kind*. In this sense, the genome is a set of conservation molecules. (emphasis Rolston's)[6]

The strength of forming environmental ethics around the issue of nature's value is that it provides a basis for a moral response to nature by and from humans. If natural entities are mere resources, then their value is realized by use. If natural resources are to be valued as aesthetic experiences, their value is realized by increased education of and experience with nature. But if natural entities are "moral others," their value is realized by moral response, actions taken by humans for their good in recognition of their good. These distinctions of value are not mere philosophical abstractions. They profoundly influence our behavior toward the environment and our management of it.

The U.S. Forest Service, traditionally an agency concerned with commodity production from national forests in the form of wood, water, and range resources for livestock, describes almost every national forest on its roadside signs as a "Land of Many Uses." Because it sees natural entities as resources, its optimal management goal is maximum sustained yield, a concept synonymous with, and some would say invented by, its founder, Gifford Pinchot, who preached, "the greatest good for the greatest number for the longest time"[7] as the moral maxim of forest management.

Unlike the Forest Service, the U.S. National Park Service, an agency commissioned by the United States Congress to protect the scenery of national parks "for the enjoyment of their visitors," places its emphasis on the education and experiences of those visitors, and its frontline foot soldiers, known to the public as rangers but within their own agency as "interpreters," bear that name as descriptive of their role of communicating or interpreting aesthetic values of natural phenomena to park visitors. In contrast, the U.S. Fish and Wildlife Service, the agency primarily responsible for saving endangered species in the United States, establishes wildlife refuges where human management is aimed at creating resources of food and habitat for protected species. In these contexts humans may engage in activities, such as bird watching and photography, that do no harm to protected species, but they are banned from disturbing nesting sites, resting cover, foraging areas, and other sensitive habitats if their presence might be detrimental. The mission of the Fish and Wildlife Service then is to promote the good of the managed species for its own sake, a transparently clear manifestation of intrinsic value in management action and mission.

As valuable, and as widely embraced, as the concept of intrinsic value is in organizing environmental ethics, it has weaknesses. Foremost among these is that although such a focus articulates the *value* of a species, thus affecting human *attitudes*, it provides no clear direction for human *action*. That is, it does not tell us what we *should do* to affirm or support the intrinsic value of nature. This deficiency has made the strategy of moral standing problematic for conservation.

"Although intrinsic value may get conservationists out of bed in the morning and into the field or up to the bargaining table," wrote environmentalist Lynn Maguire and philosopher James Justus, "it does not serve them well once they get there. Conservation requires decision-making, and here intrinsic value falls short."[8] Some, like Maguire and Justus, advocate a more nuanced use of instrumental value as the remedy for intrinsic value's shortcomings. We could call this approach the "everything is just a resource" strategy. Things we perceive as being intrinsically valuable are, in this view, merely resources of "psychic satisfaction" for the human spirit and intellect. The object's value is *really* located in the human mind, not in the object itself. The philosophical problems and limitations of this view are many, but the time for exposing them will come later. But the substantive criticism of intrinsic value remains. Even if intrinsic value acknowledges something tangible and real, it does not guide specific human interaction with nature. In this view, the problem to be solved is not a crisis of *value* (i.e., a failure to appreciate and acknowledge the worth of natural entities) but a crisis of *imagination* (a failure in the human ability to conceive of new and more constructive ways of relating to nature). This shift in emphasis leads to a radical shift in the overall strategy of environmental ethics.

THE STRATEGY OF RESPONSIBLE MORAL AGENCY

Critics of a strategy of environmental ethics framed around the first great question, "what is the basis of the intrinsic value of nature?," would agree, to a point, with Maguire and Justus. Intrinsic value is a lousy criterion for making specific environmental decisions, and that is the rub. The problem, in this view, is not how humans value (or fail to value) nature, but the way that humans *treat* nature. Therefore, environmental ethics must be organized around the second great question, what is the basis of human responsibility toward the non-human environment and how should this responsibility be carried out? Again Willis Jenkins gives this approach a memorable label in naming it "the strategy of moral agency."[9] The focus in the second strategy shifts to solving the problem of determining *why* human beings have legitimate responsibilities toward nature, *what* such responsibilities are, and *how* they should be carried out. The problem now finds very specific expression in real environmental decisions and dilemmas, namely how do humans relate themselves to nature in the mediating concepts, history, metaphors, political configurations, and other things through which humans are engaged with their environment? A strategy that focuses on moral agency makes progress in specifying the questions, but it does not necessarily get any further in directing the answers, because its fundamental question, why are humans responsible for nature, can prove, philosophically, a tough nut to crack.

Aldo Leopold, author of the environmental classic *A Sand County Almanac*, and considered by many to be the father of modern environmental ethics, had a difficult time with this question and never satisfactorily resolved it. He begins his most famous essay in *Sand County*, "The Land Ethic," by explaining the need for one. "A land ethic," wrote Leopold, "changes the role of *Homo sapiens* from conqueror of the land community to plain member and citizen of it. It implies respect for his fellow-members, and also respect for the community as such."[10] These words represent an admirable attempt at humility on the part of Earth's dominant species, but they do not get us very far in terms of establishing the basis for human responsibility for the land community. The other "plain members and citizens" don't assume these responsibilities for other species. They follow a remarkably free market, laissez-faire ecology in which each pursues its own selfish ends without regard for the ends of others. Indeed, sometimes the selfish ends of one species *are* the others, in the form of prey, for predators, or hosts, for parasites. If we take the metaphor seriously, it would suggest that human beings also could assume that their pursuit of selfish ends will ultimately provide a good outcome for all. But clearly this has not been the case in the past, nor is there any evidence that it will be in the future as human technology and Earth-altering powers increase.

Leopold was not unaware of the problem. He attempted to solve it with a time-honored, if somewhat evasive, strategy. When you find your reasoning in ideological trouble, switch metaphors. Realizing that envisioning humans as "plain members and citizens" of the biotic community provides, at best, minimal support for the justification of unique human responsibility to care for the community, he trades in this currency for a comparison of the human species to the good king Tristram of Arthurian legend. Quoting from the poem *Tristram* by Edwin Arlington Robinson,[11] Leopold recalls the words of Tristram's tutor, Gouvernail,

Whether you will or not,
You are a king, Tristram, for you are one
Of the time-sifted few that leave the world,
When they are gone, not the same place it was.
Mark what you leave.[12]

Certainly kings have responsibilities to their subjects, and good kings fulfill them, but what exactly is it that makes the human species king? Tristram was born to it by blood. Humans might claim the authority by virtue of their technological and ecological power, but power is used by kings as a basis for tyranny, not responsibility. To say that humans are somehow different from other species is at once to state the obvious and in some circles cause grievous offense or, in others, invite sarcasm and ridicule. The last can be seen in the remarks of noted environmental educator David Orr. Orr describes a class lesson in which he asks his students what rationale could be made in defense of human existence on Earth to other species, seeing that humans endanger most of them. Of their responses, Orr remarks,

> students, although finding this an interesting exercise, conclude that no good defense can be made on any terms … Almost to a person they believe that, given our intelligence and the power of our technology, we will survive. A few believe that we are made more or less in God's image, which gives us license to do whatever we want, devil take the hindmost. Otherwise articulate and intelligent, my students' confusion is, I think, representative of the larger befuddlement on the subject.[13]

We will return to Orr's perspective, and his attempts at teaching his students about human responsibility to nature, later in this chapter and at that time will examine who it is that is really befuddled in this class exercise. For the moment, however, Orr's story illustrates the dilemma of discovering the basis of human responsibility. For some, the question does not matter. After all, if humans don't assume responsibility for nature and non-human species, what other species would? But this response only begs the question. The problem remains: On what basis can humans claim a right to manage nature, even if they perform their management for nature's good? If the question has no affirmative answer, the only alternative is negation: we have none. This is the response supported by Leopold's "plain member and citizen" metaphor and by any attempts to derive the intrinsic value of nature, including humanity, from evolutionary origins. If the human species differs from other species in neither its evolutionary origins nor its evolutionary objective (survival), it cannot be expected to differ in its responsibilities, which extend only to the limits of its own self-interest. Indeed, human self-interest, perhaps more enlightened than that of a bacterium, fern, or frog, might well include some pragmatic environmental protection, but such an approach offers no incentives to save ecologically marginalized endangered species or rare environments that humans could do very well without.

But this is a view that can recoil upon itself. If humans are but "plain members and citizens" of ecological communities, "no different" than the others, then humans not only possess no responsibility to manage other species, but no authority to do so. Because people invariably live up to (or down to) their basic belief structures, the consequences of this view are increasingly manifest. When members of radical environmental groups drive ceramic spikes into trees in a logging sale or pour sand down the fuel line of a Forest Service truck, they are not engaging in thoughtless acts of vandalism or destruction of property. They are acting out a belief structure affirming that people are no more than plain members and citizens of nature and possess no basis to suppose that they should manage nature for any particular ends, especially the ends of their own interests.

Leopold's plain member and citizen metaphor has, in modern environmentalism, achieved a profound success. Just as Leopold used the device as a restraint against human arrogance toward nature, so it is used today, often in much more vitriolic rhetoric and violent means, as a reaction against "speciesism," the view that, ultimately, all of the Earth's millions of species are here to serve just one species, us. Speciesism, even in its crudest form, does at least provide a basis for human responsibility toward nature: the responsibility to manage nature responsibly for future human welfare. More subtly expressed in most cases, this view forms the basis for many of the modern ethical arguments for human responsibility. But, if it goes no further, this approach does not solve the underlying problem. Is there a valid basis for humans being responsible for the *welfare of natural entities other than ourselves*, even if fulfilling that responsibility might come at a sacrifice to us?

WHERE DO WE PUT THE GOALPOSTS? THE STRATEGY OF SELF-TRANSFORMATION

In his insightful essay "Winning and Losing in Environmental Ethics," Holmes Rolston III notes that human beings have to address the question of "winning and losing" in relating their own needs to that of the environment when it comes to making ethical decisions about the environment.[14] Economic considerations and the environment are often at odds with one another because traditional economic thinking views humans as inherently selfish and self-interested. Therefore, in their transactions with the environment, humans only "win" when they advance their own self-interest, usually at the expense of non-human environmental entities. One strategy to accomplish this, distinct from the first two we have already addressed, could be called "the strategy of self-transformation." In this third paradigm, the human self, in Rolston's words, "transforms winning by satisfying self-interest to winning by self-transformation. The once-isolated self, defending itself against the community it inhabits, is re-envisioned, extended, so that the self is smeared out in the community . . . 'Self-realization' is indistinguishable from 'self-realization of all beings.' "[15]

Deep ecology is one ethical paradigm that manifests this underlying strategy in which the human self strives for complete identification with nature. Such a strategy creates its own unique ethical and personal dilemmas. In seeing nature as a complete and unified whole, the particulars of the individual, human or otherwise, become unalterably blurred. Unable to draw an ethical line anywhere, even between living and nonliving, deep ecology is an ethical paradigm that leads to confusion, inability to make clear decisions, and moral paralysis. But the ethical dilemmas run even deeper than this. Again, to quote Rolston, the problem with deep ecology and other environmental ethics based on self-transformation is that, "The self wins by enlarging itself to include all other selves, or, put another way, the self becomes indistinguishable from all other selves."[16] But, if the human self is so enlarged that it becomes indistinguishable from its surrounding environment, it becomes extremely difficult to determine what the "right" environmental goals should be. Rolston sees this dilemma clearly: "We discover that the self is so enlarged that there is no longer any environment. Environmental ethics has made the environment unnecessary! Perhaps we should say that the environment has won, since the self is enlarged into it and all selves are realized. Perhaps we should wonder whether the environment wins if it becomes unnecessary. Winning and losing are not terms that have much meaning if we cannot distinguish self from other."[17]

The strategy of self-transformation is one that actually addresses the third and fourth great questions as one. It declares that the purpose of environmental stewardship is not to achieve a particular environmental state defined in terms of the environment, but rather for humans to achieve a personal state of transformation in which they become one with their environment. Therefore, the answer to the fourth question, what is the normative basis and pattern for environmental virtues, or behaviors of excellence toward the environment, is not based on defining a norm for the environment but on determining what behaviors are most effective at transforming the human condition into a state of unity with the environment.

The problem we are wrestling with is not a philosophical mirage. It is a real dilemma with profound implications for environmental perspective, behavior, and management. Nowhere has the problem, with all its attendant implications, become more apparent than in the science and practice of restoration ecology, a discipline that seeks to remediate harmful past and present human effects on nature by actions which restore sites or systems to predetermined states or historically normative conditions. The debate has flared out of philosophical and ethical discussion into the pages of professional journals, where it has become a bone of contention among professional restorationists precisely because a strategy of self-transformation in restoration affects practical restoration strategies of restoration management.

Following the strategy of self-transformation, some restorationists have advocated organizing ecological restoration around human interaction with nature, specifically around what have come to be called *focal practices*. In this view, modern humans immersed in a technological society are the "losers," to use the negative half of Rolston's dichotomy, because they have lost touch with their natural environment and its processes. In this state, no real restoration is possible because humans simply commodify nature as a collection of goods and services. Restoration then becomes simply the manipulation of nature to produce the goods and service commodities humans desire.

An alternative approach, articulated by restorationist Eric Higgs, is to organize restoration around human participation and organize human participation around focal practices. A focal practice, is "an activity that 'focuses' a person on things that are deeply engaging and integrates a person into a system of meaning rooted in history and place."[18] Restorationists like Higgs want to engage wider circles of public participation in the work and process of restoration in order to keep restoration itself from becoming just another technological fix for bad human actions toward nature. This is a commendable goal. Viewed in its best light, a strategy of restoration through public participation centered on focal practices would be one expression of the strategy of responsible moral agency previously reviewed. But to focus restoration on public participation and focal experience goes further and, consciously or unconsciously, embraces a strategy of human self-transformation as the ultimate answer to environmental problems, including problems of environmental ethics. This approach has the effect of both obscuring and disguising the fundamental problem to be solved, which, to recall our definition of management, is to remedy a deficiency in a natural system. The aim of focal practices, however, is to create environmentally virtuous people, and, as such, this approach can easily lose sight of what the actual deficiency of the system is. Ironically, they can also end up devaluing the very nature they want to connect people with. As Rolston observes, "the environmentally virtuous person seems to be valuing things for what they are in themselves, but in the end the primary value sought turns out to be human excellence. But if all value of and in nature is derived from virtuous actions of human agents, then nature is, after all, a kind of moral resource. This does not sound any more like such a high-souled account."[19]

A focus on self-transformation also has the tendency to blur ecological reality. Some management practices really are good for achieving or preserving particular states of nature and others are not. Maintaining or restoring variable flow rates in a U.S. Midwest river system really can be good for populations of piping plovers because of the plover's practice of building nests on sandbars. Sandbar formation is enhanced by flow variation in the river channel, whereas maintaining or creating constant flow levels in the same river tend to reduce it. Making a management decision of this kind must take into consideration what is good for piping plovers, not what kind of focal practices different management strategies might provide for optimal public participation. Indeed, management for particular needs of particular species might require technical and professional skills that few people possess and so exclude most focal practices altogether. But such skills might really be necessary for some aspects of environmental welfare.

The strategy of self-transformation is intuitively attractive as an ethical paradigm, especially in modern human culture in which growing numbers of people are now more separated and alienated from nature. It is also extremely congenial to the modern human bent toward narcissism, the tendency to define other people, creatures, and things only in relation to ourselves and the tendency to define as "real" only that which is experienced and exists within oneself. Understandably, as people begin to perceive their separation from nature, they may, with a commendably repentant spirit, begin to seek transformative experiences and processes that will reconnect them to the non-human world. If, however, they retain a narcissistic outlook that sees nature only as an experience within themselves, then we still do not have an ethic that is about "real" nature, and our "transformative experiences" might end up transforming nature in very harmful ways.

The ultimate problem with self-transformation as an organizing principle of environmental ethics, as in influential environmental paradigms such as deep ecology, is that a focus on self-transformation ultimately obscures nature by making human beings, not nature, the focus of the transformation. A preoccupation with self-transformation tends to reduce nature to becoming merely a moral resource for human virtue fulfillment. Some would argue that using nature as a moral resource is better than using it as a commodity resource, but in the end humans are still burdened with an anthropocentric point of view that obscures the reality of nature's real life and needs. The question of what will happen to non-human nature as a result of such (human) self-transformation is not directly addressed.

THE END OF NATURE: WHAT WILL BE THE FINAL FATE OF THE NATURAL WORLD?

The first four great questions are addressed in these first three fundamental strategies of environmental ethics. The final question, what is the fate of nature, is different. On its own, it does not form the basis or organizing principle for any particular strategy of environmental ethics. In fact, it is a question often conveniently ignored in many, if not most, modern approaches to the ethical problem of the environment. I choose the modifier "conveniently" because ignorance is often necessary in order to avoid difficult, and sometimes embarrassing, implications of some ethical positions on the environment that can be well-dressed in present contexts but make little or no sense when considered in light of an ethic's own assumptions about the final fate of nature.

Making morally correct decisions about the environment is not an emotionally neutral activity. To assume that ethical decisions about environmental entities are important, one must believe that such decisions are not only significant to the present but also to the future. Present faith in the significance of current environmental ethics requires an expectation of future *hope*. It requires optimism that there really will be a future for the non-human world, that the environment will still be there for future generations to enjoy. When people share such a hope for the future, not only for nature but for themselves, they have a basis for common purpose and an expectation of shared future achievement.

Armed with these expectations, present conservation actions can make sense. We see the necessity of this perspective throughout history, among the educated and the uneducated, the rural and the urban, the West and the East. As a village history from Anhui, China, instructed its readers, "Every family must take care of the mountains and waters around. Plant trees and bamboo as shelters ... Keep an eye on the environment and protect it from damage. This is a chore for people of one hundred generations to undertake."[20] But this advice is good advice only if there is a rational hope that there will be a future for "one hundred generations."

Here contemporary efforts at environmental ethics face one of their most serious obstacles. We have already seen some expression of the problem in the sentiments of Norman Levine in Chapter One. Let us hear him again:

> Some nature lovers weep at this passing [of non-human species which have become extinct] and collect money to save species. They make lists of animals and plants that are in danger of extinction and sponsor legislation to save them. I don't. What the species preservers are trying to do is stop the clock. It cannot and should not be done. Extinction is an inevitable fact of evolution, and it is needed for progress. New species continually arise, and they are better adapted to their environment than those who have died out. Extinction comes from a failure to adapt to a changing environment.[21]

But Levine has more to say, and it is now more relevant for us to hear. "Evolution exists and it goes on continually. People are here because of it, but people may be replaced someday. It is neither possible nor desirable to stop it, and that is what we are trying to do when we try to preserve species on their way out."[22]

The recent History Channel series *After People* goes even further and suggests, with admirable dramatic flair in its weekly episodes, that not only might people be replaced some day but that their replacement would be a blessing to all other life forms, and it is probably necessary for the survival of non-human life on Earth. This is the same message proclaimed in the modern (2008) remake of the 1951 science fiction movie classic *The Day the Earth Stood Still*. In the original version, an alien arrives on Earth to tell the world that the nuclear weapons humans now possess constitute a danger not only to themselves but, in their future potential, to other planets. To remove this threat, humans must learn to live together peaceably. In contrast, the 2008 version focuses on the threat humans pose to all other life on Earth. This threat of mass extinction on such a unique planet leads to the judgment of intelligent extraterrestrials that the human species must be exterminated.

One might argue that Hollywood and the History Channel do not know much about biology, but that defense would be false comfort. The Ecological Death Wish is a sentiment that is becoming increasingly mainstream in science. In 2006, the Texas Academy of Science chose University of Texas ecologist Eric Pianka as its Distinguished Texas Scientist. In addressing the Texas Academy on the occasion of receiving the award, Pianka took the opportunity to tell his audience that there was little basis for optimism regarding world conservation at the present level of human population. There was hope, however, that humans would diminish, probably suffering a crash from a future worldwide pandemic. For Pianka, this was good news because, "things are going to get better after the collapse because we won't be able to decimate the earth so much. And, I actually think the world will be much better when there's only 10 or 20 percent of us left. It would give wildlife a chance to recover—we won't need conservation biologists anymore."[23]

According to witnesses present at the talk, Pianka received a standing ovation from the academy scientists for his remarks.[24] A controversy ensued, with some claiming that Professor Pianka was advocating the extermination of the human race. The Texas Academy of Science, attempting to quell the storm of public outrage, released a statement asserting that, "Many of Dr. Pianka's statements have been severely misconstrued and sensationalized."[25] Perhaps. If Pianka is right, then, as he says, we won't need conservation biologists, with whom he self-identifies, so there goes his day job. But, as movies and television are proving, there will always be a market for good environmental entertainment, and, in that niche, Pianka will always have a place on the lecture circuit among those who can stir crowd and controversy.

Although some might view the Pianka affair as an extreme example of one scientist talking out of his hat, and others find it an overreaction from extreme right-wing, antiscientific elements of the public, those familiar with the literature of environmental ethics and conservation would hardly blush at Pianka's remarks. These ideas, usually dressed in more modest intellectual attire, have been a regular guest in many venues of environmental journals and books for the past several decades. Various environmental writers have referred to humans as "Earth's worst pest" and "a cancer on nature."[26] At the Brookfield, Illinois, zoo not far from my home, there was once a place where visitors were directed to look at "the most dangerous animal on Earth." What they looked into was not an animal display but a mirror. Steeped in this kind of thinking, some people cherish the hope that they will live to see the end of the human species. In this version of an ecological rapture, dramatized in productions like *After People*, the Earth will be saved when the human species is destroyed.

PLANNING FOR THE FUTURE: THE NATURE AND NECESSITY OF HUMAN UNIQUENESS

If such thinking reflects ecological reality, it merits consideration, if only for accurate planning for a real future event. But in the realm of environmental ethics, it hardly makes sense for the chief ethical decision-making species to look forward to its own demise as the solution to the environmental dilemma. If that is really the solution, what is the significance of *any* current ethical decision by humans about the environment, except perhaps the commendably rational decision to commit specieswide suicide? If humans are, to quote Pianka, "no better than bacteria,"[27] why should they adopt a strategy of moral responsibility toward non-human creatures? Bacteria don't.

Pianka, Hollywood, and the History Channel all make the same fundamental philosophical error in their analysis of and prescription for the environmental crisis, which is a failure to understand the difference between moral consideration and moral significance. The thinking of Pianka, the aliens in the movie, and the History Channel writers of *After People* claims that because the life of non-human species deserves moral consideration, humans should be eliminated as a threat to that life because they are only one species among many (meaning that all species have equal moral significance). But in fact, this is not the case.

The error becomes apparent when we return to our second major ethical strategy, the strategy of responsible moral agency. The doomsday scenario and ecological death wish perspective are closely tied to the same ethical problem. In order for a strategy of responsible moral agency to be plausible, there must be some basis, some ethical rationale, that gives human beings the right to make ethical decisions for nature's good. Humanity must be, in some way, different from other species for this strategy to work. And humans must not only be differ-ent *from* other species, they must have a future on Earth *with* other species in which that difference matters. Humans, in other words, must be admitted to possess *greater moral significance than non-human creatures*, not only because they have greater power to affect the lives of other creatures, but because they alone, among all species, have the capacity to ponder whether their actions toward such creatures are *right or wrong*. In other words, humans not only have freedom of action toward other creatures, but also freedom of will. They can *choose* between different courses of action, between actions they might selfishly *desire* to take for their own benefit and actions which they *ought to take* for the benefit of other species. Whether we like it or not, whether it is fashionable to admit it in today's culture or not, humans and their decisions of how to act and live on Earth must be acknowledged to have greater moral significance than the actions of other creatures. If we are not prepared to admit this, then no func-tional environmental ethic can ever be constructed.

The problem can be seen again, and further clarified, in another set-ting introduced at the beginning of this chapter. David Orr's efforts to teach his students about human responsibility for other species comes from the pages of *Conservation Biology*, the leading professional journal in its field. Here in an essay entitled "The Trial,"[28] Orr describes how he uses a particular story as a heuristic device to teach his students at Oberlin College. He asks his students to imagine an ordinary court-room. Only its participants are different. No juror in the jury box is human. Reptiles, fish, plants, microbes, mammals, insects, amphib-ians, every kind of creature is represented, and all are given the abil-ities of rational thought and speech. It is a big jury box; thousands of species are there. The judge is a wise owl, the prosecutor a cunning fox. The defendant is a human being. The defense attorney, another human, is about to address the jury with her opening remarks. The charge against the defendant is straightforward. Humans have become too numerous, dangerous, and destructive to other life forms to permit their continued existence on Earth. If found guilty, the court's sentence will be the extermination of the human race.

The defense made by the human attorney is essentially that we humans are going to try to do better:

All over the Earth, a great turning in the evolution of humankind has begun ... We now know ourselves to be a part of a larger story of life in the universe and are beginning to understand what that will require of us ... The angels of our better nature are growing more powerful in human affairs. There is now a global movement to protect species, stabilize the climate, preserve habitats for each of you, to reign in our excesses, and reduce consumption ... I ask each member of the jury to see this as dawn, not sunset; a beginning, not an end.[29]

At this point, the story ends. We are not told what the verdict will be. Will the human race be convicted or acquitted? And on what grounds?

Presumably, it is at this point that Professor Orr begins teaching his class about human responsibility for nature, but his pedagogical device severely limits what his students can learn. The essential problem of "The Trial" is this: no argument is made for human uniqueness, or for the uniqueness of human responsibility. Not only is no argument made, but the metaphor is so constructed that no argument of this kind can be permitted. Professor Orr has so constrained the venue in the court of his own classroom that some arguments have no standing before the bench. But it is precisely those arguments that are the only logical response to the dilemma that the trial poses. Further, it is only the uniqueness of human capacities that make the story of "The Trial" possible, and this is precisely what Orr removes, either by ignorance or by intentional intellectual manipulation. Again it is Holmes Rolston III, commenting on Orr's essay, who cuts to the quick:

The parable is so impossible that it restricts what it can effectively teach ... The presiding judge is a wise owl and the prosecuting attorney a cunning fox. We can tolerate that in Aesop, because everybody knows we are not describing animals but just personifying humans with wisdom or cunning. To take such personifications seriously would be to live in an animistic world, an enchanted world ... We will have to strip out all such enchantments before we begin to understand whether and how humans differ from the rest. And when we do this, there is only one species left at the council of all beings. Humans alone ponder and often worry about such things as justice, fairness, and decency for which reflection and concern there is no precedent in non-human nature.[30]

It is precisely Orr's determination to create accountability of humans to non-humans while at the same time removing any basis for human uniqueness that blinds him to the one thing that makes the question both plausible and potent. He makes the same mistake we have observed in our three previous examples, the confusion between moral consideration and moral significance. The plants and animals are morally considerable. Their interests and their lives should be taken into account in an evaluation of human behavior on this planet. But they cannot occupy the jury box and pass judgment. They cannot sit behind the bench and order these proceedings, and they cannot effectively prosecute the humans who have done many cruel and terrible things to them and to their world. Only human beings can fill those roles. Humans are unique among Earth's creatures in that they alone can be accurately described as moral agents. They alone possess the capacity to choose between right and wrong, to distinguish between what they actually do and what they *ought to do*. It is in this uniqueness of being human that lies the unique freedom that leads to unique responsibility. And this is what gives human actions toward nature unique moral significance, for humans alone possess the capacity to imagine the needs of others, including non-human others, and consider them as important, or even more important, than their own. Rolston summarizes this well:

> [T]he problem is that humans are as much apart from nature as they are a part of it, not free from nature but free in nature, transcendent in our cultures, free to choose our courses, our careers, our futures, to correct our mistakes, to repent of our sins, to conserve or to develop, to sustain development and/or the biosphere, as is no other species. That humans are a part of nature, if half the truth, is dangerous if taken for the whole truth because it does not recognize our human uniqueness and responsibility. Any solution to our challenges in environmental ethics requires a more discriminating account of who we are, and what we ought to do.[31]

A MORE DISCRIMINATING ACCOUNT– A CHRISTIAN UNDERSTANDING OF HUMAN UNIQUENESS IN NATURE AND HUMAN RESPONSIBILITY TO NATURE

The five great questions of environmental ethics are real questions, and they are important. But taken individually, each used to produce a controlling idea for a strategy of environmental ethics, they are like the blind men who tried to describe the elephant. The description they offer is honest, accurate, and sincere, but it is incomplete. The reality is something greater, and some greater vision must explain it.

In the chapters that follow, I will attempt to illustrate a larger reality. Christian faith and practice, expressed in biblical text, theology, church teaching, and Christian practice, provide it and, within it, provide an answer to each of the great questions that dominate the field of environmental ethics today. But to solve the problems that these questions address, the questions themselves must submit to a radical reorganization, for the answers that Christian faith provides come from a language and a worldview unfamiliar to these questions, a perspective that has not been part of their formation. The answers Christian faith provides will seem, at first, as the speech one hears in another language. Not only are the words different, but so is the construction of thought and image that the language conveys. All who are fluent multilinguists understand that no one language can ever be understood as simply the word-for-word translation of another. Entirely new ways of thinking are required to translate concepts unique to a given language and its culture. To this day, the Hebrew verb *hesed*, so common in the Old Testament, especially in the Psalms, has never been fully and adequately translated. We best approximate it with phrases such as tender mercy, steadfast loyalty, or loving kindness, but scholars of Hebrew will tell you that is not exactly what *hesed* means. *Hesed* is a word that has been said to attempt to define the indefinable, the nature of the love and faithfulness of God toward humanity. To understand its meaning, strength of imagination becomes as important as fluency in grammar.

As we now begin, in Chapter Three, to take up the Christian vision and understanding of what the world calls an "environmental ethic," we also enter a realm in which strength of imagination must complement logical definition. We will be traveling into a new land where the topography must be described by a new language. The traditional categories of secular orthodoxies are inadequate. If you try to use them to explain Christian thought regarding ethics of the environment, they will break in your hands. As Jesus said, men do not pour new wine into old wineskins. "If they do," he explained, "the skins will burst. The wine will run out and the wineskins will be ruined. They pour new wine into new wineskins, and both are preserved."[32] In what follows, we will be drinking new wine in environmental ethics, and we must pour it into new wineskins. Let the reader who would continue have a taste for the first, and a willingness to use the second to hold it.

NOTES

1. William James, "Is Life Worth Living," in *The Will to Believe and Other Essays in Popular Philosophy* (New York: Longmans, Green, and Co., 1931), 33–62, p. 44.

2. Ibid.

3. Quoted in Holmes Rolston III, *Philosophy Gone Wild: Essays in Environmental Ethics* (Buffalo, NY: Prometheus Books, 1986), p. 55.

4. Willis Jenkins, *Ecologies of Grace: Environmental Ethics and Christian Theology* (Oxford, UK: Oxford University Press, 2008), p. 42.

5. Holmes Rolston III, *Philosophy Gone Wild: Essays in Environmental Ethics* (Buffalo, NY: Prometheus Books, 1986), p. 111.

6. Ibid., p. 17.

7. J. Baird Callicott, "Whither Conservation Ethics?" *Conservation Biology* 4 (1990): pp. 15–20. The quote is often attributed to Pinchot, but Pinchot credited this saying to one of his contemporaries, W. J. McGee.

8. Lynn A. Macguire and James Justus, "Why Intrinsic Value Is a Poor Basis for Conservation Decisions," *BioScience* 58 (2008): pp. 910–911.

9. Jenkins, p. 46.

10. Aldo Leopold, "The Land Ethic," in *A Sand County Almanac with Essays on Conservation from Round River* (New York: Ballantine, 1970), p. 240.

11. Edwin Arlington Robinson, "Tristram," in *Collected Poems of Edward Arlington Robinson* (New York: MacMillan, 1937), pp. 595–729.

12. Ibid., p. 644. Quoted in Leopold, p. 261. Note that Leopold misquotes the poem by replacing "time-sifted" with the more familiar "time-tested." I have quoted the poem here as Robinson wrote it.

13. David Orr, "The Trial," *Conservation Biology* 20 (2006): pp. 1570–1573, 1570.

14. Rolston, "Winning and Losing in Environmental Ethics." In *Ethics and Environmental Policy: Theory Meets Practice*, eds. Frederick Ferré and Peter Hartel (Athens: University of Georgia Press), pp. 217–234.

15. Ibid., p. 223.

16. Ibid.

17. Ibid.

18. William Throop and Rebecca Purdom, "Wilderness Restoration: The Paradox of Public Participation," *Restoration Ecology* 14 (2006): pp. 493–499.

19. Rolston, "Winning and Losing in Environmental Ethics," p. 224.

20. Chris Coggins, *The Tiger and the Pangolin* (Honolulu: University of Hawaii Press, 2003), pp. 199–200.

21. Norman Levine, "Evolution and Extinction," *BioScience* 39 (1989): p. 38.

22. Ibid.

23. Eric R. Pianka, *The Vanishing Book of Life on Earth*. Available from http://uts.cc.utexas.edu/~varanus/Vanishing.Book.text.pdf (accessed

12 August 2009). Although Pianka and his supporters have repeatedly claimed that his remarks at the 2006 Texas Academy of Science meetings were misquoted or taken out of context, the quote used here reflects what Pianka has stated repeatedly in numerous public talks, many available as transcripts on various websites. Officially entitled, "The Vanishing Book of Life on Earth," the talk given at the Texas Academy of Science meeting has been commonly referred to as Pianka's "Doomsday Talk" and is one which he has repeated on multiple occasions. The text here is taken from one of Pianka's personal web pages published by the University of Texas.

24. Forest M. Mims III. "Meeting Doctor Doom," *The Citizen Scientist*, http://www.sas.org/tcs/weeklyIssues_2006/2006-04-07/feature1p/ (accessed 12 August 2009).

25. Texas Academy of Science, 2006. Official statement of the academy archived and published on http://pandasthumb.org/archives/2006/04/texas -academy-o.html (accessed 12 August 2009).

26. Quoted in Douglas S. Looney, "Protector or Provocateur?" *Sports Illustrated*, May 27, 1991, p. 54.

27. Pianka.

28. Orr.

29. Ibid., pp. 1571–1572.

30. Rolston, "Disenchanting the Rhetoric," *Conservation Biology* 20 (2006): pp. 1576–1578, p. 1576.

31. Ibid., pp. 1577–1578.

32. Matthew 9:17, *The Bible, New International Version* (Grand Rapids, MI: Zondervan, 1985).

CHAPTER 3

A Biblical Understanding of "The Environment"

And God saw all that he had made, and it was very good.

Genesis 1:31

A NEW LANDSCAPE AND A NEW LANGUAGE

We saw in Chapter Two that environmental ethics are generally organized around one or more great questions that address the intrinsic value of nature, the moral agency of responsibility of human beings toward nature, the fulfillment of the human self through appropriate interaction with nature, and the issue of nature's ultimate end. However, when we attempt to make Christian teaching on the environment fit these organizational schemes, the result is much the same as an ill-fitting corset. It may produce a shapely figure, but it can suffocate and even deform the wearer if worn for very long. Christian teaching speaks to all of these great questions, not by using the questions as categories of thought but by redefining the categories into a different kind of organization.

Christian teaching, as noted in Chapter One, is drawn from four sources: the Bible, theology, Christian tradition, and the church. We will begin with the Bible, the text Christians regard as the authoritative source on which all other sources are based. To explain *why* Christians view the Bible in this way is beyond the scope of this chapter, indeed, beyond the scope of the book, as well as a digression from its purpose. It is, however, a legitimate question, and it would be courteous to give a brief answer.

A common misconception about Christianity is that the Bible must be accepted as a divine revelation as a prerequisite to Christian faith. This is not, in fact, the case. Christians believe that the definitive revelation of God is not in a book, but in a person, Jesus Christ, whose life is known from biblical and extra-biblical, historical sources. But it is four scriptural sources, the gospels of Matthew, Mark, Luke, and John, that provide the greatest detail and insight about the person of Jesus Christ: what he said, what he taught, what he did, and who he understood himself to be. Although differences in the style and perspective among the gospel writers are obvious, a remarkably clear and self-consistent picture of Jesus Christ emerges, one which reveals his understanding of himself to be the Son of God who had become a man to save humanity. He vindicates his claim in the insights of his teachings; his power to give sight to the blind, health to the sick, and life to the dead; and his ability to die for the sins of the human race and then rise from the dead as the savior of mankind.

Although non-Christians might contest the gospel writers' claims that Jesus did these things, the point, for the moment, is, if a human witness observed Jesus saying and doing the things the gospel writers claim to have seen him say and do, then that witness has warrant to believe Jesus' claim to be the Son of God, and the definitive revelation of God, his father, to the human race. As Jesus' puts it in the gospel of John, "He who has seen me has seen the Father."[1]

If one accepts Jesus' testimony about himself, it makes sense to accept his testimony about the Bible. Jesus treats Scripture as the authoritative word of God and declares that these Scriptures, collectively, "testify of me."[2] The gospel writers accept his claim and in fact repeatedly interpret prophecies about a coming Messiah, an "anointed one," as statements about Jesus Christ. For example, the Old Testament writings of the prophet Isaiah, written seven centuries before the birth of Christ, speak of a "suffering servant" who will deliver Israel from their sins. This servant will be humble and compassionate, "a man of sorrows and acquainted with grief."[3] In describing the Messiah this way. Isaiah does not write prophecy that is easily fulfilled, since the servant is also to be the one that God will exalt to become the ruler of the world. It is a vision of integration of humility, power, and authority that human experience would be hard-pressed to imagine, much less find a good historical example of. In a remarkably prescient description of the death of the servant, Isaiah says he will be "pierced through for our transgressions"[4] and in that death, he will be "numbered with the transgressors."[5] Through his sacrifice, humanity will be saved.

As Christians find the scriptures internally consistent in both the Old and New Testaments in their descriptions of Jesus Christ, they find additional warrant in believing the scriptures because of their internal self-consistency in their description of God regarding his character and purposes. Despite being compiled over many centuries by many different writers, the Bible presents a unified and coherent picture of not only who God is, but of his purposes toward humankind and the world and of his progressively unfolding revelation of himself and those purposes to humankind. Part of the Bible's revelation of God is that one of his primary purposes is to reveal himself to human beings. His word is a principle agent to achieve that purpose. Therefore, it is consistent with this purpose that the Bible exists and has survived through many centuries to retain this constant and consistent message. As Christian philosopher Dallas Willard puts it, regarding his own reasons for believing the Bible to be an authentic revelation of God about himself, "On the divine side, I assume that God has been willing and competent to arrange for the Bible . . . to emerge and be preserved in ways that will secure his purposes for it among human beings worldwide. Those who actually believe in God will be untroubled by this."[6] And it is for these reasons, and others which space and time do not permit to detail, that Christians believe the Bible can be read in a straightforward manner, with due consideration for all modes of human communication, experience, and imagination, including and encompassing history, narrative, vision, poetry, simile, metaphor, teaching, and direct discourse. Likewise, reading the Bible intelligently requires paying attention to a particular author's historical and cultural context, as well as his literary context (i.e., understanding individual statements by how they relate to other statements that surround them) and his occasion for writing. The last element is particularly important, because the writer's *occasion* is almost always the best guide to his *purpose and intent*. By considering all of these, a Christian can recognize and learn from the Bible's historical particularity without discarding its eternal and contemporary relevance.

If we understand this perspective, we can understand the reason for beginning with the Bible as foundational for forming a Christian ethic of the environment. If we are serious in reading the Bible as a revelation by God about himself, we must discard a number of currently popular ways of reading it. If God is the Bible's primary subject, then the Bible cannot be read as a rule book for life, as it is sometimes referred to in popular Christian culture, valuable as its rules for living may be. Neither can it be treated as a manual for natural science, psychoanalysis, political theory, historical study, human relationships, or any other intellectual discipline, concern, or fad that human beings today or in times past have sought to make it. For environmental ethics, this means the Bible cannot be read as a treatise of ethical rules for understanding and caring for "the environment," for which there is, in fact, no equivalent term in Hebrew or Greek. That is why current efforts, like The Green Bible, which attempt to read all scripture through an environmental lens, are misplaced. The same error would occur if we tried to read the Bible through the perspective of one of the current great questions of environmental ethics.

No book in the Bible was written because of the *occasion* of the current environmental crisis. Therefore, we cannot simply transpose biblical texts into current conditions, environmental or otherwise, without doing our historical, cultural, and literary homework. Because the Bible is fundamentally a revelation *of God himself*, we must treat this task as its overriding occasion and purpose, and therefore it is from that perspective that we must begin. If we can develop a biblical understanding of God, we can then develop an understanding of the environment subordinate to the greater question of the nature of God, realizing, as we go, that we may have to abandon many of our current conceptions about the environment, and even the phrase itself, to understand and appreciate a truly biblical view of what we today refer to as environmental problems.

GOD AND NATURE

I have begun this chapter by stressing that the Bible is not a rule book for environmental ethics but a revelation of the person, character, and purposes of God. Yet, that caveat in place, we find that the Bible begins in a very environmentally friendly manner. The first revelation God makes of himself in the opening book of Genesis is the revelation of his relationship to nature.

"In the beginning, God created the heavens and the Earth": In these opening words of Genesis 1, a wealth of theological knowledge is revealed, along with many of the things that distinguish Judaism and Christianity from most other religions, especially pantheistic and animistic ones. The Bible begins by revealing that nature has its origin in the mind and purpose of God. Unlike most other ancient religions prevalent in the cultures and times surrounding the Hebrews, the God of the Bible did not arise from nature. He is not the outcome of cosmic processes but the author of them.

The claim of Genesis is this: God is not the same as nature. He is separate from it, neither to be identified with it and nor derived from it. Rather, nature derives its existence from the word and will of God. Therefore, God, not nature, is deserving of worship. The Bible immediately expels all attempts to construct any environmental ethic on the premise that nature is to be preserved because it is God, or contains God, or is the source of God. The Bible does not despiritualize nature but makes clear that the "spirit" of life in created things, including human beings, is not the same as the Spirit of God. Jewish environmental scholar Jeanne Kay explains, "Ancient Judaism differs from pantheism not in any inability to perceive spirits in animals and plants, but because it does not deify the spirits which it sees. Animate nature has a *nefesh* [spirit] or *ruach* [soul] as do people. But just as the Hebrew Bible does not deify human beings, it cannot deify nature."[7]

But if nature is not divine, neither is it worthless. The issue of nature's value is addressed immediately. "God saw that it was good": This simple statement, affirming the intrinsic value of nature, is repeated six times in the first 25 verses of Genesis 1. It is never used in vague or general ways, but always of particulars of the natural world: light and dark, land and sea, plants, sun and moon, birds and sea creatures, land animals and "everything that creeps on the ground." Each one is called "good."

How do we know that such goodness is a statement of nature's intrinsic value and not its utilitarian value? We know this by context, by subject, and by the cause or stimulus of the value judgment. In context, the judgments of the goodness of living and nonliving elements of nature are all made before humans are created. The goodness of these created things is not made with reference to any human use that man will find for them. This does not mean they have no utilitarian value, but that such utility is not the basis of their being good. They are good in their own right, in and of themselves. This understanding is reinforced even after humans are created. The first man and woman, Adam and Eve, are never asked to make an assessment of what they think of God's creation. God declares it good and does not invite debate. Ancient rabbinical scholars of the Talmud expressed the biblical concept this way. "Our masters taught: Man was created on the eve of the Sabbath—and for what reason? So that in case his heart grew proud, one might say to him: Even the gnat was in creation before you were there."[8]

The Bible confers the intrinsic goodness of creation in Genesis 1 not only by context but by subject. The subject making the value judgment is God. Genesis 1 shows God to be a value-able moral agent. He can discern right from wrong. In every sentence containing a predicate of value in Genesis 1, the subject performing the act of valuing is a righteous and holy God. Therefore, the reader has reason to believe that the judgment of creation's goodness is morally accurate.

Third, we know that the intrinsic value of nature is established by considering the cause or stimulus of the value judgment. The text, in its original Hebrew, does not say, of any particular created thing, simply that "It was good," or that "God said that it was good" but rather, "God *saw* [Hebrew, *ra' ah*, to see, look at, inspect or perceive, consider] that it was good" [in Hebrew, *tôb*]. The Hebrew word for good employed here is often used in conjunction with *ra*, or evil, to denote opposites, but can also be translated as pleasing, pleasant, delightful, delicious, joyful, happy, or glad. It is a powerful word. But to say that "God saw" this condition of goodness using the Hebrew word *ra' ah* is to say that God perceived such goodness in what he had made by careful inspection and reflective consideration, not casual observation. His act of seeing good in his creation is a carefully considered moral judgment upon it.

Philosopher David Hume, in his own explanation of value, said, "When you pronounce any action or character to be vicious, you *mean* nothing but that from the constitution of your nature you have a feeling or sentiment of blame from the contemplation of it."[9] That is, statements of value are only statements about your own feelings. They have no reality in the object itself. If this line of thinking is applied to Genesis 1, God is really saying that, "I feel good about what I have made when I look at it" or "What I have made stimulates feelings of goodness within me."

Hume's view of value remains popular with many modern ethicists and is often taken as an unreflective given. But this is not a biblical view, and we need to understand the difference between God's perception of value and Hume's. As C. S. Lewis explains in *The Abolition of Man*, there is another way of perceiving value in natural objects. In speaking of a statement about a waterfall in which an observer says, "this object is sublime," Lewis notes:

> Even if it were granted that such qualities as sublimity were simply and solely projected into things from our own emotions, yet the emotions which prompt the projection are the correlatives, and therefore almost the opposites, of the qualities projected. The feelings which make a man call an object sublime are not

sublime feelings but feelings of veneration. If *This is sublime* is to be reduced at all to a statement about the speaker's feelings, the proper translation would be *I have humble feelings*. If this view ... were consistently applied it would lead to obvious absurdities ... to maintain that *You are contemptible* means *I have contemptible feelings*; in fact that *Your feelings are contemptible* means *My feelings are contemptible*.[10]

It is clear in the Genesis text that God is not making a statement about his feelings but about a quality of the object itself. To recognize this fact is to recognize an important idea regarding the Bible's theory of value about natural objects. Namely, the intrinsic value ascribed to a natural entity is locatable *within the object itself*, although it requires a rational mind, whether divine or human, to perceive the existence of it.

If we understand these dimensions of value inherent in the statements of Genesis 1, we can understand the judgment of environmental ethicist J. Baird Callicott quoted earlier in Chapter One: "The Judeo-Christian Stewardship Environmental Ethic is especially elegant and powerful. It also exquisitely matches the requirements of conservation biology." Callicott bases his view especially on the question of intrinsic value. "The Judeo-Christian Stewardship Environmental Ethic confers objective intrinsic value on nature in the clearest and most unambiguous of ways: by divine decree."[11]

GOD AND MAN

THE IMAGE OF GOD

Most of Genesis 1 addresses the creation, and the value, of non-human nature. But the chapter closes with a statement about the creation of human beings and the nature of being human. "Then God said, 'Let us make man in our image, according to our likeness; and let them rule over the fish of the sea and the birds of the sky and over the cattle and over all the Earth, and over every creeping thing that creeps on the Earth.' God created man in his own image, in the image of God he created him; male and female he created them. God blessed them and God said to them, 'Be fruitful and fill the Earth; and rule over the fish of the sea and over the birds of the sky and over every living thing that moves on the Earth.' "[12]

The phrase "in our image" is not to be understood as God making human beings look like him or that human beings can do the things that God does. Rather, in the time and culture in which the text was written, images served rulers as symbols of authority, and images were used in worship as a means through which the deity acted. As Old Testament and Hebrew language scholar John Walton explains, "the deity's work was thought to be accomplished through the idol. The Hebrew word *selem* ("image") is a representative in physical form, not a representation of physical appearance . . . The image is a physical representation of divine (or royal) essence that bears the function of that which it represents; this gives the image-bearer the capacity to reflect the attributes of the one represented and act on his behalf."[13] Thus, the text is stating that God is making human beings a representative of himself to non-human creation and will act through them to accomplish his purposes for the creation.

CULTIVATING AND KEEPING

We have seen in Chapter Two that much of modern environmental ethics is divided along one major fault line: whether the appropriate ethical strategy is to emphasize the value of nature or to emphasize the moral agency of human beings. The recurring problem of environmental ethics has been its failure to connect a moral estimate of nature's value with specific prescriptions of how humans should *behave* toward nature. As ethicist Willis Jenkins puts it, "Without the simultaneous purchase on natural description and moral agency, the ethicist bears the burden of providing and justifying an additional mediating concept [between value and moral agent] to impress the action-shaping force of an intrinsic value attribution."[14]

Together, Genesis 1 and 2 provide the needed simultaneous purchase. After humans have been made in the image of God and commanded to rule the creation as representatives of God, they are given prescriptive tasks of how to express their authority. "Then the Lord God took the man and put him into the Garden of Eden to cultivate it and to keep it."[15] The story of Genesis 1 and 2 depicts the world as the temple of God, and the Garden of Eden is established for the first human habitation as the inner sanctuary. In this arrangement, the fact that humans are made in the image of God gives them the capacity to act as a priest, mediating between God and the natural world. Again Walton discerns the contextual meaning well:

> The verbs *abad* ("work") and *shamar* ("take care of") are terms most frequently encountered in discussions of human service to God

rather than descriptions of agricultural tasks. . . . When the verb [*abad*] does not take a direct object, it often refers to work connected with one's vocation . . . The verb *shamar* is used in the contexts of the Levitical responsibility of guarding sacred space as well as for observing religious commands and responsibilities . . . since there are other indications that the garden is being portrayed as sacred space, it is likely that the tasks given to Adam are of a priestly nature—that is, caring for sacred space. In ancient thinking, caring for sacred space was a way of upholding creation.[16]

In the juxtaposition of Genesis 1 and 2, we have clear connection between the intrinsic value of nature and the moral agency of human beings that is essential for the formation of a meaningful environmental ethic. God's creation is intrinsically good. Human beings, made in the image of God, have unique capacities to represent God's intention to creation, along with unique authority from God to carry them out. In these few verses we find answers to three of the most important questions of environmental ethics. What is the basis for assuming an intrinsic value of nature; what gives humans the right to exercise authority over nature; and what is the moral responsibility of human beings to nature? The Genesis answer: nature is intrinsically valuable because of divine perception and decree. Humans exercise authority over nature because they are unique in being made in God's image and endowed with the capacity of moral judgment, and they are given the authority to exercise such moral judgment as representatives of God on Earth. The nature of their responsibility is to serve and protect (the better translations of the verbs, rather than cultivate and keep) what God has made. In his original created state, man has the capacity to know good and evil but in actuality knows only good. He is free from inherent desire to do evil, and is postured in his own will to pursue good and follow God's directives in doing so.

As nature's existence is derived from God's work, so human authority over nature is derived from being made in God's image and in pursuing a care and use of the Earth deemed proper by God. It is on this single point that critics of the Christian tradition make their most serious errors. For David Orr, the problem "The Trial" could not effectively address is resolved if a correct understanding is clear. Humans alone have the capacity to be morally responsible agents to nature, and humans alone have responsibilities to nature that transcend their own needs. They are not on trial before other species but before God, who has given them the mandate by which they will be judged.

Similarly, it is on this same point that Lynn White, Jr. makes his most egregious mistake. The error is subtle, but extremely significant, and resides in two closely connected statements. "No item," wrote White, "in the physical creation had any purpose save to serve man's purposes." A few sentences later, White seems to repeat himself by saying, "Christianity ... insisted that it is God's will that man exploit nature for his proper ends."[17] As essayist Wendell Berry perceived, the fundamental error lies in White's inability to see the critical difference between "man's purposes" and "man's proper ends."[18] The proper ends of the human effort, as defined in Genesis 1 and 2, are to use uniquely human capacities to rule over nature for its service and protection, benefiting not only human life but all other life as well. Man's purposes, on the other hand, have become, in our modern world, something quite different than his proper ends. The Bible reveals the origin and nature of these differences in Genesis 3.

CREATION AND JUDGMENT–THE FAILURE OF HUMAN MORAL AGENCY IN THE CREATED ORDER

THE CORRUPTION OF THE AUTHORITY AND IMAGE OF GOD

As the Bible will reveal in the chapters and books that follow Genesis, God is a righteous being possessing clear and inerrant understanding of right and wrong. Further, he is committed to doing right, to establishing justice in both the human and the non-human world. Because humans are the agent-representatives of God, their actions, for good or evil, will affect the created order, as well as God's view of and response to it.

In Genesis 3, the first man, Adam, and first woman, Eve, succumb to a temptation to disobey the sole prohibition God has placed upon them, that they should not eat the fruit of one tree, the tree of the knowledge of good and evil. Disobeying, they eat the fruit and come into possession of the knowledge of evil. Combined with their freedom of will as beings made in the image of God, they now are altered in their very nature, armed with a knowledge of how to disobey God combined with a will inclined to act out their disobedience. The consequences for the creation are immediate and severe. "Cursed is the ground because of you," God says to Adam. "In toil you will eat of it all the days of your life. Both thorns and thistles it shall grow for you; and you will eat the plants of the field; by the sweat of your face you will eat bread, till you return to the ground, because from it you were taken; for you are dust, and to dust you shall return."[19]

The work of humanity, which was to be a labor of joy and significance sharing the purposes of God toward creation, now becomes one of drudgery and, often, futility. It will now take all the labor man can muster to meet his own needs and stay alive. A creation formerly responsive to his activity and initiative is now, in biblical terms, set against him, and what it grows of itself will not be what he wants or needs. No longer to enjoy the dignity of their original vocation to serve and protect creation, the man and woman are cast out of the garden and forbidden to return. They will now discover the "privilege" of self-fulfillment, a toilsome and laborious life that must be centered on their own interests rather than God's. But the power of sin, the human inclination to do evil, has been set loose into the world and cannot be recalled. The humans have not lost their power to dominate nature, but they will no longer be inclined to do so for God's purposes, and harm will come to creation because of this perversion of their original vocation.

God's Judgment Against Creation

After Genesis 3, the biblical story begins to show the effects of sin in the world in multiple aspects of human life. It takes only another three chapters for God to reach a logically inescapable conclusion: "Then the Lord saw that the wickedness of man was great on the Earth, and that every intent of the thoughts of his heart was only evil continually. The Lord was sorry that he had made man on the Earth, and He was grieved in his heart. The Lord said, 'I will blot out man whom I have created from the face of the land, from man to animals to creeping things and to birds of the sky; for I am sorry that I have made them.' "[20]

If the ecological death wish observed in Professor Pianka, *After People*, and the Hollywood film *The Day the Earth Stood Still* is prevalent in many circles today, it is well to remember that God thought of it first. The creation is ruined, and the sin of man cannot be recalled. Yet God, who is not only morally blameless but compassionately creative, devises a plan that combines judgment and preservation, to be manifested in the life of a man named Noah. A flood will come that will serve as an instrument of judgment and an agent of cleansing: "Then God said to Noah, 'The end of all flesh has come before me; for the

Earth is filled with violence because of them [humans]; and behold I am about to destroy them with the Earth. Make for yourself an ark of gopher wood . . . and of every living thing of all flesh, you shall bring two of every kind into the ark, to keep alive with you; they shall be male and female.' "[21] And Noah began his task.

The flood comes. Noah's civilization and its human population are destroyed. But when the waters have receded, God sets a contractual agreement in place between himself and his creation. Known by theologians as the Noachian Covenant, its terms are expressed by God in this way, "Now behold, I myself do establish my covenant with you and with your descendants after you; and with every living creature that is with you, the birds, the cattle, and every beast of the Earth with you; of all that comes out of the ark, even every beast of the Earth. I establish my covenant with you; and all flesh shall never again be cut off by the water of the flood. . . . "[22]

The covenant described displays the intrinsic value of creation God established in Genesis 1. Because his creatures are good, they are treated as moral subjects. Because Noah is a man, made in the image of God, he acts as creation's representative to God in receiving the covenant, yet all living things are parties to it. Although not moral agents like Noah, the animals are moral *subjects* whom God considers worthy of inclusion in the covenant. They are given the equivalent of *rights* of covenant protection under the arrangement God describes. They become covenant partners with God. In judgment, God has destroyed human and non-human life. But in mercy, he has preserved the Earth's biodiversity and the role of humanity as its guardian, and he has reaffirmed the value of his creation, including his non-human creation, by elevating it to the status of a protected party in his covenant to preserve the Earth.

God's judgment against human sin in the flood is incomplete and provisional. Sin is not eliminated from the world, for it is present in Noah and his family, as in all humans, and its manifestations and effects are soon evident. What God has done is to create a pro tempore arrangement that protects and preserves the world from his appropriate judgments against sin until a time when a more complete redemption can be accomplished, when God will place himself, in a much more personal way, between a sinful world and his judgment against it. As the Bible continues it revelation of God, it also reveals that the sin which God condemns is not a psychological event in the human mind but a destructive force affecting all creation, human and non-human. Because sin affects not only the human race but every created thing, all creation stands in need of redemption and restoration. Therefore God includes consideration of non-human creation in establishing a people dedicated to himself, the nation of Israel, and in the laws that govern their life which would begin to form a pathway to a lasting redemption for the world.

A BIBLICAL UNDERSTANDING OF "THE LAND ETHIC"

As God continues his work of revealing himself to human beings, the channels of that revelation become increasingly specific. God calls out one man, Abram, from Ur of the Chaldeans,[23] which is probably in the region that today lies within the nation of Iraq. The call of Abram can be placed in the first half of the second millennium before the birth of Christ, probably between 1600 and 1800 BC. In God's revelation of himself to Abram, he promises that he will make of Abram "a great nation, and I will bless you, and make your name great, and so you shall be a blessing."[24] This promise is not abstract. God promises Abram not only a legacy of many descendants but a physical place for them to live, a land which would become their own by his direct provision. "Go forth from your country, and from your relatives and from your father's house, to the land which I will show you."[25] This land was Canaan. It would, in time, become the physical location of the nation of Israel and bear that name, even as it does today.

In the years that followed, God changed Abram's name from "exalted father" (Abram) to "father of a multitude" (Abraham), in anticipation of the promise that would be fulfilled in Abraham's many descendants. The land itself was central to the promise God had made to the nation and a critical part of his revelation of himself to the Israelites.

As this promised land was considered the ultimate fulfillment of God's blessing on an obedient people, the ultimate punishment for disobedience and rebellion against God was banishment and exile from the land. So the Jewish prophet Moses, who led Abraham's descendents to Canaan after they had suffered a long period of slavery in Egypt, spoke on behalf of God as he told the Israelites, as they were preparing to enter Canaan, "If you walk in my statutes and keep my commandments so as to carry them out, the I shall give you rains in their season, so that the land will yield its produce and the trees of the field will bear their fruit. Indeed, your threshing will last for you until grape gathering, and grape gathering will last until sowing time. You will thus eat your food to the full and live securely in your land."[26] Likewise the penalties for disobedience also are closely tied to the land-human relationship. "But if you do not obey me, and do not carry out all these commandments, . . . I will make the land desolate so that your enemies who settle in it will be appalled over it. You, however, I will scatter among the nations. . . . Then the land will enjoy its Sabbaths all the days of the desolation, while you are in your enemy's land; then the land will rest and enjoy its Sabbaths."[27]

This is God's second version of *After People*. But what is this "land Sabbath" referred to in this text? If we understand this concept, we will understand much of how God views land and how he views human treatment of it.

THE LAND SABBATH

English philosopher John Locke espoused a theory of the value of land based entirely on what humans generated from it:

Though the earth and all inferior Creatures be common to all men, yet every man has a property in his own person; this nobody has any right to but himself. The labour of his body and the work of his hands, we may say, are properly his. Whatsoever then he removes out of the state that nature hath provided, and left it in, he hath mixed his labour with, and joined to it something that is his own, and thereby makes it his property.[28]

According to Locke, land has no value until a person improves it. For its natural products, Locke shows nothing but contempt, "*Bread* is more than Acorns, *Wine* than Water, and *Cloth* or *Silk* than Leaves, Skins, or Moss."[29] From this view, Locke developed a theory of private property that made the landowner the holder of inalienable property rights that no king or government could usurp. The land and all its use belonged to the landowner by virtue of his investment of himself in it.

This is not a biblical view of land, but it is necessary to understand Locke's ideas, still dominant in modern culture as the basis for property rights, so that we may understand the contrasting view of land and property expressed in the Bible as God reveals his intentions and purposes for the land he has created. Moses speaks for God as he instructs the people on land use, explaining the concept of "the land Sabbath":

> When you come into the land which I shall give you, then the land shall have a Sabbath to the Lord. Six years you shall sow your field, and six years you shall prune your vineyard and gather its crop, but during the seventh year the land shall have a Sabbath rest, a Sabbath to the Lord. . . .[30]

God goes on to give instructions, not only for the land Sabbath to be observed every seven years but for a special observance in the year after the seventh sabbatical year (every fiftieth year):

> You shall thus consecrate the fiftieth year and proclaim a release through the land to all its inhabitants. It shall be a jubilee for you, and each of you shall return to his own property, and each of you shall return to his family . . . The land, moreover, shall not be sold permanently, for the land is mine; for you are aliens and sojourners with me.[31]

God's theory of property rights is different from Locke's. God does not impute ownership or rights of land to people because of their efforts. Rather, he sees their efforts as merely a "cooperative contribution," and a lesser one at that, to his own effort of making the land fruitful. Further, he includes the land within the provision of Sabbath rest. This is in part to benefit the land itself and the non-human creatures that live on it: "Even your cattle and the animals that are in your land shall have all its crops to eat."[32]

For people, an important purpose of the land Sabbath was to strengthen their faith in God and his ability to provide for them:

> But if you say, what are we going to eat on the seventh year if we do not sow or gather in our crops? Then I will so order my blessing for you in the sixth year that it will bring forth the crop for three years. When you are sowing the eighth year, you can still eat old things from the crop, eating until the ninth year when the crop comes in.[33]

The curse of the fall was that man would eat bread by the sweat of his face (Genesis 3:19). The blessing of the land Sabbath was that God's people would eat bread by the work of God while they rested from labor and the land rested from cultivation. The blessing of obedience would be not only continued residence on the land but an increasing experience of learning how to live by faith in the provision of God. Further, the Year of Jubilee, observed every fiftieth year, was to be an explicit recognition of God's ownership of the land, symbolic of a recognition of the control and autonomy of God over the universe, including the Earth. In this revelation, the land Sabbath is instituted so that God's people can recognize God as the land "owner," and his work, not their own, as the source of their provision.

These texts reveal God's intentions that, for people, blessing does not come from accumulation of real estate but from obedience to God's commands. But to place the emphasis on the human element in these statements is to do injustice to the text. The statements about the land Sabbath itself do not treat people as the subject. God does not say, "You shall give the land a Sabbath rest," but rather, *The land shall have* a Sabbath to the Lord" (emphasis mine). God treats that land as the subject of the action that is carried out. He views the land, in terms familiar to environmental ethicists, as morally considerable, an entity that can be treated rightly or wrongly by people, and therefore to be protected by divine provision through the institution of a Sabbath rest. The people of Israel benefit from the land Sabbath, but it is the land which receives it.

The significance of the land Sabbath is revealed in the severity of the punishment for breaking it. God has told his people that if they ignore his laws, including the land Sabbath, deportation and exile will be their punishment. In fact, the Israelites failed to observe God's command for the land Sabbath, at least after the institution of their monarchy, a period of about 490 years. They turned from God and worshipped idols, and they failed to establish a just and righteous community that would have revealed the nature and character of God. The promised penalty for disobedience was enacted. The final words of the book of II Chronicles close the story:

> Those who had escaped from the sword he [Nechudadnezzar, the Babylonian king and conqueror of Jerusalem] carried away to Babylon. . . . *to fulfill the word of the Lord by the mouth of the prophet Jeremiah, until the land had enjoyed its Sabbaths. All the years of its desolation it kept Sabbath until seventy years were complete.*[34] (emphasis mine)

Christopher Stone, in his classic work *Should Trees Have Standing,*[35] argues for giving legal rights to environmental entities like trees, animals, or ecosystems. Stone is careful to define what having rights constitutes in a legal sense. Something has rights if legal action can be instituted *at its behest*. In granting relief, the court must *take its injury into account*, and relief granted must *run to the benefit of the entity*. The revelation of II Chronicles 36 follows this understanding of rights in redressing the sins of the people against the land. Taking action on the land's behest to establish justice for it, God acts to see that the people are removed from it. In granting relief, God takes the injury of the land into account (its lack of rest) so that the type and length of punishment (rest for the land for 70 years, equal to the number of Sabbaths taken from it) run to the benefit of the injured party, the land. Although God's revelation of himself establishes the intrinsic value of his creation in Genesis 1, his institution of the land Sabbath, and his punishment for failing to obey it, adds depth to our understanding of what it means to impute value to nature.

The land Sabbath is exemplary of a pervasive biblical concept, that God views non-human nature as a morally considerable entity. The value of nature is neither a utilitarian calculation nor a philosophical abstraction. Nature exists under the sovereign control and care of God just as humanity does. Because nature is as much his subject as human beings, we can understand why God "speaks" to nature as he does to people, and so gives nature its own commands, laws, and rights. For example, the first use of the phrase "be fruitful and multiply" is not in a command given to humans (Genesis 1:28) but to birds and aquatic creatures (Genesis 1:22). As we have already seen, non-human creatures are explicitly included in God's covenant of protection for the Earth (Genesis 9:8–17). Likewise, non-human creatures are commanded to praise God for his greatness and goodness (for example, Psalm 148:7–10). As the land is given opportunity for a Sabbath of appropriate time scale in years, domestic animals are enjoined to observe the Sabbath with humans on its appointed day (Deuteronomy 5:14). But as non-human nature is subject to moral consideration under God's statutes and provision, so it is subject to his judgment against the evil that is within it. Although this evil did not originate in or from nature, nature is nevertheless affected by it. This relationship is captured in the words of the prophet Hosea. Speaking against the sins of the people of Israel, Hosea cries,

> Listen to the word of the Lord, O sons of Israel, for the Lord has a case against the inhabitants of the land, because there is no faithfulness or kindness or knowledge of God in the land. There

is swearing, deception, murder, stealing and adultery. They employ violence, so that bloodshed follows bloodshed. *Therefore the land mourns, and everyone who lives in it languishes along with the beasts of the field and the birds of the sky, and also the fish of the sea disappear.*[36] (emphasis mine)

In its work of revealing the nature and character of God, the Bible also unfailingly reveals sin to be a force of destruction in the natural world. Once set in motion, it destroys all things it touches, including non-human life. That is why the Bible presents human crimes against individuals and society as also being crimes against the environment (land) in which the crimes are committed. As Jeanne Kay explains, "The concept is crucial for understanding why the Bible threatens to punish misdemeanors in business or interpersonal relations with drought or eviction from the land. In the Bible, all moral and immoral deeds have positive or negative impacts on the land on which they are perpetrated, and the land responds accordingly."[37] Because non-human nature suffers from the effects of sin just as humans do, it stands in the same need of redemption as humans. That need brings us to the final topic we must consider to understand a biblical view of the environment.

NATURE'S REDEMPTION

The story of the Fall in Genesis 3 reveals the origin of evil in the world, and the story of Genesis 6–8 is God's judgment against that evil. The covenant of Genesis 9 established a provisional arrangement to protect the world from destruction in the face of God's judgment against the evil within it, and a system of animal sacrifices for sin likewise provided a provisional arrangement for the people of Israel to atone for sins they continued to commit. But these arrangements could not serve as permanent solutions, for both failed to rid the world of evil or fundamentally change human nature toward good. Against this need, the New Testament marks a turning point in its revelation of God's strategy and action to redeem the good world he had created from the evil that had entered it. For a student of the Bible, the turn is not unexpected, but long foreshadowed and foretold. This was the hope of the Messiah, a deliverer sent from God who would save God's people from their sins.

Speaking of the Messiah, the prophet Isaiah wrote, "The Spirit of the Lord will rest on him, the spirit of wisdom and understanding, the spirit of counsel and strength, the spirit of knowledge and the fear of the Lord, and he will delight in the fear of the Lord."[38] But the coming of the Messiah will not only reorder human society, but non-human creation as well. Isaiah continues, "the wolf will dwell with the lamb, and the leopard will lie down with the young goat, and the calf and the young lion and the fatling together, and a little boy will lead them ... They will not hurt or destroy in all my holy mountain, for the Earth will be full of the knowledge of the Lord as the waters cover the sea."[39]

The Messiah will inaugurate a new kingdom marked by acknowledgment of God's sovereignty and obedience to his commands. This kingdom is described in a real landscape, populated by animals and people. The prophet Hosea describes the redeemed environment as a place, as well as an arena of changed human relationships among nature, God, and man:

> In that day I will also make a covenant for them [God's people] with the beasts of the field, the birds of the sky and the creeping things of the ground. . . . It will come about in that day that I will respond, declares the Lord, I will respond to the heavens and they will respond to the Earth, and the Earth will respond to the grain, to the new wine and to the oil, . . . and I will sow her for myself in the land. I will also have compassion on her who had not obtained compassion, and I will say to those who were not my people, you are my people! And they will say, You are my God![40]

The Bible asserts that sin continues in the world because human beings are unresponsive to God's revelation of himself to them, and, in that state, are disobedient to his commands. But just as part of the curse of such disobedience was that nature would become unresponsive to human effort and intention, so the redemption God provides will be marked by "responsiveness" among humans, nature, and God. But who would or could accomplish this?

The New Testament introduces the one who brings the promised redemption. The Messiah comes in the person of Jesus Christ. In his actions, Jesus demonstrates the abilities consistent with and expected of a God who rules nature as a sovereign. He changes weather patterns with a word, calming wind and waves in a storm by simply saying, "Hush, be still" (Mark 4:39). He commands the movements of animals, domestic and wild (Mark 5:13, John 21:6) and heals diseases in human bodies and replaces sickness with health (Luke 8:43–48).

He teaches that people are uniquely important to God, but does so by showing the breadth of God's care for all creatures, "Look at the birds of the air, that they neither sow nor reap, nor gather into barns, and your heavenly father feeds them. Are you not worth much more than they? . . . "[41]

To save the world from its own sin, Jesus, the Son of God, sacrifices himself as a final and complete offering for sin, suffering death as a victim of a Roman crucifixion, and then rises from the dead, vindicating his claim as the Messiah. From this resurrection, a new religion, Christianity, arises out of Judaism. It adherents declare that forgiveness of sin is no longer provisional and no longer requires the maintenance of repeated sacrifices of animals, as was the custom in Judaism. Rather, in the words of the chief apostle of Christianity, Paul of Tarsus, "having been justified by faith, we have peace with God through our Lord Jesus Christ."[42]

It is sometimes perceived (because Christians sometimes mistakenly declare) that such redemption equates with the personal salvation of human beings. This is a part of what the Bible reveals about Christ's work, and it is a part human beings are naturally and intensely interested in. But the work of Christ's redemption is not only personal but cosmic and must be so, because of the need for redemption that exists in the entire creation. It is Paul who again explains it well:

> For by him [Christ] all things were created, in the heavens and on Earth . . . all things have been created through him and for him. He is before all things, and in him all things hold together. . . . For it was the Father's good pleasure for all the fullness to dwell in him, and through him to reconcile all things to himself, having made peace through the blood of his cross; through him, I say, whether things on Earth or things in heaven.[43]

The recurring two-word phrase of this passage, all things, is also a recurring two-word phrase in the original Greek text, τά πάντα. Paul asserts, first, that Jesus Christ created τά πάντα (Colossians 1:16). Second, Jesus Christ sustains τά πάντα (Colossians 1:17). And the "all things" that Jesus created and sustains are the very same "all things" that he reconciles "through the blood of his cross" (Colossians 1:20).

The New Testament shows the means through which the Old Testament's revelation of the need for redemption in both humans and nature is accomplished. They are linked in the person of Jesus Christ, who is the creator of both, and restored (saved) to right relationship with God because he is the redeemer of both. Paul therefore describes the atonement's effects in cosmic terms that achieve reconciliation between God and the created order. The atonement, the death of Christ, is the means through which Christ redeems the cosmos he created.

Such understanding is grounds for hope of creation's eventual redemption: "For the anxious longing of creation waits eagerly for the revealing of the sons of God. For the creation was subjected to futility, not willingly, but because of him who subjected it, in hope that the creation itself will be set free into the freedom of the glory of the children of God. For we know that the whole creation groans and suffers the pains of childbirth together until now."[44]

This promise of creation's redemption is the basis for the hope expressed by Simon Stuart and other conservation biologists in their response to David Orr (Chapter One). Remember their words, "Every time we celebrate a conservation success story such as the recovery of the white rhinoceros in southern Africa, we are strengthened in this present hope that God is working with us to redeem his creation; furthermore, these present successes are a very real foretaste of even greater things to come on that day when God will fully restore all that He has made."[45] In these statements, these biologists see and affirm the vision the apostle John described at the end of the Bible, in the book of Revelation. "Then I saw a new heaven and a new Earth; for the first heaven and the first Earth passed away ... And he who sits on the throne said, 'Behold, I am making all things new ...' "[46] And in the Bible's final words, we are presented with its answer to the last great question: What is the fate of nature? The Bible's answer is that the fate of nature is its redemption in the kingdom of God. Nature has a future. And because nature has a future, present conservation effort is both significant and appropriate to God's future purposes for it.

It has been said, perhaps by a cynical historian, that early Christians were expecting the return of Jesus, and what appeared was the church. This statement is true. The work and teaching of Jesus Christ, the savior and redeemer of both humans and nature, is carried forward by this institution, the Christian church.

NOTES

1. John 14:9, NASB.
2. John 5:39, NASB.
3. Isaiah 53:3, NASB.
4. Isaiah 53:5, NASB.

5. Isaiah 53:12, NASB.

6. Dallas Willard, *The Divine Conspiracy* (San Francisco: HarperSanFrancisco, 1998), p. xvi.

7. Jeanne Kay, "Concepts of Nature in the Hebrew Bible." In *Judaism and Environmental Ethics*, ed. Martin D. Yaffe (Lanham, MD: Lexington Books, 2001), p. 101.

8. Nahum Glatzer, ed., *A Jewish Reader* (New York: Schocken Books, 1961). Quoted in David Ehrenfeld and Philip J. Bentley, "Judaism and the Practice of Stewardship." In *Judaism and Environmental Ethics*, p. 126.

9. David Hume, *A Treatise on Human Nature, Volume 1: Texts*. ed. D. F. Norton and M. J. Norton (Oxford, UK: Clarendon Press, 2007), p. 301.

10. C. S. Lewis, *The Abolition of Man or Reflections on Education with Special Reference to the Teaching of English in the Upper Forms of Schools* (New York: MacMillan, 1978), p. 15.

11. J. Baird Callicott, "Conservation Values and Ethics." In *Principles of Conservation Biology*, ed. Gary K. Meffe and C. Ronald Carroll (Sunderland, MA: Sinauer Associates, 1994), pp. 24–49, 36.

12. Genesis 1:26, NASB.

13. John Walton, *Genesis, The New NIV Application Commentary* (Grand Rapids, MI: Zondervan, 2001), pp. 130, 131.

14. Willis Jenkins, *Ecologies of Grace: Environmental Ethics and Christian Theology* (Oxford, UK: Oxford University Press, 2008), p. 45.

15. Genesis 2:15, NASB.

16. Walton, pp. 172, 173. I have changed Walton's expression of the Hebrew verbs by transliterating their spelling using English alphabetical characters. In his own text, Walton omits the vowels and inserts special characters to fully capture the written form of the verbs in Hebrew.

17. Lynn White, Jr., "The Historical Roots of Our Ecologic Crisis," *Science* 155 (1967): pp. 1203–1207, 1205.

18. Wendell Berry, "The Gift of Good Land." In *The Gift of Good Land: Further Essays Cultural and Agricultural by Wendell Berry* (New York: North Point Press, 1982), p. 269.

19. Genesis 3:17–19, NASB.

20. Genesis 6:5–7, NASB.

21. Genesis 6:13–14, NASB.

22. Genesis 9:9–11, NASB.

23. Genesis 11:28, NASB.

24. Genesis 12:2, NASB.

25. Genesis 12:1, NASB.

26. Leviticus 26:4–5, NASB.

27. Leviticus 26:14, 32–34, NASB.

28. John Locke, "The Second Treatise of Civil Government," Chapter V, "Of Property," in *Two Treatises of Government*, ed. Thomas I. Cook (New York: Hafner Press, 1947), p. 134.

29. Ibid., Sections 37, 42.
30. Leviticus 25:2–4, NASB.
31. Leviticus 25:10, 23, NASB.
32. Leviticus 25:7, NASB.
33. Leviticus 25:20–22, NASB.
34. II Chronicles 36:19–21, NASB.
35. Christopher Stone, *Should Trees Have Standing? Towards Legal Rights for Natural Objects* (Los Altos, CA: William Kaufmann, 1974).
36. Hosea 4:1–3, NASB.
37. Kay, p. 96.
38. Isaiah 11:2–3, NASB.
39. Isaiah 11:6–7, 9, NASB.
40. Hosea 2:18, 21–23, NASB.
41. Matthew 6:26, NASB.
42. Romans 5:1, NASB.
43. Colossians 1:16–17, 19–20, NASB.
44. Romans 8:19–22, NASB.
45. Simon Stuart and others, "Conservation Theology for Conservation Biologists—An Open Letter to David Orr," *Conservation Biology* 19 (2005): pp. 1689–1692, 1690–1691.
46. Revelation 21:1, 5, NASB.

CHAPTER 4

The Church and the Environment

I believe in God, the Father Almighty, the Maker of heaven and Earth.

The Apostles' Creed, Second century AD

THE EARLY CHURCH AND THE ENVIRONMENT– CREATION AND NATURAL REVELATION

The first century world into which the Christian church was born had no concept of an environmental crisis and no sense of need to develop an environmental ethic. Hence, no one should be surprised if neither is addressed in the writings of Christian leaders of this period. But a more fundamental question is relevant, stated with clarity by the historian Lynn White, Jr., "What did Christianity tell people about their relations with the environment?"[1]

From Judaism, Christianity inherited a view that God was the creator of a good world that was an active witness and revelation of his glory and power. In the words of Psalm 19, it was a world in which, "The heavens are telling the glory of God; the skies proclaim the work of his hands."[2] Paul affirmed theologically what the Psalmist expressed poetically, "For since the creation of the world, his [God's] invisible attributes, his eternal power and divine nature, have been clearly seen, being understood through what has been made. Therefore, they [unbelievers] are without excuse."[3] The patriarch Clement of Alexandria, writing to Christians at Corinth, told them,

For in His overwhelming might He has set up the heavens, and by His unsearchable wisdom He has put them in order. He has separated the earth from the surrounding water and placed it on the solid foundation of His own will; and He has called into existence the animals that move in it by His own arrangement.[4]

If Christians shared with Jews the view of the world as a creation of God and an active revelation of his character and attributes, they were more explicit in their understanding of precisely how God had chosen to create the world and reveal himself in it, and this increasing clarity is achieved through explication of the Trinity, that God exists as three persons: Father, Son, and Holy Spirit. This is a difficult concept, beyond human experience, but one so essential the apostle John is willing to throw his readers straight into this deep end of theology, "In the beginning was the Word, and the Word was with God, and the Word was God. He was in the beginning with God. All things came into being through him, and apart from him nothing has come into being that has come into being. . . . " As the prologue continues, John follows a chain of logic to reveal that this Word, God's agent of creation, was Jesus Christ, and John is an eyewitness of this revelation of the Word as a human being, "And the Word became flesh and dwelt among us, and we beheld his glory, glory as of the only begotten of the Father, full of grace and truth. . . . For the law was given through Moses. Grace and truth were realized through Jesus Christ."[5]

John opens his gospel to address Jewish and Greco-Roman readers in terms both would understand, speaking to questions each considered significant but to which each had different answers. Writing in Greek, John calls this Word the *logos*. Among the Greeks, Stoic philosophers named the *Logos* (which they all but personified) as the principle of divine reason (*logos spermatikos*) which caused the natural creation to flourish and grow. But Greek philosophy, exemplified in Aristotle and Plato, held that the world had always existed, that it had no beginning. Thus, in such a world view, the *Logos*, although important in causing continued growth in creation, was not its source and certainly not to be identified as a person.

Jews, on the other hand, would identify the Word as the creative agent of God, for that is how Genesis describes God bringing the world into being ("And God said, let there be light. And there was light."),[6] but they too would not naturally assume that the word possessed a personal and distinct nature from God. To the Greeks, John asserts that the *Logos*, not the world, is pre-existent. It is this *Logos* that brings the world into being. To both audiences, John demonstrates that this Word is God the Father's agent of creation, revealed in human form as the person of Jesus Christ.

In many religions, such as Islam, the idea that God would become a man is not considered merely false but positively disgusting, something the Almighty would never do. To take human form would be beneath his dignity. To Christians, however, this *incarnation* of God in flesh shows both the unrelenting determination of God to fully reveal himself to creation, as well as the depth of love he bore the world and the lengths he would go to save it. Jesus explained the situation saying, "For God so loved the world [*cosmos*, the entire physical universe] that he gave his only begotten Son, that whoever believes in him shall not perish, but have eternal life. For God did not send the Son into the world to condemn the world, but that the world might be saved through him"[7] In the Noachian Covenant, God's provisional symbol of protection of the world against his judgment was a rainbow, a symbol of his personal presence (Ezekiel 1:28, Revelation 4:3). In the New Testament, the protection is no longer symbolic and provisional but personal and permanent. Indeed, it is no longer protection at all, but salvation and redemption.

This incarnational understanding of God's redemptive action had two profound effects on the thinking of early Church patriarchs. First, it gave them a high view of matter and the material world. Matter was not to be worshipped, but it was the divine means through which God chose to be present to human beings in the world as well as the means through which he would save the world. Second, it provided them with a vision of redemption for the entire universe, achieved through a human being, Jesus Christ, whose sacrifice was of such cosmic consequence that the entire creation would be redeemed through him.

THE PATRIARCHS–THE DIGNITY OF MATTER AND THE REDEMPTION OF CREATION

The first-century church was birthed in a hostile environment. Suspect and often persecuted by Roman authorities for its demands of ultimate allegiance to Christ rather than the emperor, it was internally beset with heresies that could have altered its most basic doctrines, and externally threatened by a world steeped in pagan animism, the deification of nature and natural objects.

One of the most pervasive and corrosive of heresies that threatened the infant church was Gnosticism, a loose body of beliefs united by the idea that the material world was evil and only the spiritual was good. Human beings were viewed as composite life forms consisting of divine souls trapped in physical bodies. Like Christians, Gnostics asserted that man had to find an escape from his sinful predicament, but, unlike Christians, Gnostics believed only the spirit would be saved, not the body. Through an elaborate system of secret rituals and knowledge, Gnostics hoped they would eventually escape a sinful material world and enter into a fully spiritual, nonmaterial state. Ironically, in its identification of matter and the physical body as evil, Gnosticism taught its adherents that physical sins, that is, anything done with the human body itself, were of no consequence. Thus, Gnosticism sanctioned and even encouraged actions traditionally regarded as immoral, even by pagans. But, to Christians, the most serious error of Gnosticism was its belief that God had no relationship with the physical world and took no responsibility for it.

Unlike Gnosticism, Christianity did not teach a divided "body-soul" nature, but rather that believers in Christ would be physically resurrected in a glorified, but still in some sense physical, body (I Corinthians 15:35–44, Philippians 3:20–21). Further, Christianity did not see matter or the material world as evil but as good. The human body was understood as a temple of God (I Corinthians 6:19) to be presented to God as a living sacrifice. Paul uses this term in contrast to the sacrifice of a dead animal, which can perform no service to God. Instead, Paul tells his readers that the human body is to be used as an instrument of good; therefore they are to present their bodies to God "as living sacrifices, which is your spiritual service of worship."[8]

In distinguishing Christian faith from Gnosticism, the Patriarchs were explicit, even vehement, in their clarity of expression. The Christian affirmation of the material world was coupled with an imminent expectation of the return of Christ and the redemption of all creation accomplished through him. Athanasius, writing in the fourth century AD, said, "It is well, then, in treating of this subject, to speak first of the creation of the universe, and of God its Artificer, in order that one may duly perceive that its re-creation has been wrought by the Word who originally made it. For it will not appear at all inconsistent for the Father to have wrought its salvation in Him through whom He made it."[9]

Paul repeatedly affirms in his letters that Christ's work as Redeemer affects all of creation and is sufficient in its scope and power to accomplish the redemption of every created thing (Colossians 1:15–20). The second-century theologian Irenaeus developed perhaps the most extensive theology of this idea through his theory of "recapitulation," in which Christ embodies all of creation in his incarnation in order to reclaim it from the effects of sin. Jesus, wrote Irenaeus, "recapitulates all things in Himself, so that, as the Word of God rules over the super-celestial, spiritual, and invisible, so He has primacy over the visible and the corporeal."[10]

As elements of Aristotelianism and Neo-Platonism entered Christian theology in subsequent centuries, the early emphasis on the value of creation and the redemption of all of creation in Christ began to fade. The Greek philosopher Aristotle taught that all things had been created for use by man. Plato taught that material objects were imperfect representations of perfect forms that existed in a spiritual realm. Some of the patriarchs, like Origen, embraced these ideas, teaching not only that everything on Earth was made for man but that the world itself was evil and a manifestation of the effects of sin. But this was not a normative view in the church. Augustine, Bishop of Hippo in the fourth century AD, argued against the idea that all non-human creation had been made only for man's use. "It is not with respect to our comfort or discomfort, then, but with respect to their own nature, that created things give glory to their Maker,"[11] wrote Augustine. He explained further with a humorous analogy:

> If an unskilled person enters the workshop of an artificer he sees in it many appliances of which he does not understand the use, and which, if he is a foolish fellow, he considers unnecessary. Moreover, should he carelessly fall into the fire, or wound himself with a sharp-edged tool, he is under the impression that many of the things there are hurtful; whereas the craftsman, knowing their use, laughs at his folly. And thus some people presume to find fault with many things in this world, through not seeing the reasons for their existence. For though not required for the furnishing of our house, these things are necessary for the perfection of the universe.[12]

Basil, Bishop of Caesarea, gave attention to creation through his homilies on the first chapter of Genesis. He shared Augustine's view that all things were not made for man, especially animals, whom he

called "our brothers" because they shared, with humans, a common
creator, and, in that sense, a common "Father." His understanding
that non-human creatures possessed a good of their own, and a value
in the sight of God, is revealed in one of his prayers:

> O God, enlarge within us the sense of fellowship with all living
> things, Our brothers the animals to whom Thou gavest the Earth
> as their home in common with us. We remember with shame that
> in the past we have exercised the high dominion of man with
> ruthless cruelty so that the voice of the Earth, which should have
> gone up to Thee in song has been a groan of travail. May we real-
> ize that they live not for us alone, but for themselves and for
> Thee. And that they love the sweetness of life even as we, and
> serve Thee better in their place than we in ours.[13]

Here, in only a few words, Basil deftly addresses the issues of right
relationships between humans and animals, God's provision for animals, the correct understanding and use of human dominion over
nature, and the intrinsic value of animals for their own sake in the
sight of God. In another prayer for animals, Basil, again with elegance
and brevity, affirms the New Testament doctrine of the redemption of
all creation by praying

> For those, O God, the humble beasts, that bear with us the bur-
> den and the heat of day,
> And offer their guileless lives for the well-being of mankind;
> And for the wild creatures, whom Thou hast made wise, strong
> and beautiful,
> We supplicate for them Thy great tenderness of heart,
> For Thou hast promised to save both man and beast, and great is
> Thy loving kindness,
> O Master, Savior of the world.[14]

THE PROBLEM OF PAGAN ANIMISM

If Gnoticism attempted to subvert Christianity by teaching that the
material world was sinful and not truly "real," the surrounding culture
attempted to destroy it by teaching that nature and natural objects
were the home of spiritual beings, with each spirit requiring its own
distinctive obeisance, worship, and sacrifice. Contrary to the assertion
of Lynn White, Jr., this spiritual enchantment of the environment did

less to preserve nature from destruction than it did to promote immoral and debased behavior in humans. Speaking of the decline of the Roman civilization, the British essayist G. K. Chesterton noted that the Roman Empire

> ultimately suffered from the same fallacy [as Greek civilization] in her religious tradition; which was necessarily in no small degree the heathen tradition of nature worship. What was the matter with the whole heathen civilization was that there was nothing for the mass of men in the way of mysticism, except that concerned with the mystery of the nameless forces of nature, such as sex and growth and death.... What happened to the human imagination, as a whole, was that the whole world was colored by dangerous and rapidly deteriorating passions; by natural passions becoming unnatural passions.[15]

The apostle Paul says the same more directly, "Professing to be wise, they become fools, and exchanged the glory of the incorruptible God for an image in the form of corruptible man and of birds and four-footed animals and crawling creatures."[16]

Faced with these conditions, the church prescribed strong medicine. That medicine was asceticism, a practice of strict self-denial which, in some cases, led saints to live their lives in places so desolate that they would rarely see any living thing, and thus not be tempted to worship nature. Again to quote Chesterton,

> It was no good telling people to have a natural religion full of stars and flowers; there was not a flower or even a star that had not been stained. They had to go into the desert where they could find no flowers or even into the cavern where they could see no stars. Into that desert and that cavern the highest human intellect entered.... and it was the very wisest thing to do.... Whatever natural religion may have had to do with their beginnings, nothing but fiends now inhabited those hollow shrines. Pan was nothing but panic. Venus was nothing but venereal vice.[17]

In such an environment, Christianity developed strong ascetic elements, not against nature but against nature worship. Yet the early emphasis on the goodness of creation still persisted beyond the Patriarchal period even as the church continued to stress that matter and nature were not divine and not objects of worship. St. John of

Damascus, writing in the seventh century, expressed this distinction with clarity and theological skill:

> I do not worship matter, I worship the Creator of matter who became matter for my sake, who willed to take his abode in matter; who worked out my salvation through matter. Never will I cease honoring the matter that wrought my salvation. I honor it, but not as God ... Because of this I salute all remaining matter with reverence, because God has filled it with his grace and power. Through it my salvation has come to me.[18]

CREATION AND THE MEDIEVAL CHURCH

THE MONASTIC ORDERS—DEFINING THE HUMAN RELATION TO CREATION IN COMMUNITY

Under the Roman Emperor Constantine, criminal penalties against Christians within the Roman Empire were removed and the government restored confiscated Church property. What began as toleration evolved into favoritism, as Constantine began to give political and monetary aid to the Christian church, support the building of cathedrals, give privileges to Christian clergy, and promote Christians to high office. His reign marked a turning point in Christian history, changing the relationship between the Christian church and the state from animosity to privileged position that led to a functional union between them, and to the beginnings of the Roman Catholic Church. With the elevation of the church to this favored status, the monastic tradition began to flourish and expand. Religious orders no longer had to fear persecution or confiscation of property, and so could work, serve, and preach openly and could retain property essential to sustaining permanent residences for their members.

In this more favorable political climate Benedict of Nursia established a monastery at Monte Cassino in southern Italy. Benedict taught that "Idleness is the enemy of the soul."[19] Thus, "the brothers should have specified periods for manual labor as well as for prayerful reading."[20] And if, from poverty and lack of gifts from benefactors, monks had to grow and harvest their own food, Benedict asserts that, "They must not become distressed if local conditions or their poverty should force them to do the harvesting themselves. When they live by the labor of their hands, as our fathers and the apostles did, then they are really monks."[21] Benedictine monks were not preservationists. In their labor, they intervened in nature as farmers and landscapers, but they sought not to exploit nature rapaciously but to order it productively. Thus, in a practical manner by the work of their hands, the Benedictines affirmed the goodness of the Earth which God had made, and from which they derived their daily bread.

The early monastics sometimes withdrew from the world in order to avoid the temptations of the flesh, but, although ascetic and disciplined, they did not despise the natural world around them. A twelfth-century Cistercian monk, viewing the landscape around the Cistercian monastery at Clairvaux, spoke of how the river that meandered near the monastery nourished the fish, watered the crops and trees, and fed a nearby lake. The Cistercian did not simply describe these conditions, but endeavored, with gratitude, to list all the services provided by the stream, which he described variously as "friendly," "faithful," and "kindly," for the purpose of giving "thanks due to it."[22]

By this time, the church's ascetic disciplines had produced their desired effect. They purged the western world of pagan animism and nature worship and of the moral depravity that had accompanied it. With this success, the church had cleared the way for a reengagement with nature that did not make it an object of worship but a revelation of God and a gratefully acknowledged provision for humankind. By the Middle Ages, the church had begun to practice Rogation Days, observed for three days before Ascension Day (40 days after Easter). During Rogation Days, priests would go about the fields of landowners and peasants blessing the land and its harvest and praying for its continued bounty. [23]

In his failure to understand the church's struggle against nature worship and animism, Lynn White, Jr. makes some of his greatest errors of interpretation in "Historical Roots." In his discussion of the calendar art of the Middle Ages, White wrote, "In older calendars, [before 830 AD] the months were shown as passive personifications. The new Frankish calendars, which set the style for the Middle Ages, are very different: they show men coercing the world around them—plowing, harvesting, chopping trees, butchering pigs. Man and nature are two things, and man is master."[24]

The passive personifications White refers to were usually Greek or Roman gods and goddesses, such as the Roman deity Janus, the god of beginnings and endings, who was associated with the month of January. The reason these minor deities ceased to be portrayed on calendars was because no one believed in them anymore. Freed from the superstitions and fears of animism and nature worship, people, guided by the church's teaching, saw nature as a real and good gift of God. In that understanding, they also saw the joy and dignity of their own labors in it. To suggest that slaughtering pigs or gathering acorns represent humans "coercing the world around them" is simply silly, and would mean that every human civilization on the planet, even the most primitive, is constantly engaged in a ruthless exploitation of the natural world. Neither did the church teach such a doctrine. Actual studies of Bible commentaries of the Middle Ages on passages like Genesis 1:28 ("fill the Earth and subdue it, and rule over the fish of the sea and the birds of the sky . . . ") rarely show interest in learning how to dominate the Earth, but instead are usually directed to understanding God's covenant with mankind or with understanding the implications of human sexuality.[25]

The simple practice of priests and monks moving about the countryside blessing the fields and harvests veils a far greater change that Christian teaching and practice were making on the understanding of the human relationship to nature compared to that of pagan animism. The monasteries that formed the centers of religious communities, from which the monks went forth and to which they returned, were communities in which members appreciated the blessing and provision of nature and were actively grateful for it. This led to a continuance of careful agriculture practices to sustain both the community and the landscape in which it resided.

By the late Middle Ages, Christian monasteries had not only grown in number and presence in the landscape but also in religious and cultural influence. Some were becoming centers of learning and scholarship. In these, some of Christianity's greatest saints and scholars were nurtured. One of the most influential was Thomas Aquinas.

THE INTELLECTUAL FOUNDATION—THOMAS AQUINAS AND THE NATURE OF CREATION

Thomas Aquinas was the foremost scholar of medieval Catholicism. A priest of the Dominican Order in the thirteenth century, the second part of Aquinas's name is derived not from family but from residence, Aquino, modern day Lazio in Italy. As a youth, he acquired the nickname "the dumb ox," perhaps because he was large by physique and silent by temperament. Aquinas more than made up for his oral silence through his writings, the most famous of which is *Summa Theologica*, a summary of his answers to the greatest philosophical and theological questions of his time. In *Summa*, Aquinas begins with God, his nature and existence, and the relationship between God and man, especially how man became estranged from God and how he may return to God through Christ. Aquinas organized his work into sections, divided the sections into questions (what we might today call issues) and the material on questions into articles (which we might more readily recognize as essays).

In section I, question 20 is "Whether Love Exists in God?" Aquinas examines God's relationship to his creation. In doing so, he constructs an argument for the intrinsic goodness and value of nature.

> God loves all existing things. For all existing things, in so far as they exist, are good, since the existence of a thing is itself a good: and likewise whatever perfection it possesses. Now it has been shown above (Q[uestion] 19, A[rticle] 4), that God's will is the cause of all things. It must needs be, therefore, that a thing has existence, or any kind of good only inasmuch as it is willed by God. To every existing thing, then, God wills some good. Hence, since to love anything is nothing else than to will good to that thing, it is manifest that God loves everything that exists.[26]

Aquinas then explains why God's love for his creation is superior to any love that humans could generate for it.

> Since our will is not the cause of the goodness in things, but is moved by it as by its object, our love, whereby we will good to anything, is not the cause of goodness; but conversely its goodness, whether real or imaginary, calls forth our love, by which we find that it should preserve the good it has, and receive besides the good it has not, and to this end we direct our actions: whereas the love of God infuses and creates goodness.[27]

Thus, God's love is not a *response* to the good qualities of non-human creatures but an active force that *inspires* good in them; it expresses itself by desiring their preservation and providing for their needs.

In *Summa*, Aquinas makes five arguments for the existence of God. His fifth and final argument to demonstrate God's existence is the orderly governance of the natural world. Here Aquinas again takes up God's work in creation. Specifically, why are there many things and not just one thing? If God is One, do these different things come from God as a reflection of his goodness? Or is such diversity an imperfection, a deviation from God's goodness in a sinful world? Aquinas answers:

> God brought many things into being in order that his goodness might be communicated to creatures and represented in them; and because this goodness could not be adequately represented by one creature alone, God produced many and diverse creatures, so that what was wanting to one in the representation of divine goodness might be supplied by another. For goodness which in God is simple and uniform, in creatures is manifold and diverse. Hence the whole universe together participates in the divine goodness more perfectly, and represents it better than any single creature whatever.[28]

Further, says Aquinas, God creates diversity so that his divine goodness may be shared among created things in their interactions with one another. Not only is the diversity of non-human creatures good, but so are the purposes they follow to secure their own interests. Not only is God the creator of the universe, he is also the creator and originator of every purpose which each creature pursues in the course of living the life God has given to it. Therefore, every purpose which a creature follows that is intrinsic to its own nature can be described as a good purpose. Although each creature pursues its own purposes, the interaction of these purposes is ultimately cooperative and mutually beneficial: "Though God is the first pattern of all creatures, creatures can be secondary patterns for each other. God is the ultimate goal of all creatures, but creatures can also serve each other ... The order of the world consists in creatures acting on, patterning themselves on, and serving one another."[29]

Everything, says Aquinas, "acts for an end: otherwise one thing would not follow more than another from the action of the agent, unless it were by chance."[30] But God works for an end that is truly unique and different. He is unselfishly motivated toward the good of his creations, and all creation will ultimately move toward this end. As Aquinas puts it, God

> intends only to communicate his perfection, which is His goodness; while every creature intends to acquire its own perfection, which is the likeness of the divine perfection and goodness. Therefore, the divine goodness is the end of all things. ... All things

desire God as their end, when they desire some good thing, whether this desire be intellectual or sensible, or natural, i.e. without knowledge; because nothing is good and desirable except forasmuch as it participates in the likeness to God. . . .[31]

Aquinas is criticized by some modern environmental ethicists because some statements in *Summa* suggest that all creatures were created for man's use. But these critics only reveal that they do not fully grasp the extent of what Aquinas envisions as "use," nor his depth of imagination in considering what sorts of relationships humans can participate in with other creatures. Aquinas is thinking not only of utilitarian purposes, such as the use of beasts for food or to carry burdens, but the use humans can find for beasts to enjoy them as they are and see in the biodiversity of God's creatures a reflection of the perfection and purposes of God. Additionally, Aquinas notes that not all kinds of use of creatures were appropriate or wise.

Creatures of themselves do not withdraw us from God, but lead us to him; for *the invisible things of God are clearly seen, being understood through what has been made* (Romans 1:20). If then, they withdraw men from God, it is the fault of those who use them foolishly ... And the very fact that they can thus withdraw us from God proves that they came from him, for they cannot lead the foolish away from God except by allurements of some good they have from him . . .[32]

FRANCIS OF ASSISI

If Aquinas provided intellectual warrant for valuing God's creation, it was the monastic orders of the church and their leaders that provided its expression. Religious orders established monasteries as centers for contemplation, prayer, worship, and learning. To sustain themselves, they also needed to interact effectively and sustainably with the world around them. Even in religious orders in which monks were itinerant, making a living by asking for alms (begging), interaction with the non-human environment was inescapable. This interaction was not only significant to their own needs, but to people they were called to serve.

As in the Patriarchal period, the medieval world had no concept of an ecologic crisis, so the religious orders did not address one. Most focused their ministries primarily on the human condition, but we find cases in which awareness of the natural world becomes important.

Lynn White, Jr. noted this in *Historical Roots*, citing the example of Francis of Assisi, whom he offered "as a patron saint for ecologists."[33] But what did Francis and his followers believe and do that supports this commendation?

Francis was the son of a wealthy cloth merchant, Peter Bernadone of Assisi, near modern Umbria in central Italy. As a young man, Francis developed a reputation for high living and elegant tastes, along with admirable generosity to the poor. At age 24, Francis took part in a war that broke out between his own city of Assisi and neighboring Perugia. He was captured in battle and imprisoned. Eventually returning home, Francis suffered a long period of illness that, combined with his experience in the war, began to alter his view of life.

Francis had little formal education, but had been instructed by priests in his youth and was familiar with Christian doctrine. Increasingly striving to follow the example of Jesus, Francis began to devote himself to the care of the poor and the sick, especially persons affected with the dreaded skin disease of leprosy, which was common at that time in his region. Within two years after he had begun this ministry, Francis is credited with having restored three churches and gained a personal following of 12 disciples. Within 11 years, his order had grown to more than 5,000 members.[34]

The Franciscans differed from most other orders in their vow of abject and complete poverty. They were itinerant, having no permanent monastery, but wandering from town to town, begging alms. But it would be incorrect to ascribe these practices to traditional asceticism. Rather, they were carefully calculated strategies Francis employed to make himself and his followers more effective at spreading the gospel of Jesus Christ. We see this logic in the way Francis answered his bishop about the conditions of the members of his order. The bishop, upon gaining a firsthand knowledge of the circumstances in which Francis and "the Little Brothers" were living—without comforts, without possessions, eating whatever they could get, and sleeping in the open on the ground—was horrified. He urged Francis to make some provision for acquiring possessions for their needs. Francis replied, "If we had any possessions, we should need weapons and laws to defend them."[35] In this simple reply lay the genius of Francis's movement. Because there was nothing in the world the Franciscans depended on, nothing could hold or hinder their work. In this, Francis saw himself and his followers as freer than ordinary men, ready, at a moment's notice, to go wherever God might direct them. Thus, Francis and his followers were constantly "in" nature, intimately connected with it and relying upon it, whether for finding berries to eat along their journeys or a tree in a forest under which to sleep. It was this mode of life, coupled with his understanding and experience of nature, which made Francis particularly sensitive to understanding the unique relationship of every created thing with God.

Stories of Francis and his work include many instances of healing the sick and other miracles, as well as what would be called today revivals, with entire communities and towns turning to Christ in response to his preaching. People who heard Francis preach or pray were deeply moved by his tender heart, his transparent simplicity, and his profound insight into the nature of God. The surviving writings of Francis include songs (canticles) he composed for worship. In these, we see a man who identified not only with people, with but all creation. Anyone who reads Francis directly will recognize that Francis was not a "nature lover" in the modern sense of the term. As one of his biographers, G. K. Chesterton noted,

> Saint Francis was not a lover of nature. Properly understood, a lover of nature was precisely what he was not. The phrase implies accepting the material universe as a vague environment, a sort of sentimental pantheism ... the hermit might love nature as a background. Now for Saint Francis nothing was ever in the background. He saw everything as dramatic, distinct from its setting, not all of a piece like a picture but in action like a play.[36]

Francis saw in each creature a dignity and value in its relation to God, and a spirit that was unique to it, not in a pantheistic sense but in its own relation to God as one of his creatures. Following the example of Psalm 19 ("The heavens are telling the glory of God, and their expanse is declaring the work of his hands ... "), Francis composed "Canticle of the Creatures," sometimes called "Canticle of the Sun." Here he begins with his own praise to God and continues, through the use of repeated couplets, in an exhortation for a variety of created things to join him and add their praises to the chorus:

> Most High, all-powerful, all-good Lord,
> All praise is Yours, all glory, honor and blessings.
> To you alone, Most High, do they belong;
> No mortal lips are worthy to pronounce Your Name.
> We praise You, Lord, for all Your creatures,
> especially for Brother Sun,

Who is the day through whom You give us light.
And he is beautiful and radiant with great splendor,
Of You Most High, he bears your likeness.[37]

As the canticle continues, Francis exhorts praise to God from
"Sister Moon," "Brother Wind," "Sister Water," "Brother Fire," and
"Sister Mother Earth," finally calling upon death itself to praise God,

We praise You, Lord, for Sister Death,
from whom no-one living can escape.
Woe to those who die in their sins!
Blessed are those that She finds doing Your Will
No second death can do them harm.[38]

Francis did not simply contemplate the non-human creation in
abstract ways. He interacted with it poignantly and powerfully.
We see examples of this in *The Little Flowers of Saint Francis of Assisi*,
a collection of stories about Saint Francis and his associates compiled
about 200 years after his death based on oral traditions of Francis's
work that had survived to that time. The stories tell of how important
people became his followers, of his long fasts and prayers, and of his
moving sermons that convinced many to follow Christ. *The Little
Flowers* also contains accounts of Francis's interaction with nature.
In one case where Francis is called to preach to the residents of a castle
called Saurviriano, his preaching is interrupted by the twittering of
swallows residing in the castle's walls. Francis commands the swallows, as Jesus did the wind and waves (Mark 4:39), to be quiet until
he has finished preaching, and, in the words of the author of *The Little
Flowers*, "the swallows obeyed him; and he preached in that place with
such fervor that all the men and women in that castle, from devotion,
would have followed after him."[39]

Of all Francis' miracles described in *Little Flowers*, the one that most
clearly captures his view of the dignity of non-human creatures is the
story of the wolf of Gubbio, a "very great, terrible and fierce wolf, which
not only devoured animals, but even also men,"[40] Gubbio is a small
town in north-central Italy on the southwest slope of the Apennine
Mountains. Francis, hearing of the ravages of the wolf, is moved with
compassion for the townspeople and their livestock and travels to
Gubbio. Going into the forest in search of the wolf, he finds it, greets
the creature with the sign of the cross, and addresses the wolf with
these words: "Come hither, Brother Wolf; I command you in the

name of Christ Jesus, that you do no manner of evil either to me or to any other man."[41] And the wolf, which had been running toward Francis with his jaws open, "came meekly as any lamb, and laid himself down at the feet of Saint Francis."[42]

Francis then rebukes the wolf for killing beasts without God's permission, and worse: "you have dared to kill men, made in the image of God, and all the people cry out."[43] But at this point Francis shows his characteristic courtesy and compassion, even to an animal, saying, "But I desire, Brother Wolf, to make peace between you and them, so that you offend no more; inasmuch as it pleases you to keep this peace, I promise you that I will see to it that your living shall be given to you continually, so long as you shall live, by the men of this country forasmuch as I am well aware that hunger has caused you every crime."[44]

Francis charges the wolf to follow him back into the village, where the contract they have reached is to be ratified by the townspeople. The wolf obeys, and Francis, acting a bondsman between the wolf and the people, confirms the agreement. Francis, however, also uses the occasion to preach to the people. As fearful as the wolf is, says Francis, it "can but kill the body, so much more therefore should ye fear the jaws of hell. . . . Turn then, my Beloved, unto God, and repent worthily of your sins." In response, "all began to cry aloud unto heaven, praising and blessing God, that had sent unto them Saint Francis."[45]

Lynn White, Jr. attempted to portray Francis as a heretical radical, lucky to escape persecution by church authorities. "The prime miracle of Saint Francis," wrote White, "is that he did not end up at the stake. . . ."[46] Such interpretation aids White's claim that "establishment Christianity" never understood or approved of Francis, and that his theology was heretical, but this view has no basis in fact. Less than two years after his death, Pope Gregory IX canonized Francis and commissioned Brother Thomas of Celano, a friend and associate of Francis, to write an account of his life. In his charge, Gregory not only commissioned Thomas to honor the saint through this writing, but to instruct readers about the importance of Francis' life and his pathway to holiness.[47] These instructions are hardly intelligent tactics if the church was trying to stamp out "the Franciscan doctrine of the animal soul," as White called it.[48] Francis never proposed such a doctrine. He was not concerned with saving animal souls but with respecting whatever creature was presented to him, for he recognized each existed in relationship to God, just as he did.

Nature, the Monastic Tradition, and the Catholic Church

The consideration of nature in theology and holy living did not die with Francis but continued in his order through its future leaders, like Bonaventura, who became the leader of the Franciscans in 1257. More theologically erudite than Francis, if less charismatic, Bonaventura described six stages of ascent to the knowledge of God in his book, *The Mind's Road to God*. The contemplation of God in nature, said Bonaventura, is the first. All creatures lead the mind to contemplate God because they are "shadows, echoes and pictures, the traces, simulacra, and reflections of that First Principle most powerful, wisest, and best; of that light and plenitude; of that art productive, exemplifying, and ordering, given to us for looking upon God."[49]

Here Bonaventura shows a strong strain of neo-Platonism, perceiving the value of creatures not in themselves, as Aquinas taught and Francis demonstrated, but in the "perfection" of the forms they only imperfectly represented. Nevertheless, Bonaventura in no way demeans nature or offers any warrant to abuse it.

With the onset of the Reformation, Christian thought was recast in ways that weakened authority of church tradition and elevated the authority of the Bible itself. Reformed theologians removed the emphasis on good works as a means of salvation and replaced it with the precept of salvation by faith alone. The Reformation's rallying cry, *Sola Scriptura, Sola Fides* (Scripture alone, faith alone) summarized these critical distinctions. With its renewed emphasis on faith, there was within the Reformation a strain of "otherworldliness" that tended to devalue non-human nature and the importance of its study. But with their renewed attention to the Scripture as the authoritative rule of faith and practice, reformers also rediscovered the importance of biblical doctrines about creation.

Of all Reformation leaders, Martin Luther is most recognized and synonymous with the establishment of Protestantism as an independent expression of Christian faith. Luther, like Catholic theologians before him, had no environmental crisis to address. He had bigger fish to fry in his debates and conflicts with the Catholic Church. But Luther, through his attention to Scripture, did begin to assert biblical teachings about creation that had diminished or altogether disappeared in Catholic thought. Chief among these was a renewed emphasis on a right understanding of human dominion over nature and the redemption of non-human nature in Christ. Of all reformers, Luther

communicates the greatest sense of sorrow over the present relationship of humanity to nature. Referring to God's charge to humans to
rule and subdue the Earth, Luther wrote, regarding the human capacity to rule nature, that

> All our faculties today are leprous, indeed dull and utterly dead.
> Who can conceive of that part, as it were, of the divine nature,
> that Adam and Eve had insight into all the dispositions of all
> animals, into their characters and all their powers? What kind of
> a reign would it have been if they had not had this knowledge?
> Among the saints there is evident in this life some knowledge of
> God. Its source is the Word and the Holy Spirit. But the knowl-
> edge of nature—that we should know all the qualities of trees and
> herbs, the dispositions of all the beasts—is utterly beyond repair
> in this life.[50]

In his sorrow over the loss of a right relationship between humans
and nature, Luther considered human technology not a way to restore
the pre-fall state, but as an evidence and fruition of sin:

> What we achieve in life, however, is brought about, not by the
> dominion which Adam had but through industry and skill. Thus
> we see the birds and the fish caught by cunning and deceit; and
> by skill the beasts are tamed. . . . Therefore even now, by the
> kindness of God, this leprous body has some appearance of the
> dominion over the other creatures. But it is extremely small and
> far inferior to that first dominion, when there was no need of skill
> or cunning, when the creature simply obeyed the divine voice
> because Adam and Eve were commanded to have dominion over
> them. Therefore we retain the name and word "dominion" as a
> bare title, but the substance itself has been almost entirely lost.[51]

Not all of Luther's theological expressions were in Bible commentaries. His remarks on the redemption of nature, while equally well
grounded theologically, are sometimes placed in ordinary conversation. When asked if dogs, particularly his own dog Tölpel, would
inhabit heaven, Luther answered, "Certainly, for there the earth
would not be without form and void. Peter said that the last day would
be the restitution of all things. God will create a new heaven and a new
earth and new Tölpels with hide of gold and silver. God will be all in
all; and snakes, now poisonous because of original sin, will then be

so harmless that we shall be able to play with them."[52] These are simple and homely statements, yet in them, Luther not only addresses the concept of creation's redemption, but explains the words of Peter, which some have taken as reason to believe that the present Earth will be destroyed, as statements referring to the Earth's redemption and renovation.[53]

Luther was not unique in his rediscovery of biblical concepts defining the human relationship to creation. John Calvin, the Swiss reformer, often falls under criticism in environmental circles for his unequivocal statements that the Earth and all it contains were made for man. This view, not original with Calvin, reflects an Aristotelian rather than a Christian understanding of nature. Yet even while laboring under this misconception, Calvin demonstrates a thoroughly biblical understanding of human dominion and stewardship far from simple utilitarianism and provides no basis for an abuse of nature. In his *Commentaries on the First Book of Moses Called Genesis*, Calvin writes on Genesis 2:15 ("Then the Lord God took the man and put him into the garden of Eden to cultivate it and keep it"[54]):

> The custody of the garden was given in charge to Adam, to show that we possess the things which God has committed to our hands, on the condition that, being content with a frugal and moderate use of them, we should take care of what shall remain. Let him who possesses a field, so partake of its yearly fruits, that he may not suffer the ground to be injured by his negligence: but let him endeavor to hand it down to posterity as he received it, or even better cultivated. Let him so feed on its fruits, that he neither dissipates it by luxury, nor permits it to be marred or ruined by neglect. Moreover, that this economy, and this diligence, with respect to those good things that God has given us to enjoy, may flourish among us; let everyone regard himself as the steward of God in all things which he possesses.[55]

If Luther and Calvin display a biblical understanding of dominion and stewardship, it is John Wesley who takes the doctrine of creation's redemption to new levels of theological understanding and ethical application. One example is expressed in Wesley's sermon, "The General Deliverance," based on Romans 8:19–22. In this text, Paul describes the entire creation waiting "eagerly for the revealing of the sons of God" because "the creation itself will be set free from its slavery to corruption into the freedom of the glory of the children of God."[56]

In explaining this passage, note the surprisingly modern tone of Wesley's words as he addresses ethical issues still relevant today and answers charges of God being cruel to his creatures:

> May it not answer another end; namely, furnish us with a full answer to a plausible objection against the justice of God, in suffering numberless creatures that never had sinned to be so severely punished? They could not sin, for they were not moral agents. Yet how severely do they suffer!—yea, many of them, beasts of burden in particular, almost the whole time of their abode on Earth; so that they have no retribution here below. But the objection vanishes away, if we consider that something better remains after death for these poor creatures also; that these, likewise, shall one day be delivered from this bondage of corruption, and shall then receive an ample amends for all their present sufferings.[57]

What does await these creatures after death? Wesley explains,

> The whole brute [animal] creation will then ... be restored, not only to the vigour, strength and swiftness which they had at their creation, but to a far higher degree of each than they ever enjoyed. ... And whatever affections [qualities, skills, and abilities] they had in the garden of God, will be restored with vast increase; being exalted and refined in a manner which we ourselves are not now able to comprehend.[58]

Wesley concludes with a practical discussion on the proper treatment of and regard for animals by humans:

> One more excellent end may undoubtedly be answered by the preceding considerations. They may encourage us to imitate Him whose mercy is over all his works. They may soften our hearts towards the meaner creatures, knowing that the Lord careth for them. It may enlarge our hearts toward those poor creatures, to reflect that, vile as they appear in our eyes, not one of them is forgotten in the sight of our Father which is in heaven.[59]

These examples are illustrative of a Reformed understanding of the interaction of humanity and nature. The reformers had no environmental crisis to address, but they explored and developed the biblical concepts of dominion, stewardship, intrinsic value, and redemption in regard to the interactions of people and nature.

As the Reformation changed people's relationship to the church, the Industrial Revolution, which had its beginnings in the latter portion of the Reformation period, changed the human relationship to nature. It is in these latter changes that we find some of the most difficult challenges and most dangerous threats to the non-human world. How did Christian theology and practice speak to the Industrial Revolution? Was the church its opponent, its advocate, or only a silent and ineffectual witness of its harmful effects?

NOTES

1. Lynn White, Jr., "The Historical Roots of Our Ecologic Crisis," *Science* 155 (1967): pp. 1203–1207, 1205.

2. Psalm 19:1, NASB.

3. Romans 1:19–20, NASB.

4. Clement, "The Letter to the Corinthians." In *The Apostolic Fathers*, trans. Francis X. Glimm, Joseph M. F. Marique, and Greald C. Walsh (New York: Cima, 1947), p. 35.

5. John 1: 1–3, 14, 16–17, NASB.

6. Genesis 1:3, NASB.

7. John 3:16–17, NASB.

8. Romans 12:1, NASB.

9. Athanasius, *On the Incarnation of the Word of God*, trans. T. Herbert Bindley (London: Religious Tract Society, 1903), pp. 42–43.

10. Irenaeus, *The Scandal of the Incarnation: Irenaeus Against the Heresies*, ed. Hans Urs von Balthasar, trans. John Saward (San Francisco: Ignatius Press, 1981), p. 63.

11. Augustine, *The City of God Against the Pagans*, ed. and trans. R. W. Dyson (Cambridge, UK: Cambridge University Press), p. 503.

12. Quoted in Thomas Aquinas, *Summa Theologica* Volume I (New York: Benziger Brothers, 1947), p. 352.

13. Quoted in Sean McDonagh, *The Greening of the Church* (Maryknoll, NY: Orbis, 1990).

14. Ibid.

15. G. K. Chesterton, *Saint Francis of Assisi* (Peabody, MA: Hendrickson, 2008), pp. 16–17.

16. Romans 1:22–23, NASB.

17. Chesterton, pp. 18–19.

18. Quoted in James A. Nash, *Loving Nature: Ecological Integrity and Christian Responsibility* (Nashville, TN: Abingdon Press, 1991), p. 109.

19. Benedict, *The Rule of Saint Benedict in English*, ed. Timothy Fry (Collegeville, MN: Liturgical Press, 1982), p. 69.

20. Ibid.

21. Ibid.

22. Summarized in Jame Schaefer, *Theological Foundations for Environmental Ethics: Reconstructing Patristic and Medieval Concepts* (Washington. DC: Georgetown University Press, 2009), p. 46.

23. Roderick Nash, *The Rights of Nature: A History of Environmental Ethics* (Madison: University of Wisconsin Press, 1989), p. 98.

24. White, p. 1205.

25. Elspeth Whitney, "Christianity and Changing Concepts of Nature: An Historical Perspective," in *Religion and the New Ecology: Environmental Responsibility in a World in Flux*, ed. David M. Lodge and Christopher Hamlin (Notre Dame: University of Notre Dame Press, 2006).

26. Thomas Aquinas, *Summa Theologica*, Vol. I. trans. Fathers of the English Dominican Province (New York: Benzinger Brothers, 1947), p. 115.

27. Ibid.

28. Ibid., p. 246.

29. Quoted in Denis Edwards, *Ecology at the Heart of Faith* (Maryknoll, NY: Orbis, 2006), p. 90.

30. Thomas Aquinas, *Summa Contra Gentiles*, quoted in Michael S. Northcutt, *The Environment and Christian Ethics* (Cambridge, UK: Cambridge University Press, 1996), p. 229.

31. Thomas Aquinas, *A Summa of the Summa: The Essential Philosophical Passages of St. Thomas Aquinas' Summa Theologica Edited and Explained for Beginners*, ed. Peter Kreeft (San Francisco: Ignatius Press, 1990), p. 191.

32. Ibid., pp. 220–221.

33. White, p. 1207.

34. Regis J. Armstrong and Ignatius C. Brady, trans., *Francis and Clare: The Complete Works* (New York: Paulist Press, 1982).

35. Chesterton, p. 80.

36. Ibid., pp. 67–68.

37. Francis of Assisi. Text is in the public domain. Accessed at the website of The Prayer Foundation, http://www.prayerfoundation.org/canticle_of_brother_sun.htm. Accessed February 2, 2010.

38. Ibid.

39. Anonymous, *The Little Flowers of Saint Francis*, ed. Louise Bachelder, trans. Abby Langdon Alger (Mount Vernon, NY: Peter Pauper Press, 1964), p. 24.

40. Ibid., p. 31.

41. Ibid.

42. Ibid.

43. Ibid.

44. Ibid., pp. 31–32.

45. Ibid.

46. White, p. 1206.

47. Armstrong and Brady, p. 14.

48. White, 1207. White himself attributes this phrase to Sir Steven Ruciman, but gives no reference.

49. Bonaventura, *The Mind's Road to God*, trans. from the Latin by George Boas (New York: Liberal Arts Press, 1953), quoted in Clarence J. Glacken, *Traces on the Rhodian Shore* (Berkeley: University of California Press, 1967), p. 238.

50. Martin Luther, *Luther's Works, Volume I, Lectures on Genesis Chapters 1–5*, ed. Jaroslav Pelikan (St. Louis: Concordia Publishing House, 1958), p. 66.

51. Luther, p. 67.

52. Quoted in Scott Ickert, "Luther and Animals: Subject to Adam's Fall?" In *Animals on the Agenda*, ed. Andrew Linzey and Dorothy Yamamoto (Urbana: University of Illinois Press, 1998), pp. 90–99, 91.

53. The text Luther is referring to is II Peter 3:10. "But the day of the Lord will come like a thief, in which the heavens will pass away with a roar and the elements will be destroyed with intense heat, and the Earth and its works will be burned up." Luther, with his knowledge and command of Greek, knew that the verb translated in many English Bibles as "burned up" is the Greek *heurethēsetai*, derived from the Greek *heureskein*, "to find" and from which is derived the transliterated Greek-English expression, "Eureka" or "I found it." A better translation of this verb in the oldest manuscripts is therefore "discovered," "laid bare," "revealed," "found" or "found out." That is, Luther would have understood Peter to be saying that in the final judgment of God preceding its ultimate redemption, the Earth and its works will be "revealed." Therefore, this is not a statement describing the destruction of the Earth but of the purging and cleansing nature of its judgment prior to redemption. In fact, the 1985 version of Luther's German Bible (*Deutsche Bibelgesellschaft Stuggart*) translates the phrase as "the Earth and the works upon it will find their judgment." A more recent Dutch translation puts it as "the Earth and the works upon it will be found." In light of the significance of this verse, and the extremely different impression that is given from "burned up" compared to "revealed" or "found," ethicist and language scholar Steven Bouma-Prediger called this case "perhaps the most egregious mistranslation in the entire New Testament." Steven Bouma-Prediger, *For the Beauty of the Earth: A Christian Vision for Creation Care* (Grand Rapids, MI: Baker Academic, 2001), pp. 76–77.

54. Genesis 2:15, NASB.

55. John Calvin, *Commentaries on the First Book of Moses Called Genesis* (Grand Rapids, MI: Eerdmans, 1948), p. 125.

56. Romans 8:19, 21. NASB.

57. John Wesley, "The General Deliverance," in *The Works of John Wesley*, Vol. VI (Grand Rapids, MI: Zondervan, 1958), p. 251.

58. Ibid., p. 249.

59. Ibid., pp. 251–252.

CHAPTER 5

The Industrial Revolution and the Church: The Real Historical Roots of the Ecologic Crisis

Man has too long forgotten that the earth was given to him for usufruct alone, not for consumption, still less for profligate waste.

George Perkins Marsh, *Man and Nature*[1]

THE INDUSTRIAL REVOLUTION–RADICAL CHANGES IN TECHNOLOGY, ECONOMICS, AND ATTITUDES

When I first read these words of George Perkins Marsh in his environmental classic *Man and Nature* (1864), I had to look up "usufruct." This obscure noun is defined in my well-worn dictionary as "the legal right of using or enjoying the profits of something belonging to another."[2] Written in the United States at the height of nineteenth-century optimism in industrial progress and the prosperity that would surely result from it, Marsh's words did not find a receptive audience. Marsh's subject was not theology but the record of human destruction of the natural systems of the Earth, an analysis of the tragic consequences of this destruction on past civilizations, and a warning that a similar fate could befall the present generation if it did not recognize the dangers of modern industrialization and change its ways. But here, in his introductory chapter, Marsh makes a cryptic but incisive remark about *why* human beings should not do these things to the Earth: The Earth does not belong to man, and has not been given him to do with as he wills.

From the first century to the late Middle Ages, church leaders, scholars, and reformers had established that the usufruct Marsh refers to was grounded in the knowledge that humans were subject and subordinate to God, both in their nature and their desires. In their elaboration of this fundamental relationship, three ideas dominate. First, the physical world is neither eternal nor divine, neither to be taken for granted nor worshipped. It is a creation of a sovereign, eternal God. People can enjoy the fruits of the Earth, but they do not own them. Second, the non-human world is good, valuable in and of itself. Among its creatures man is unique, created in the image of God, to know and understand the world in limited ways, and to carry out God's intentions toward the world as his representative to non-human creation. Third, all creation has been scarred by human disobedience to God and suffers from the effects of sin that such disobedience has loosed into God's good creation. Therefore, all creation is included in God's plan and purpose of redemption that will one day remove the effects of sin and restore humans and nature to a right relationship with God. That Marsh should note this point, almost offhandedly, as if everyone knew it, suggests that the Christian church, for all its shortcomings, had made this truth widely known.

From the first to the eighteenth century, human culture, art, invention, science, knowledge, and literature advanced slowly, but with a continuity that made the past relevant to the present. The writings of Hippocrates continued to be important to practicing physicians. The principles used by engineers of the second and third centuries were still used to build cathedrals in the fifteenth. Italian philosopher Machiavelli consulted the Roman constitution for his writings on political science in the sixteenth century. But this continuity was about to come to a rapid and intellectually violent end through a radical transformation of the way in which humans would restructure their technology, their economy, and their use and sources of energy. And these changes would transform the human relationship to nature. This transformation, although its foundations had been being laid for centuries in the past, began in earnest from 1700 to 1900, a period that has been called the Industrial Revolution. The past became only a source of history, not a source of education. As historian C. M. Cippola expresses it, by the mid-nineteenth century "the past was not merely past—it was dead."[3]

One of the most critical changes occurred in the human relationship to energy. Again Cipolla addresses it precisely: "The Industrial

Revolution opened up a completely different world of new and untapped sources of energy such as coal, oil, electricity and the atom, exploited by means of various mechanisms—a world in which Man found himself able to handle great masses of energy to an extent inconceivable in the preceding bucolic age ... the Industrial Revolution can be defined as the process by which society gained control of vast sources of inanimate energy...."[4]

Since the early Middle Ages, people had been improving techniques of harnessing water and wind power to grind grain, pump water, and tell time, but these developments had been slow with respect to history and benign with respect to nature. Flowing water and moving wind are indirect forms of solar energy. The *stock* of such energy was large, but the *flow* or *rate* at which it could be used was slow. One cannot speed up the hydrologic cycle or change the direction and velocity of air currents. But if one could learn to use a form of energy that was different, that was stock limited, but flow abundant, all that would change. The process of making iron is one such example.

For millennia humans had known how to make iron, but the process requires intense heat. Heat was produced from burning wood, but heat generated this way is relatively low, and the iron produced, by modern standards, was of poor quality. Further, the process was limited by an environmental effect, deforestation. As wood is used in large quantities in making iron, forests disappear, wood becomes scarce, and making iron becomes increasingly unfeasible.

As early as the tenth century AD, people in both European and Asian cultures had attempted to replace wood with coal, but the coal produces noxious gases, fumes, and hazardous solid by-products that make it dangerous to use. In the late Middle Ages, iron manufacturers began to refine the so-called *coking process*, a technique in which coal could be burned in an airless furnace, driving off most of its volatile gases, water, and tar. The residue, called coke, is more stable, can be burned with little or no emission of gases, and is used as a fuel for heating furnaces to make iron. The higher temperatures generated from using coke, along with other desirable properties, increase the quality of iron produced and the size of the blast furnaces used to forge it. Coal then became the raw material to produce coke. With large deposits of coal near the surface in many European countries, it became possible to make increasing amounts of high-quality iron at faster rates, a significant contributing factor to industrial development.

CAPITALISM AND THE ORGANIZATION
OF MARKETS

Most people in most of the world today cannot imagine a nonmar-
ket economy, except in the now-defunct and deservedly ridiculed
examples of formerly communist countries who tried to manage their
economies through central planning. But for much of history, mankind had no conception of markets as we understand them today. Just
as changes in technology played a critical role in changing the human
relationship to nature from the seventeenth century onward, so did
changes in the organization of local and national economies.

Capitalism needs three things to operate effectively, all of which
were in limited use or nonexistent until the late Middle Ages. First,
capitalism requires economic decisions to be organized through the
use of markets (individual bargaining decisions). Second, it requires
the institution of private property and a way of enforcing rights associated with private property so that accessibility and use of resources
needed for production can be made exclusive to an individual or group
and thus becomes part of the individual bargaining decisions needed
for market organization. Finally, capitalism requires surplus production to be used for reinvestment to create greater productive capacity.[5]
Such changes in economic behavior profoundly affect human use and
organization of resources and, therefore, the human relationship to
nature. The market becomes the model not only for economic activity
but for human relationships. In a market-modeled society, work
becomes the central human activity. Man no longer works to live.
He lives to work.

Throughout the middle ages, land was the basis of wealth, as it was
also the basis of work. Populations were rural and dispersed, for
human energy and productivity came directly through and from plants
and animals. As technology developed the capacity to harness ever
increasing quantities of energy for work from coal and, in time, oil
and natural gas, the production process could be centralized in single
locations. The market model for exchange of goods also became the
model for organizing labor, and the emergence of the labor market,
with labor demand greatest in urban centers of production, drew rural
populations into cities. Relations between managers and laborers,
which in past ages might have been based on land tenure, historic
family relationships, or personal loyalties, were now organized on
market principles in which labor was but another good to be bought

and sold. For skilled and productive workers, this arrangement increased wealth. But the less skilled and less productive were less marketable and therefore often unemployed. The cumulative effect was part of the reason for an increase in the number of poor even at a time of growing national wealth.

TECHNOLOGY AND ECONOMY: UNEXPECTED EFFECTS OF INDUSTRIALIZATION

The modern proverb among environmentalists, "you can never do just one thing," was all too true during the Industrial Revolution. Technologies developed or applied for one goal often proved more useful in attaining previously unforeseen objectives, with the result that entirely new, hitherto unimagined markets were created. Natural entities formerly considered worthless were transformed into valuable resources. The history of the railway is one example.

Railways had been developed before there were trains. By the sixteenth century, miners had learned that a horse could pull a heavy load more easily if provided with a smooth, level track to walk on and if the wheels of the cart were set on metal rails, reducing the friction between the wheel and its surface. Thus, the first rail cars were pulled not by trains, but by horses.[6]

As coke, derived from coal, provided an alternative source of heat, mining coal to make coke became more profitable. Surface pits to remove coal became deeper, eventually striking groundwater that flooded the pit, threatening to end the mining operation. Pumps, powered by horses, were installed to remove the water, but at some mines, the quantity of water flooding the pit was so great it took hundreds of horses to operate the pumps. Thus arose demand for a mechanically powered device that could remove water and replace horses. James Watt is well known as the inventor of the steam engine. Less well known is that one of the steam engine's first applications was to remove water from mining pits. Watt and others then realized that a steam engine could also replace the horse as the means to move the coal from the pit. And if the steam engine could power a device that could run on the already existing rails, the prospects of transporting the coal to new markets would be expanded.

So it was in England, and later throughout Europe, that the first railroads were developed, not to carry people from place to place, but to carry coal from mine to market. As historian Samuel Lilley noted, commenting on an early rail line in England from Stockton to Darlinton, "Nobody foresaw how the carriage of coals and merchandise would create its own passenger traffic—soon amounting to five or six hundred a week."[7] Previously, coach traffic between these towns carried 14 or 15 passengers per week. Without intention or plan, railroad builders created the first commuters, and this commuter traffic, not the transport of coal, became the principal source of railway income. As a result, the network of railroads, originally envisioned as a small number of lines connecting coal fields with neighboring cities, spread throughout all of England to take people from one place to another.[8] Work was separated from residence, and life from community.

This example is one illustration of many unintended and unforeseen effects of industrialization and capitalist, market-centered economic reorganization. But what intellectual engine fueled the development of the technologies that supported both? To understand that basis, we turn to the writings of Francis Bacon.

FRANCIS BACON AND SCIENTIFIC INDUCTION– KNOWLEDGE OF NATURE IS POWER OVER NATURE

At the height of his political career from 1613 to 1621, Francis Bacon was Lord Chancellor of England under King James I, and bore the additional titles of Counsel Learned Extraordinary to His Majesty, King's Solicitor-General, His Majesty's Attorney General, Counselor of Estate, and Keeper of the Great Seal of England. Even at an early age, Bacon began to consider what his life mission should be:

> I therefore asked myself what could most advantage mankind, and for the performance of what tasks I seemed to be shaped by nature. But when I searched, I found no work so meritorious as the discovery and development of the arts and inventions that tend to civilize the life of man ... Above all, if any man could succeed. ... in kindling in nature a luminary which would, at its first rising, shed some light on the present limits and borders of human discoveries, ..., it seemed to me that such a discoverer would be called the true Extender of the Kingdom of Man over the universe, the Champion of human liberty, and the Exterminatory of the necessities that now keep men in bondage.[9]

No one can fault Bacon for lack of ambition. Despite the pomposity of his prose, Bacon, in his writings on philosophy, particularly in *The Advancement of Learning* and *Novum Organum*,[10] contributed an original idea, an early expression of the inductive method to gain new knowledge in science. Bacon asserted knowledge should be acquired "not by *arguing* but by *trying*." "There are," said Bacon,

> and can be only two ways of searching into and discovering truth. The one flies from the senses and particulars to the most general axioms, and from these principles, the truth of which it takes for settled and immovable, proceeds to judgment and to the discovery of middle axioms [deductive reasoning, from the whole to a part]. And this way is now in fashion. The other derives axioms from the senses and particulars, rising by a gradual and unbroken ascent, so that it arrives at the most general axioms last of all. This is the true way, but as yet untried [i.e., inductive reasoning, from the part to the whole].[11]

Bacon was an advocate of progress and of technology as its agent. "Neither the naked hand nor the understanding left to itself can effect much. It is by instruments and helps that the work is done, which are as much wanted for the understanding as for the hand. And, as the instruments of the hand either give motion or guide it, so the instruments of the mind supply either suggestions for the understanding or cautions."[12]

With his emphasis on progress and technology, Bacon also believed in application. Knowledge was a resource to be used for specific ends. It is this perspective that has led many to attribute to Bacon the saying "knowledge is power." And the power that Bacon sought was power over nature. Bacon himself never used those exact words, but he does say something like it: "Human knowledge and human power meet in one; for where the cause is not known the effect cannot be produced."[13]

Of all historical figures, Bacon is most often the villain or foil for those who argue that the developments of the Industrial Revolution were the primary cause of the environmental crisis, and that the methods and machines of the Industrial Revolution sprang from a Baconian attitude toward nature as something to be controlled by man. Bacon is often credited with the saying that nature must be "tortured" to give up her secrets, the knowledge of which then becomes the resource to craft power against her. In fact, Bacon never used such language. The phrase was employed later by one of his admirers, Gottfried

Wilhelm von Leibniz, writing in praise of the use of experimentation which Bacon commended. Leibniz failed to distinguish, as Bacon did, between the concept of torture and the experimental process of agitating or provoking a state of nature in pursuit of examining a hypothesis.[14]

Bacon is himself a person of tragic-comic ironies. In one of his works he quotes Proverbs 28:20, "He that maketh haste to be rich shall not be innocent,"[15] yet is himself later charged, in 1621, with accepting bribes in his office as Lord Chancellor and loses his position.[16] He advocates the method of induction through experimentation, yet conducts only one experiment in his life, which results in his death. Baconian scholar Matthew Thomas writes,

> While driving from Highgate to London he conceived the idea that dead flesh might be preserved longer if kept very cold. With Bacon to conceive was to execute. He alighted from his carriage, procured a chicken from a nearby house, killed it, and packed it in snow. The weather was very cold, and due to the exposure to which he was subjected, he caught a severe cold which swiftly led to his death. . . . Thus by a peculiar irony of fate the founder of the experimental method was hurried to his death by conducting an experiment, the only one on record which he himself ever performed.[17]

Bacon is often invoked to link Christian faith to the abuses of the industrial age because he stated his goals for science and technology in theological terms. "Only let the human race recover the right over nature which belongs to it by divine bequest," he wrote, "and power be given it; the exercise thereof will be government by sound reason and true religion."[18] The "right" he refers to is God's word to humans in Genesis 1:28, "Be fruitful and multiply, and fill the Earth, and subdue it; and rule over the fish of the sea and the birds of the sky and over every living thing that moves on the Earth." Recall that Reformation theologians like Luther saw that, as a result of the Fall, the damage done to the human capacity to rule nature was "utterly beyond repair in this life."[19] Luther had in mind a knowledge that permitted understanding and empathy. Bacon envisioned a knowledge of causes and effects, which could be controlled to produce an intended result: "For man by the fall fell at the same time from his state of innocency and from this dominion over creation. Both of these losses however can even in this life be in some part repaired; the former by religion and faith, the latter by arts and sciences."[20] "It is a restitution," wrote Bacon, "and reinvesting (in great part) of man to the sovereignty and power ... which he had in his first state of creation."[21]

In these assertions, Bacon was not espousing a biblical doctrine but a Christian heresy called Pelagianism. Pelagius, a fifth-century Christian teacher and contemporary of Augustine, taught that Adam's original sin did not corrupt human nature but only set a bad example for those who came after. Human will, choosing a right path, was sufficient to live a life leading to salvation. Jesus set a good example through his teaching and manner of life, but his death was not necessary for salvation.

The church condemned Pelagius and his teaching, but Bacon committed the same error in different form, arguing that science and technology, rather than direct human effort, could correct the loss of human dominion over nature. Bacon did not speak for any church or group of Christians, but his ideas are often identified with Christianity because he expressed them in theological motifs. This identification has been used to support the claim that Christian beliefs about nature were responsible for environmental destruction.

Bacon's writing on the use of induction as a new method of knowing in science was his most original philosophical contribution. Inductive reasoning does not, in itself, necessarily lead to any conclusions or practices that would harm nature. Nonetheless, the inductive method formed an important component of a belief structure that emphasized progress, mechanization, and applied scientific investigation, all characteristics of the early industrial period in the western world. Bacon, although not an adept theologian, is not the environmental villain he is often portrayed to be. His stated aims, for all his verbosity and pomposity, were to better the common welfare of mankind. He did not see scientific inquiry or the knowledge gained from it as boundless, but limited by restraints set in place by God.

The restraints on scientific inquiry and technology that Bacon desired and envisioned, restraints he understood as needed, given the reality of human sinfulness and of God as Sovereign Creator and King of the universe, were rarely observed in the years that followed. The Industrial Revolution spawned a myriad of forms of environmental pollution and degradation never seen before. How did the Christian church respond?

THE INDUSTRIAL REVOLUTION AND THE
CHRISTIAN COMMUNITY–PROTESTANTISM
AND CAPITALISM

In his classic sociological treatise, *The Protestant Ethic and the Spirit of Capitalism*, the nineteenth-century political economist and sociologist Max Weber advanced a revolutionary idea about the relationship between religion and the development of capitalism. Weber believed the teachings of Protestantism, particularly Calvinism, were prerequisites for the development of capitalist economies and capitalist-based societies. He based his theory on three key ideas.

First, Protestantism, in all its forms, gave increased emphasis and dignity to ordinary life and work. It rejected the Catholic concept that priests and other church workers were engaged in a higher calling than those engaged in ordinary tasks. The Reformers argued that any legitimate and lawful work, pursued by a disciple of Jesus Christ, could and should be performed to the glory of God.

Second, Calvinism, more specifically, gave its followers a radically different understanding of Christian calling than Catholicism, or even other strains of Protestantism. To a Calvinist, one's calling is not something that one is born to by place, family, and circumstance but rather a divine vocation that is worked out interactively with God to discover God's will in life. The pursuit of the calling is to glorify God and produce good works as evidence of faith and salvation. One is not to labor for wealth, but prospering in one's calling is a sign of God's favor, and the profit derived thereof is to be frugally saved or reinvested in the calling in order to become even better at it and more productive in it, to the glory of God. Weber argued that this concept of a calling created a rationale for the specialization of labor, a sanctification of continuously renewed profit, and a tendency to reinvest such profit in increasing one's productive capacity (that is, capital reinvestment and accumulation).

Puritanism, the most extreme expression of Calvinism, stressed worldly asceticism. The believer was to avoid excesses of emotion, enthusiasm, and sensuality that would lead to sins of the flesh. Work was glorified by calling, but one's earnings from that work were never to be spent on selfish personal pleasures, ostentatious dress, or lavish dwellings. The ideal was one of unpretentious simplicity. But the now-sanctified combination of hard work in a specialized calling with diligent frugality and avoidance of self-centered expenses produced ideal conditions for accumulation of wealth, maximizing efficiency of effort while minimizing unnecessary expense.

Protestant leaders themselves saw the effects of these tendencies, effects that they did not intend, much less approve. John Wesley, speaking, in his case, of Methodists, noted, "For the Methodists in every place grow diligent and frugal; consequently they increase in goods. . . . We ought not to prevent people from being diligent and frugal; we must exhort all Christians to gain all they can, and to save all they can; that is, in effect, to grow rich."[22] It should be noted that, when read in its context, Wesley is speaking of the irony of the situation. He is not advocating that Methodists be taught to desire riches, but that the acquisition of riches is an unintended and, for Wesley, undesired consequence of the biblical teachings of diligence and frugality.

There is an intuitive appeal, and some circumstantial evidence, that made Weber's thesis attractive in its time. In the nearly 150 years since its publication, historians still consider Weber's work a classic in its field, but most would now say that Weber's case is over-stated, and more of historical than analytical value today. To be fair, Weber himself was a diligent scholar and nuanced writer. He was careful to distinguish between capitalism per se and what he called "the spirit of capitalism." For Weber, this is a distinction with an important difference. Weber did not claim that Calvinism was the cause of capitalist structures, markets, or philosophies. Rather, Calvinism gave capitalism a spirit or rationale that legitimated the pursuit of profit as a rational activity in pursuing the calling of God in one's life. This rationalization gave capitalism an "energy" that it could not have otherwise possessed and without which it would not have supplanted older, more traditional economic systems. Weber never connects Protestantism with environmental harm (the idea that the environment could be harmed by capitalistic market activity does not even seem to have occurred to Weber or to almost anyone else in the nineteenth century). Nevertheless, Weber asserts that changes in the understanding of work and calling aided in significant ways by changes from Catholic to Protestant understandings of Christian faith and were contributing factors to shifts from traditional to capitalist economic systems that changed the human relationship to nature. Most elements of the church were unaware of these effects as they were happening or of the role they were playing in these cultural changes. But there were leaders and voices in the Christian community that saw the dangers, and they spoke and acted against them.

THE INDUSTRIAL REVOLUTION AND THE
CHRISTIAN COMMUNITY–VOICES OF DISSENT

The Industrial Revolution brought changes, though long in preparation, that came with incredible speed. In human cultures, rapid
change is rarely accompanied by wise foresight. As we have seen, railways originally conceived to haul coal ore proved more profitable as
transportation systems for people, leading to a rapid and unexpected
growth of rail systems throughout Europe.

Industrial production produced industrial by-products. Noxious
fumes were released into the air, poisonous effluents into rivers, toxic
wastes into soil. Landscapes changed. The church, although commendably attempting to address the needs of growing numbers of
poor and unemployed workers immigrating to cities from rural communities, was taken by surprise at both the nature and rapidity of
industrial progress. Often the church was not merely unprepared but
inexcusably complicit in its failure to speak against the abuses to
humans and nature that industrialization brought. But voices within
the church, and informed Christians working and writing in other
fields, began to understand the dangers of such changes, and they
began to speak, write, and act.

In 1788 Gilbert White, pastor of the Church of Saint Mary's in the
village of Selbourne, England, published his records of more than two
decades of natural history study under the title *The Natural History and
Antiquities of Selbourne*. His book was, in many ways, a simple and
unpretentious journal of an amateur naturalist who never traveled far
from home, observed ordinary plants and animals in his surrounding
countryside, and never invoked the pretension of professional expertise or scientific credentials. Yet White's humble but insightful observations, his penetrating discernment about the causes of ordinary
events in nature, and his personal warmth and wry humor drew many
people, who had formerly been ignorant and oblivious to nature, into
study and relationship with the non-human world around them. The
keen observer with attention to the details of seemingly inconsequen-
tial things is seen in White's description of a tortoise kept as a pet by a
neighbor in his village:

When it [the tortoise] first appears in the spring it discovers very
little inclination towards food; but in the height of summer grows
voracious: and then as the summer declines its appetite declines;
so that for the last six weeks in autumn it hardly eats at all. Milky

plants, such as lettuces, dandelions, sow-thistles, are its favourite dish. In a neighbouring village one was kept till by tradition it was supposed to be an hundred years old. An instance of vast longevity in such a poor reptile![23]

What does all this have to do with human relationship to nature? White's writings, compiled during the early stages of the Industrial Revolution in England, offered no specific appeals to conserve nature. There was no incentive to do so because, at that time, the English countryside seemed to have plenty of nature left in it. Neither does his work, as first glance, appear to be a protest of any kind. But White's work was, in many ways, subtly subversive of the market-centered acquisitiveness and human-centered worldview that was becoming entrenched in an industrial-centered landscape and culture. As a Christian, White understood that nature was, in every respect, "good," made so in its original state by God. Therefore there was warrant to enjoy nature for its own sake. And anyone could do so, if nature was at hand. But nature enjoyed must be nature attended, and that meant forsaking the alternative. At the beginning of his work, White extends this invitation to the reader in a poem:

> See, Selborne spreads her boldest beauties round
> The varied valley, and the mountain ground,
> Wildly majestic! What is all the pride,
> Of flats, with loads of ornaments supplied?—
> Unpleasing, tasteless, impotent expense,
> Compared with Nature's rude magnificence.[24]

Here White compares "Nature's rude magnificence" to the "unpleasing, tasteless, impotent expense" that was ripening as the fruit of industrialization. And it was the latter that he found deficient.

Two hundred twenty years later, White's work remains one of the classics of natural history. But in its immediate context, White's book was the spearhead of a much larger social phenomenon, the "back to the land" movement that began to grow as landscapes were increasingly blighted by industrialization and attendant pollution. Critics of the industrial revolution and its consequences began to find their voice as the effects of industrialization intensified, and those voices began to rise.

Not all protests took literary form. Many occurred in factories and streets, sometimes turning into hand-to-hand combat between

civilians and soldiers. In England, the Luddites became a powerful
protest movement in the early nineteenth century, primarily composed of textile workers and artisans who believed that industrialization was leaving them unemployed. The name Luddite came from
one Ned Ludd, a weaver, who in 1779 smashed two knitting frames
in what was described as a fit of passion. The act came to symbolize
the frustration of weavers and other industrial workers with various
forms of technology that was replacing their traditional skills in
favor of faster and greater production. Breaking a knitting frame,
or any kind of machinery, was viewed as industrial sabotage, and
penalties were severe. In some cases the sentence was death. Ned
Ludd's act became a proverb, such that whenever frames were
sabotaged, people would jokingly say that "Ned Ludd did it."
By 1811 such sentiments had become an organized social protest,
often taking violent forms. Mills and factory machinery were
burned. There were full-scale battles with the British army, and
one mill owner was assassinated.

The Luddites show no connection to the Christian church or
Christian faith, and the increasingly violent and criminal nature of
their actions ultimately resulted in the loss of public and moral support for their cause. But the conditions against which they protested
were real and deeply symptomatic of the frustration occurring among
many segments of the working class during the Industrial Revolution.
Christian pastors, denominational leaders, and theologians were not
equipped to fully understand the effects that industrialization was
bringing, but Christian scientists and social critics did, and they took
leadership roles in such protests.

The leading physicist of the British Empire, Michael Farraday, was
a devout Christian who belonged to a small religious community
called the Sandemanians, who were strong believers in a literal interpretation of Scriptures. Farraday served as a deacon and elder in his
church, devoting many hours to visiting the sick and destitute. His
faith formed the basis and motivation of a long career of public service
to the British government, one in which he often undertook difficult
assignments at his own expense. There was no such term as "environmental scientist" in the nineteenth century, but Faraday may have
been the first. In 1846, working with geologist Charles Lyell, he produced a detailed report on an explosion in a coal mine that killed
95 men. Faraday and Lyell provided a meticulous forensic investigation that revealed that coal dust had contributed to the severity of
the explosion. Although reforms were still decades away, Faraday

and Lyell's report provided the foundation for future regulations in the mining industry designed to improve the safety and health of miners.

It was in the context of his scientific expertise and his concern for national and public welfare that Farraday became increasingly concerned over the deteriorating conditions in the Thames River in London and began to make firsthand investigations into the quality of the water in it. The results alarmed him. In an editorial to the London *Times*, he wrote, "surely the river which flows for so many miles through London ought not to be allowed to become a fermenting sewer. . . . If we neglect this subject, we cannot expect to do so with impunity; nor ought we to be surprised if, ere many years are over, a hot season gives us sad proof of the folly of our carelessness."[25]

SOCIAL CRITICISM INSPIRED BY CHRISTIAN CONVICTION

If a Christian physicist like Faraday provided the beginnings of a scientific understanding of the effects of industrialization, it was a Christian essayist who provided the most scathing denunciations of its social, economic, and moral consequences. John Ruskin was unquestionably the harshest critic of industrialization of his time. His critiques were not only poignant and penetrating but theologically well informed. In an essay entitled, "The White-Thorn Blossom," written in the form of a letter and addressed simply to "My Friends," Ruskin begins with words from the Song of Solomon.

For lo, the winter is past,
The rain is over and gone,
The flowers appear on the earth,
The time of the singing of birds is come,
Arise, O my fair one, my dove,
And come.[26]

"I fear for you," Ruskin wrote, "the wild winter's rain may never pass, —the flowers never appear on the earth; —that for you no bird may ever sing; for you no perfect Love arise, and fulfill your life in peace."[27] As he develops his case against industrialization, Ruskin drives his barbs deeper with specific examples that ridicule the so-called "achievements" of industrial science as meaningless and foolish.

Speaking of the construction of a railway through a beautiful valley connecting the towns of Bakewell and Buxton, he continues,

> There was a rocky valley between Buxton and Bakewell, once upon a time, divine as the Vale of Tempe ... You cared ... but for cash (which you did not know the way to get): you thought you could get it by what the *Times* calls "Railroad Enterprise." You enterprised a railroad through the valley—you blasted its rocks away, heaped thousands of tons of shale into its lovely stream. The valley is gone, and the Gods with it; and now every fool in Buxton can be at Bakewell in half-an-hour; and every fool in Bakewell at Buxton; which you think a lucrative process of exchange—you Fools Everywhere.[28]

Ruskin notes that things might have been different.

> You can bring rain where you will, by planting wisely and tending carefully; —drought where you will, by ravage of woods and neglect of soil. You might have the rivers of England as pure as the crystal of the rock; beautiful in falls, in lakes, in living pools; so full of fish that you might take them out with your hands instead of nets. Or you may do always as you have done now, turn every river of England into a common sewer, so that you cannot so much as baptize an English baby but with filth, unless you hold its face out in the rain; and even *that* falls dirty.[29]

Of capitalism of his time, Ruskin is even more severe: "You were ordered by the Founder of your religion to love your neighbor as yourselves. You have founded an entire science of Political Economy, on what you have stated to be the common instinct of man—the desire to defraud his neighbor." Ruskin ends with an appeal, offering to give 10 percent of his own income in combination with any who will help him try to reclaim

> some small piece of English ground, beautiful, peaceful, and fruitful. We will have no steam engines upon it, and no railroads. . . . When we want to go anywhere, we will go there quietly and safely, not at forty miles an hour in the risk of our lives ... we will have plenty of flowers and vegetables in our gardens, plenty of corn and grass in our fields,—and few bricks.[30]

Today we would call Ruskin's ideas a proposal for a land conservancy. Although his own effort did not succeed, many such proposals were developed in England and in other parts of Europe, and some achieved their ends, like the efforts in England to preserve the historic and beautiful Lake District. Many of these efforts were spurred by motives similar to Ruskin's, and many of these grew from the Christian concepts of a good creation, a humanity made in God's image, and a dignity in tending and caring for the Earth.

CHRISTIAN MINISTERS AND NATURALISTS FORM THE FIRST ORGANIZATION TO SAVE SPECIES

Gilbert White was only one among many of his fellow clergy who became serious students of natural history, the better to understand the work of God as manifested in his creation. One of these was the Reverend Francis Orpen Morris. Beginning his work at the church at Nafferton in East Yorkshire, England in 1844, Morris developed a reputation in science through his books on natural history, especially bird identification, which included *A Guide to the Arrangement of British Birds*, *A History of British Birds*, and *A History of the Nests and Eggs of British Birds*. Through his studies he made acquaintances with many of the best scientists and naturalists in England, including John Cordeaux, a naturalist who studied the migrations of birds, especially their migrations along the coastline near Dunham and Yorkshire.

Through their studies, both men had become increasingly alarmed over the effects that hunting was having on seabirds and shorebirds, particularly in the spring when the birds were preparing to breed. Shooting and egg collecting were unregulated at that time, and, by the 1860s, an estimated 120,000 birds were being killed annually by shooting or trapping between April and August in just one 18-mile stretch of coastline between Bridlington and Scarsborough.

Determined to act, Morris petitioned the House of Commons to impose a heavy tax on guns, hoping this would curtail the especially heavy loss of seabirds and shorebirds in coastal areas. The Reverend Henry Frederick Barnes, Morris's superior, came to his aid and with Cordeaux began working to stop the slaughter. Barnes used his influence to convene a meeting of local clergy and naturalists where, gaining their support, he established the Association for the Protection of Sea Birds (APSB) in 1868. At the same time Barnes began meeting with local landowners to persuade them to prevent hunters from crossing their property to gain access to areas where birds were breeding and nesting. Barnes added political and social clout to the effort by gaining the support of his own superior, the Archbishop of York, as well as several members of Parliament. His contacts in Parliament sponsored the Sea Birds Preservation Act, which became law in June 1869 and enforced a closed season from April through August. The first prosecution under the Act took place in Bridlington on 10 July 1869, when Mr. Tasker, of Sheffield, was fined £3 19s for shooting 28 birds.[31]

The APSB served as a model for hundreds of similar organizations that were later formed in the United Kingdom, the United States, and Europe. A second major effort in conservation, the creation of parks and nature preserves, was also a response to the threats of an increasingly industrialized society. The roots of that concept were influenced by people who drew deeply on a Christian understanding of nature.

NATURE AND THE NATURE RESERVE–THEOLOGICAL PROVOCATION AND PRACTICAL EXAMPLE

The British naturalist John Ray, whom historians have called "the father of natural history," was also known for his Christian faith and writings in theology. Ray asserted that, contrary to Calvin, the only sense in which everything in the world was made for man was that everything was worthy of his study. "There is greater depth of art, and skill, in the structure of the meanest insect," wrote Ray, "than thou art able for to fathom or comprehend."[32] Ray devoted an entire book, *The Wisdom of God Manifested in the Works of Creation* (1691), to proving the existence and characteristics of God through the revelation of his work in nature, particularly with respect to animals and plants. Here Ray noted that "it seems to me highly absurd and unreasonable, to think that Bodies of such vast Magnitude as the Fixed Stars, were only made to twinkle to us ... And, I believe there are many species in Nature, even in this sublunary World, which were never yet taken notice of by Man, and consequently of no Use to him, which we are not to think were created in vain. ..."[33] Ray did believe that all creatures had a use for man, but not in a utilitarian sense. Rather, their use was to lead human beings to "exercise our

Wits and Understandings, in considering and contemplating them, and so afford us Subjects of admiring and glorifying their and our Maker." It was this understanding of the use of nature and its creatures that also led Christian leaders, teachers, and theologians to recognize the value of experiences in nature, and of preserving nature in its natural state.

As the Industrial Revolution was changing the landscape of Europe at the beginning of the eighteenth century, the United States, then a possession of Great Britain, was still little more than a collection of coastal colonies bordered by a vast and unknown interior wilderness. Jonathan Edwards (1703–1758), today considered America's most original and important philosophical theologian, was then serving as a pastor, teacher, and missionary to Native Americans. It was Edwards' sermons that later sparked the most widespread religious revival in American history, the First Great Awakening, in the 1730s and 1740s. His many books, including his most famous, *Religious Affections*, still guide and inspire Christians today.

Although Edwards loved books and the joy of private contemplation in the comforts of his own study, his description of his conversion and development as a Christian, particularly his growth in his awareness of God and intimacy with God, come primarily from his experiences in nature. In *Personal Narrative*, he describes one such experience that happened while walking in the New Jersey countryside, "As I was walking there and looking up into the sky and clouds, there came into my mind so sweet a sense of the glorious majesty and grace of God, that I know not how to express. I seemed to see them both in a sweet conjunction . . . it was a sweet and gentle and holy majesty; and also a majestic meekness."[34]

Edwards goes on to explain from this and other experiences that it is the natural world which tempers God's glory, enabling the human eye to behold what would otherwise be inaccessible to our weak gaze. In his *Narrative*, Edwards continues his explanation:

> The appearance of every thing was altered; there seemed to be, as it were, a calm sweet cast, or appearance of divine glory, in almost every thing. God's excellency, his wisdom, his purity and love, seemed to appear in every thing; in the sun, moon, and stars; in the clouds, and blue sky; in the grass, flowers, trees; in the water, and all nature; which used greatly to fix my mind. I often used to sit and view the moon for continuance, and in the day, spent much time in viewing the clouds and sky, to behold the sweet

glory of God in these things; in the meantime, singing forth with a low voice my contemplations of the Creator and Redeemer.[35]

Although these were expressions of personal experiences, they were grounded, for Edwards, like Ray, in a theology that saw nature as good in and of itself. But Edwards moved beyond Ray in his understanding that a proper attitude of one's self to others, including non-human others, was part of the foundation of Christian virtue. In his book *The Nature of True Virtue*, Edwards distinguished the highest virtue as the characteristic of *benevolence*, or love for things in general, as opposed to love of self and things that pertain to one's self. In this effort Edwards implied, and laid the groundwork for believing, that virtue as a person and as a community, even a community as large as America, depended on our *beneficence* toward our natural environment (effort directed toward the needs of the environment itself) rather than our *exploitation* of it (effort directed toward using the environment to meet our own needs, to love ourselves).[36]

Edwards' admonition to cultivate virtue through benevolence, combined with his theology of nature as a revelation of God, were taken to heart in the nineteenth century by the influential Boston preacher, William Henry Harrison Murray (1840–1904). Murray, who came to be known popularly as "Adirondack Murray," extolled the virtues of New York's Adirondack Mountains and their forests. He urged his hearers to (temporarily) leave the comforts of their urban homes and go into the wilderness where they would be renewed in spirit and, just as Edwards had implied, become more virtuous and moral people through their experiences in nature. Murray was even more explicit than Edwards that moral virtue was formed through contact with wilderness. Thousands followed his advice. Although the popular press often referred to these adventurers as "Murray's Fools," Murray's preaching about the Adirondacks was the single most important stimulus in the development of the Adirondack Great Camp movement, in which many urbanites, especially among the wealthy, established homes in the Adirondacks arranged in the model of the so-called Great Camp, which featured multiple, different log cabins arranged at a single location for different uses, such as sleeping, dining, storage, and blacksmithing. It did not occur to Murray (or anyone else at that time) to argue for the preservation of the Adirondacks, which then seemed an inexhaustible wilderness. But Murray did accomplish something much like Gilbert White, although in a different way, in motivating thousands to see nature as a subject of moral and aesthetic value which they could experience and enjoy firsthand.

As Murray was influencing the large urban centers of the east, another individual, John Muir, was, at about the same time, beginning to discover the wilderness of the western United States and see the need and value of its preservation. Muir emigrated, with his father and brothers, to the United States from Scotland while still a child. Growing up in southern Wisconsin in the 1840s and 1850s, in a place not far removed from a wilderness condition, Muir reveled in the joys of exploring nature. Raised by stern Calvinist parents, Muir had committed all of the New Testament, and much of the old, to memory by the time he was 12. His most powerful religious experiences, however, would not come from his memorization of scripture but from his experiences in nature. The environmental historian Roderick Nash describes one of these early in Muir's life, when, engaging in draft dodging to avoid conscription into the U.S. army during the Civil War, Muir fled to Canada. Nash writes:

> He followed a lonely trail into a wet and darkening swamp, where he suddenly came upon a cluster of rare white orchids, miles from anywhere and so beautiful that he 'sat down beside them and wept for joy.' Reflecting later on the experience, Muir realized that his emotion sprang from the fact that the wilderness orchids did not have the slightest relevance to human beings. Were it not for Muir's chance encounter, they would have lived, bloomed, and died unseen. Nature, he generalized, must exist first and foremost for itself and for its creator. Everything had value. 'Would not the world suffer,' he concluded, 'by the banishment of a single weed?'[37]

Muir was an eloquent and persuasive writer, and his articles in major newspapers and national magazines urged Americans, as Murray had, to (temporarily) leave the cities and enjoy the wilderness. As his experiences in nature were religious, his writing used religious language and biblical images to express his concerns, as exemplified by the title of one of his early and most influential articles in the Sacramento, California, *Record-Union* titled, "God's First Temples: How Shall We Preserve Our Forests?" Muir framed the struggle for conservation in biblical and ethical terms, not simply as a choice between competing claims about the use of resource, but in terms of right versus wrong relationships to nature. Muir expressed the conflict as a fundamental struggle of good versus evil. After the establishment of Yosemite National Park in California, but still in the heat of the conflict over the use of the Sierras, Muir wrote:

> The smallest forest reserve, and the first I ever heard of, was in the Garden of Eden; and though its boundaries were drawn by the Lord, and embraced only one tree, yet even so moderate a reserve as this was attacked. And I doubt not, if only one of our grand trees on the Sierra were reserved as an example and type of all that is most noble and glorious in mountain trees, it would not be long before you would find a lumberman and a lawyer at the foot of it, eagerly proving by every law terrestrial and celestial that the tree must come down. So we must count on watching and striving for these trees, and should always be glad to find anything so surely good and noble to strive for.[38]

There are scholarly works on Muir which create more confusion than insight about his personal beliefs. Pantheist and transcendentalist environmental scholars display an almost frenzied eagerness to claim Muir as one of their own, a discontented Calvinist who rebelled against his father's stern disciplines (and sterner beatings) to a proto-type deep ecologist, seeing not simply God in nature but nature as God. Muir's own words do not convey the kind of pantheistic tran-scendentalism characteristic of Emerson or Thoreau, or of modern deep ecologists. Muir was not a theologian, nor a spokesman for any Christian church or sect, and his lack of orthodoxy is most clearly seen in his consistent reference to nature as unfallen, demonstrating that he did not take a biblical view of the Fall's effect on creation or its need for redemption. Although his theological objectivity was slipshod, his thoroughly biblical perspective was a powerful inspiration to his moral thinking. His view of nature as a good creation was a biblical one, and his unshakable conviction that it was *right* to protect God's creation (a term which Muir used as often as nature) permitted him to frame conservation as a matter of moral choice, not political or eco-nomic expediency. His inspirational work and writings galvanized a new movement the United States: *preservationism*. The broad popular support he won by framing environmental issues in moral terms led not only to the protection of individual areas like Yosemite but to the formation of an entirely new U.S. government agency, the National Park Service, whose mission would be to preserve America's natural heritage for the benefit of future generations.

Ultimately, Muir's preservationism would be supplanted by the more utilitarian concept of *conservation*. As the U.S. government became the leading force in environmental initiative, it predictably redefined the mission in nonreligious, democratic, and utilitarian terms as "the greatest good for the greatest number for the longest time," a strategy that, stripped of religious connotations, could appeal to all citizens. But was this in fact the case? Did conservation and environmentalism actually prosper without a religious tradition or a theological context in which to ground them?

THE SEPARATION OF CHURCH AND STATE AND THE SEPARATION OF RELIGION AND SCIENCE

The Reformation did not denigrate the importance of creation as a revelation of God, or the fact that the same creation was an object of God's redemptive plan and purpose. In many ways, Protestant leaders like Luther, Calvin, Wesley, and others elevated both doctrines and inspired renewed attention to nature and its preservation. In the United States, however, Protestantism took a course that tended to disengage American Protestants, especially evangelical Protestants, from considering nature as a source of revelation and from engaging concerns for the welfare of the natural world.

We have already noted the writings of Jonathan Edwards as an example of an intellectual Protestant and evangelical leader who gave serious attention to nature and its role in revealing the character of God. But Edwards was, in many ways, the last of his breed. As the American republic embraced its new concept of complete separation of church and state, it changed the dynamic of interaction between churches and public life. Because churches consistently lost influence and audience in U.S. public institutions from the mid-nineteenth century onward, revivalism became the dominant vehicle for spreading and expanding church influence. Revivalism promoted a new style of church leadership, one that emphasized a leader's directness, accessibility, personality, and popularity. It did not emphasize a leader's intellectual credentials or his place in social, governmental, or academic hierarchy. Thus, revivalism provided opportunity for charismatic popular leaders to have great effect in converting many to Christian faith, but it encouraged a spirit of individualism and urgency in religious thinking, not collective deliberation and reflection.

To be successful, a revival had to have elements of mass appeal. Therefore the questions addressed by the preacher were not, as for Luther, Calvin, and other early Reformation leaders, questions of theology, social order, or political arrangement, but questions more contemporary and individualistic in nature, often driven by popular thinking. Leaders planning a revival often considered most immediately, "What do people want to hear?" or "What is the greatest concern of the common man today?" Because revivals were based on popular preaching aimed at emotional response and immediate conversion, they did not emphasize reflective consideration of larger theological issues, or of how to apply biblical ideas to society at large.

Revivals also tended toward an antitraditional attitude. Since evangelical leaders were defined by popularity and personality, they did not place a high value on theological tradition or opinions of past Christian leaders, however learned and devout. This emphasis tended to cut the theology of revivals off from the accumulated learning of past Christian intellects and traditions, including traditions that had given serious attention to the human relationship to nature. With revivalism, the nineteenth century saw a decline in the influence of Christian thinking in U.S. colleges and universities. Originally established mainly by Christians for education designed to build faith and character, the better to understand the person of God and the means of obeying him, state land grant universities became the dominant presence in U.S. higher education as federal legislation gave them increasing resources and influence. These larger universities adopted a German organizational model of education that de-emphasized training for moral character and increased emphasis on research and innovation. As a result, Christian teaching and scientific discovery were increasingly separated. As Christian thinking lost influence in the present world, evangelical Christians became more focused on the world to come and more estranged from engagement in issues that concerned the world in which they lived.

Even as these changes occurred, the federal government began taking an expanding role in conservation, reframing the ideals of conservation out of the biblical and moral language of men like John Muir and into secular language of utilitarian benefit and national interest. In such a climate, evangelicals developed an understandable distrust of both the government and the university. These, however, were the primary sources of understanding environmental and conservation problems. Evangelical disengagement from government and academia also led to a parallel disengagement from concerns about conservation and the environment. Such disengagement did not, contrary to White, necessarily result in an antienvironmental attitude among evangelical Protestants, but it did discourage an active consideration of the kinds of environmental and conservation problems that scientific discovery began to illuminate, and that government agencies would increasingly attempt to regulate.

The estrangement between American evangelicals and environmental conservation created by these historical trajectories limited the influence and engagement of evangelicals in matters of conservation and environmental concern. This estrangement is being diminished today through developments we shall explore in succeeding chapters, but its effects are still with us. They are the root causes of much of the current tension between evangelical Christians and the conservation community, tensions that cannot be resolved without repentance on both sides, and we shall consider the steps needed for such repentance in the final chapter. In contrast, churches with stronger institutional structures, especially Roman Catholics and mainline Protestants, retained sufficient engagement with academic communities and government agencies, combined with habits of application of Christian truth to wider social contexts. These remained more involved with conservation and its moral and social implications, and began speaking to the ethical dimensions of environmental problems, often in advance of scientists and managers.

NOTES

1. George Perkins Marsh, *Man and Nature*, ed. David Lowenthal (Seattle: University of Washington Press, 2003), p. 36.
2. *Webster's Seventh New Collegiate Dictionary* (Springfield, MA: G. C. Merriam and Company, 1971).
3. Carlo M. Cipolla, "Introduction." In *The Industrial Revolution 1700–1914*, ed. Carlo M. Cipolla (New York: Barnes and Noble, 1976), p. 9.
4. Ibid., pp. 7, 8.
5. Murray Jardine, *The Making and Unmaking of Technological Society* (Grand Rapids, MI: Brazos Press, 2004), p. 34.
6. Samuel Lilley, "Technological Progress and the Industrial Revolution." In Cipolla, op. cit., p. 205.
7. Ibid., p. 207.
8. Ibid., p. 209.
9. Francis Bacon, *Bacon Selections*, ed. Matthew T. McClure (New York: Charles Scribner's Sons, 1928), p. ix.

10. The phrase *Novum Organum* was one chosen by Bacon because his aim was to refute the ideas of Aristotle, particularly in the manner in which science was investigated. Aristotle's writings on logic had been collected in a single work called the *Organon*. Bacon saw his work as a "new" (Latin, *novum*) *Organon*, but, in properly declinated Latin, the correct phrase, when the two words are used together, is *Novum Organum*.

11. Bacon, p. 283.

12. Ibid., p. 279.

13. Ibid., p. 280.

14. Nieve Matthews, *Francis Bacon, The History of a Character Assassination* (New Haven: Yale University Press, 1996).

15. Bacon, p. 56.

16. Historians are now generally agreed that the investigation and trial associated with these charges was politically motivated by Bacon's enemies, not by any real evidence of corruption in Bacon's conduct or judicial decisions. His "confession" has been reexamined in detail and appears to be more of an explanation of specific charges against him than an admission of guilt, but it was used by his enemies to substitute for evidence against Bacon, which they did not possess. For a detailed account of this and other important events in Bacon's life, see Nieves, op cit.

17. Matthew T. McClure, "Introduction," in Bacon, p. xiii.

18. Bacon, p. 372.

19. Martin Luther, *Luther's Works, Volume 1: Lectures on Genesis Chapters 1–5*, ed. Jaroslav Pelikan (St. Louis: Concordia Publishing House, 1958), p. 66.

20. Bacon, p. 431.

21. Bacon, *Religious Meditations:* "On the Interpretation of Nature." In *The Works of Francis Bacon*, ed. James Spedding, Robert L. Ellis, and Douglas D. Heath (New York: Houghton Mifflin, 1900), cited in John Passmore, *Man's Responsibility for Nature: Ecological Problems and Western Traditions* (New York: Charles Scribner's Sons, 1974), p. 19.

22. Quoted in Luke Tyerman, *The Life and Times of John Wesley M. A, Founder of the Methodists* (London: Hodder and Stoughton, 1871), p. 520.

23. Gilbert White, *The Natural History and Antiquities of Selbourne*, ed. Grant Allen (Herefordshire, UK: Wordsworth, 1996).

24. Ibid.

25. Michael Farraday, "Observations on the Filth of the Thames," *The Times* (London, 7 July 1855). Available at http://www.chemteam.info/Chem-History/Faraday-Letter.html. Accessed 25 September 2009.

26. Song of Solomon 2:11–13.

27. John Ruskin, *The Genius of John Ruskin*, ed. John D. Rosenberg (New York: George Braziller, 1963), p. 363.

28. Ibid., pp. 368, 369.

29. Ibid., pp. 370, 371.

30. Ibid., p. 373.

31. Cited in Fred Van Dyke, *Conservation Biology: Foundations, Concepts, Applicatons.* 2nd ed. (Dordrecht, The Netherlands: Springer, 2008).

32. John, Ray, *The Wisdom of God Manifested in the Works of the Creation* (Oceanside, New York: Dabor Science Publications, 1977), p. 180.

33. Ibid., p. 177.

34. Jonathan Edwards, *Personal Narrative*, cited in Alistair McGrath, *The Reenchantment of Nature: The Denial of Religion and the Ecologic Crisis* (New York: Doubleday, 2002), p. 13.

35. Ibid., cited in McGrath, p. 13.

36. Mark Sagoff, *The Economy of the Earth*, 2nd ed. (Cambridge, UK: Cambridge University Press), p. 186.

37. Roderick F. Nash, *The Rights of Nature: A History of Environmental Ethics* (Madison: University of Wisconsin Press, 1989), p. 39.

38. John Muir, "Address on the Sierra Forest Reservation," *Sierra Club Bulletin* 1 (1896): pp. 275–277.

CHAPTER 6

The Theological Response to the Ecologic Crisis

> That those who affirm the divinity of the Creator should come to the rescue of His creature is a logical consistency of great potential force.[1]
>
> Wendell Berry

FILLING A MORAL VACUUM–THE CONSERVATION MOVEMENT IN THE TWENTIETH CENTURY

In the United States, the increasing role of the federal government in conservation brought enormous financial and political resources to bear in the preservation of the natural environment, but not without moral cost. Under Theodore Roosevelt, the twenty-sixth president of the United States (1901–1909), the twentieth century began with the government's aggressive acquisition of western lands as forest reserves, lands that would become, in time, the foundations of the U.S. system of national forests. With the guidance and counsel of Gifford Pinchot, chief of the Division of Forestry (which would later become the U.S. Forest Service), President Roosevelt not only acquired western lands as forest reserves in large quantities but did so with a management philosophy for their use already in hand. Pinchot is today credited as being the author of the so-called Resource Conservation Ethic.

The Resource Conservation Ethic was in many ways ideally suited to provide the means of expressing normative goals in conservation for a strong, secular federal government. Its twin intellectual pillars were equity and efficiency. That is, resources should be available and distributed to all citizens, not only citizens of the present genera-tion but those of generations to come. In this way, the Resource Con-servation Ethic recognized an early version of what we would today call transgenerational rights or, more simply, the rights of future generations. Second, the Resource Conservation Ethic affirmed that it was wrong to use resources wastefully. Waste was understood to mean that which could have been used to benefit humankind but was not. In this kind of thinking, an old growth forest in which trees were not adding significant new biomass per individual each year was wasted if it was not cut.

Pinchot himself was no unreflective secularist, but a man of deep religious convictions. When he began his education at Yale he intended a career in medicine or ministry. He was a deacon of his class of 1889, which meant he was in part responsible for conducting regu-lar Sunday and weekday prayer meetings. When he graduated, the Yale Young Men's Christian Association (YMCA) offered him the position of general secretary (equivalent to president), and he very nearly took the job. Following instead a career path in forest manage-ment, Pinchot understood his work as stewardship, and the mission of stewardship was the betterment of mankind both now and for all gen-erations to come.[2] What Pinchot called the "one gigantic single prob-lem" of his work was to perfect the science of forest management to the point that national forests would forever provide a sustained yield of resources to the citizens of the United States. "As far as I knew then or have since been able to find out," he wrote, "it had occurred to nobody, in this country or abroad, that here was one question instead of many, one gigantic single problem that must be solved if the gener-ations, as they came and went, were to live civilized, happy, useful lives in the lands which the Lord their God had given them."[3]

Thus Pinchot saw himself as a steward of the Earth for future generations and for God. But his concept of stewardship contained no vision of an intrinsic value of nature in its own right, and his professional side, as a servant of the people employed by the U.S. government, made it unthinkable for him to express this goal in moral or biblical terms, as John Muir almost invariably did. There-fore, Pinchot, ever the faithful public servant, framed the value of stewardship in terms of efficiency, equity, and human benefit, an equation that stripped stewardship of any moral appeal or ethical authority and would in time create a moral vacuum of insipid and uninspired conservation policy, a vacuum that others would step forward to fill by other means.

If the Resource Conservation Ethic was less than morally inspiring, it was nevertheless admirably enforceable, for values established by federal agencies were codified into law, and programs that affirmed and enhanced approved conservation values were provided with special sources of funding. Thus the Pittman-Robertson Act of 1937 placed special taxes on firearms and ammunition to create funds for wildlife management and preservation, just as the Dingell-Johnson Act of 1950 would do for fish populations through taxes on fishing equipment. The federal government strengthened the power of enforcing the values of the Resource Conservation Ethic not only through laws and designated revenues but through the creation of new government agencies with explicit missions and mandates to manage resources according to such values, including the U.S. Forest Service (1905), the U.S. Fish and Wildlife Service (1940), and the Bureau of Land Management (1946), complete with their own law enforcement officers and agents.

Such efforts brought stability to the U.S. conservation effort, which became a model for many countries around the world, and there were notable successes in the number of acres of forests and rangelands brought under agency administration, increases in populations in many game and nongame species, and relatively constant supplies of valuable resources, such as timber, to national production. But although such an approach provided many benefits, its effect on the development of an environmental ethic, and especially one affecting the attitudes and behaviors of ordinary citizens, was, in many ways, detrimental. In a culture of conservation created primarily by a federal government, any sense of human obligation or duty to nature came to mean nothing more than following the rules. If there was no rule concerning a particular environmental behavior or resource use, there was no obligation. Thus, obligations to nature were simply understood as those things one had to do to avoid being subject to the threat of punishment by the government.

The shortcomings of such an approach began to become apparent near the end of the first half of the twentieth century, as the moral vacuum of conservation rulekeeping was increasingly perceived. The wildlife ecologist and conservation ethicist Aldo Leopold took this approach to task in his essay, "The Land Ethic." Satirically summarizing the conservation education of the 1930s and 1940s, Leopold wrote, "the content is substantially this: obey the law, vote right, join some organizations, and practice what conservation is profitable on your own land. The government will do the rest. Is not this formula too easy to accomplish anything worthwhile? It defines no right or wrong, assigns no obligation, calls for no sacrifice, implies no change in the current philosophy of values. In respect of land-use, it urges only enlightened self-interest. Just how far will such education take us?"[4] Leopold's answer was, not very. "In our attempt to make conservation easy," Leopold concluded, "we have made it trivial."[5]

BRIEF GLIMPSES OF HEAVEN

Leopold's life work was to replace such triviality with a genuine ethic that would change "the role of *Homo sapiens* from conqueror of the land-community to plain member and citizen of it. It implies respect for his fellow members, and also respect for the community as such."[6] The outcome was *A Sand County Almanac*, published posthumously after Leopold's untimely death, which occurred while fighting a neighbor's brush fire in 1948. As a young man, Leopold had read and been impressed with the book *The Holy Earth*, by noted botanist Liberty Hyde Bailey. *The Holy Earth* (1915) was an early attempt to establish a land ethic rooted in established moral principles. "A man cannot be a good farmer unless he is a religious man,"[7] said Bailey. True to his word, he frames his effort squarely within the Judeo-Christian tradition, starting with Genesis 1:1. "'In the beginning God created the heaven and the earth.' This is a statement of tremendous reach." Bailey continued, "It sets forth in the fewest words the elemental fact that the formation of the created earth lies above and before man, and that therefore it is not man's but God's."[8] Ironically, Bailey expressed hostility to Christian faith in many of his other writings, affirming a more general pantheism that fit better with the creeds of Freemasonry in which he had been raised. But finding no better alternative for moral authority in *The Holy Earth*, Bailey invoked Judeo-Christian scripture to support his claim.

If he was not always intellectually consistent as a theologian, Bailey also was no ordinary botanist. After graduating from the Michigan Agricultural College (now Michigan State University) in 1882, where he studied agriculture and horticulture, Bailey was only 30 years old when he took up his first academic post at Cornell University in 1888 and founded Cornell's College of Agriculture. Bailey was also the principal founder of the American Horticultural Society and authored 65 books, more than 1300 articles, and more than 100 scientific papers. We note these things about Bailey not to rewrite his eulogy, but to appreciate his stature in the field of horticulture and understand his fundamental motivation—a love for land and rural life. Bailey was the leader of the Country Life Movement, an American movement analogous to England's Back to the Land movement of the eighteenth and nineteenth centuries. Both movements emphasized the virtues of rural life in contrast to what Bailey considered the corrupting and impersonal culture of the city. Bailey was an advocate of the family farm, in contrast to farming as a corporate enterprise, because he shared American ideals, dating back to Thomas Jefferson, that a society of rural, independent farmers living and working on their own land was the fundamental basis of a virtuous community.

Despite the fact that he rejected Christian teaching at many levels, Bailey, in *The Holy Earth*, repeatedly turned to the Bible as his source of moral authority and of specific precepts to guide the proper care of the Earth, for here he found the clearest principles on which to build a tradition of agricultural conservation. "Man is given the image of the creator," wrote Bailey, "even when formed from the dust of the earth, so complete is his power and so real his dominion ... One cannot receive all these privileges without bearing the obligation to react and to partake, to keep, to cherish, and to co-operate."[9]

Other voices followed Bailey, invoking biblical teaching as a basis for environmental stewardship. One was William Lowdermilk, Assistant Chief of the U.S. Soil Conservation Service during the 1930s. Lowdermilk traveled widely in the Mediterranean Basin, seeing many of the same depleted soils and now dysfunctional ecosystems that had moved George Perkins Marsh to pen his environmental classic, *Man and Nature*, in 1864. While in that part of the world, Lowdermilk, in June of 1939, made a speech on Jerusalem radio entitled, "The Eleventh Commandment." Here he asserted that if God had foreseen the thoughtless ravages which human beings would impose upon the Earth, he would have added an eleventh commandment to the original 10. Drawing on Bailey's term, "the holy earth," the wording Lowdermilk proposed for commandment eleven was

> Thou shalt inherit the holy earth as a faithful steward, conserving its resources and productivity from generation to generation. Thou shalt safeguard thy fields from soil erosion, thy living waters from drying up, thy forests from desolation, and protect the hills from overgrazing by thy herds, that thy descendants may have abundance forever. If any shall fail in this stewardship of the land, thy fruitful fields shall become steep stony ground

and wasting gullies, and thy descendants shall decrease and live in poverty or perish from off the face of the earth.[10]

His address appeared in print a year later in *American Forests*, the official magazine of the Society of American Foresters.

Had Lowdermilk been a better theologian, he might have hesitated to accuse God of a lack of foresight, and had he been a better student of the Bible, he would have realized that everything he had placed in this modern day commandment had been addressed in various biblical texts, sometimes in almost the same words (see Chapter 3). There is certainly a healthy dose of presumption in adding a new commandment to scripture, but Lowdermilk's aim was the same as John Muir's, to frame issues of conservation as matters of moral choice, not economic self-interest. Lowdermilk's fundamental claim was that religion should be the basis for an ethic of conservation.

In the year following the publication of Lowdermilk's address, the 1941 Malvern Conference of the Church of England named "respect for the earth" as a major component of its Christian Strategy report, which described how the church should respond to the most important problems of society. The author of this report, Reverend V. A. Demant, stated the problem in uncompromising terms. "The earth upon which we live," he said, "is being drained of its power to support plant, animal and human life, by the breaking of its vital reproductive cycle under the spur of capitalist aggressiveness . . . Humanist man has treated the earth just as he has behaved towards Almighty God; he has lived on it without recognizing his dependence; he has used the life it has given him to turn against it in aggressive self-dependence and exploitation. . . ."[11] Demant urged that the Earth be treated as a moral subject and its care a question of moral significance.

In the years that followed, Christian voices continued to speak to the care of the Earth from theological perspective. One of these was Daniel Day Williams, Associate Professor of Christian theology in the Federated Theological Faculty of the University of Chicago and the Chicago Theological Seminary, and later Professor of Theology at the Union Theological Seminary in New York City. In his book *God's Grace and Man's Hope* (1949), Williams stated, in a chapter entitled, "The Good Earth and the Good Society," that Christian hope was sustained by, and expressed itself in, a reverent and grateful love for the Earth. Prophetically anticipating some of the same language that Lynn White, Jr. would use to describe what White considered a Christian attitude toward nature, Williams identified the cause of the environmental problem as an abuse of science and technology. He wrote:

> When man regards nature only as something to be exploited for immediate gain without concern for the whole good it is meant to serve, he loses even his capacity to make full use of nature. A scientific conquest of nature without the sense of reverence will always turn against us. Mind becomes calculating, practical, sure of its capacity to dominate. Yet this imperial confidence of man the exploiter has nothing to serve. It loses the zest of life. It has no power to see it whole. That is much of what is wrong with man's spirit today. Sheer control over life for the sake of control is self-defeating. The good earth is good only as we love it in the using of it.[12]

Like Bailey, who preceded him, and like Lowdermilk and Williams, who were his contemporaries, Aldo Leopold strove to develop an ethic of authentic moral authority to overcome the triviality of enlightened self interest that characterized the conservation ethics of his day. But he did not follow Bailey, Lowdermilk, or Williams in grounding his appeals in Christian ethics. Leopold based his own ethic on ecology and evolution and an attitude for proper treatment of land evolving through moral extensionism from ethics that once considered only human beings as moral subjects. This kind of extension Leopold saw as "an evolutionary possibility and an ecological necessity."[13] Contrasting his approach to an ethic based on utilitarian economic value with reference to Wisconsin, his state of residence, Leopold wrote, "Of the 22,000 higher plants and animals native to Wisconsin, it is doubtful whether more than 5 percent can be sold, fed, eaten, or otherwise put to economic use. Yet these creatures are members of the biotic community, and if (as I believe) its stability depends on its integrity, they are entitled to continuance."[14] For Leopold, the question of value was resolved by a creature's contribution to community stability, as well as by its evolutionary history and its tenure on the land. This evolutionary aspect is developed in his essay "Marshland Elergy," which he wrote in tribute to the sandhill crane, a species he deeply admired but which he expected to be exterminated, at least from Wisconsin, in the not too distant future:

> Our appreciation of the crane grows with the slow unraveling of earthly history. His tribe, we now know, stems out of the remote

Eocene. The other members of the fauna in which he originated are long since entombed within the hills. When we hear his call we hear no mere bird. He is the symbol of our untamable past, of that incredible sweep of millennia which underlies and conditions the daily affairs of birds and men.[15]

Leopold's land ethic was a sincere attempt to change the human conscience toward land, but his writings languished in obscurity and without effect for many years after his death. The discovery of Leopold's land ethic began in the 1960s even as the emerging environmental crisis raised its relevance to unforeseen importance.

"The Land Ethic" essay became prominent at this time because the environmental crisis caught both science and ethics unprepared to deal with the types and complexities of problems never before encountered. "The Land Ethic" was prescient in its understanding of the fundamental problem as a failure to treat land as a moral subject. Thus it was and has remained a significant consciousness-raising device in American culture. But Leopold never actually accomplished his fundamental goal: to establish an ethical relationship between human beings and the land on the foundation of secure moral and ethical principles.

As the environmental crisis caught the philosophical and scientific community unprepared for the problems to be faced and solved between humans and their environment, it surprised the Christian church in the same way. But as there were voices, like Leopold's, who had sounded unheeded warnings ahead of their time, so there were theologians in the church who had begun to speak to these things before the majority of people realized their dilemma.

PROPHETIC VOICES–THE BEGINNINGS OF THE MODERN THEOLOGICAL DEVELOPMENT OF A JUDEO-CHRISTIAN STEWARDSHIP ETHIC

An odd-looking man, clad in a black coat under a black beret, shuffles among the lanes of Chicago's Hyde Park, looking at least a little lost if not positively homeless. In this time, the later years of his life, he is virtually blind, yet seeing far more than others with his inner eye. With these words I summarize some of the description that church historian Martin Marty offered of his distinguished colleague, theologian Joseph Sittler, who taught, first at the Chicago Lutheran

Seminary and later at the University of Chicago's Divinity School.[16] Sittler was one of the first modern theologians to take environmental problems seriously. He did so not only because he recognized, far in advance of others, that such problems were growing in number and extent, but because he clearly understood biblical themes and ancient teachings of the church about creation that we have already explored. Speaking one Sunday in 1953 at the University of Chicago's Rockefeller Chapel, Sittler drew his congregation's attention to those problems through a reference to a contemporary book called *Our Plundered Planet* (1948), and addressed them with these words:

> When man relates himself to nature as one who plunders her, he ultimately destroys what he uses. When nature is regarded only as an inexhaustible warehouse of oil, ore, timber and all other materials, then she is ruthlessly plundered. This problem cannot be solved by economics, for the disposition to plunder is not an economic problem at all. It is the creation of a lust grown rapacious; and lust and rapacity are problems of the spirit of man before they ever become events of economic history.[17]

The next year there appeared the first of his many writings on the problem, "A Theology for Earth," published in *The Christian Scholar*. In this seminal essay Sittler brings a critique against the greatest theologians of his day, Rienhold and Richard Neibuhr, Richard Kronner, and John Bennett, who had produced a theology (neo-orthodoxy) that treated the earth and the creation as meaningless in the plan and purpose of God. In this writing, Sittler not only attacked a theology which took no notice of creation, but also predicted the rise of non-Christian eco-theologies which would fill the vacuum that the church left void. "When Christian orthodoxy," wrote Sittler,

> refuses to articulate a theology for earth, the clamant hurt of God's ancient creation is not thereby silenced. Earths' voices, collective of her lost grace and her destined redemption, will speak through one or another form of naturalism. If the Church will not have a theology *for* nature, then irresponsible but sensitive men will act as midwives for nature's unsilenceable meaningfulness, and enunciate a theology *of* nature. For earth, not man's mother—which is a pagan notion—but, as St. Francis profoundly surmised, man's sister, sharer of his sorrow and scene and partial

substance of his joys, unquenchably sings out her violated whole-
ness, and in groaning and travailing awaits with man the restoration of all things.[18]

"A Theology for Earth" was the first of what would become a
wealth of writings on the theology of the environment and the problems of pollution that remained the subject of Sittler's attention
throughout the years until his death in 1987. His theological rubric
was framed around simple but profound biblical concepts. First,
Sittler taught that God's grace was manifest to human beings primarily through nature, the creation in which every person moved
and lived, the same creation in which God became incarnate in Jesus
Christ. But Sittler went further. He argued that the reality of the natural world as the theatre of God's grace could be verified in human
experience by taking actions on behalf of nature for her good. In other
words, nature would provide examples and manifestations of God's
grace to human beings if properly cared for and nurtured by them.
This is a theme common in biblical texts, especially in the Psalms,
such as Psalm 104, where God "causes grass to grow for the cattle,
and vegetation for the labor of man, so that he may bring forth food
from the earth."[19] Second, the Christ who became incarnate in nature
is both the creator and redeemer of the entire universe, a *cosmic Christ*,
such as Paul describes in Ephesians and Colossians, who has the
power to redeem not only individual lives but all of creation from
the curse and consequences of sin.

This theme is evident in what has come to be regarded as Sittler's
most influential work, not an article or book but an address given to
the World Council of Churches (WCC) in 1961, "Called to Unity."
Sittler does not argue in this address for changing theology from
being redemption-centered to nature-centered, but rather that the
"circumference of redemption" (Sittler's phrase) be properly expanded
to embrace the whole of creation, just as it is described in Paul's letters
to the Romans, the Ephesians, and the Colossians. Like Leopold,
Sittler was a moral extensionist. But unlike Leopold, he grounded the
extensionism not in the premise that ethics evolved over time, but
rather that the word of God revealed in the past time warranted such
extension in the present. Basing his address on Colossians 1:15–20,
the doxology Paul wrote in praise of Jesus Christ who redeems "all
things through the blood of his cross," Sittler told the delegates of the
WCC that

A doctrine of redemption is meaningful only when it swings through the larger orbit of the doctrine of creation. For God's creation of earth cannot be redeemed in any intelligible sense of the word apart from a doctrine of the cosmos which is his [man's] home, his definite place, the theatre of his selfhood under God, in cooperation with his neighbor, and in caring relationship with nature, his sister.... Unless the reference and the power of the redemptive act includes the whole of man's experience and environment, straight out to its farthest horizon, then the redemption is incomplete.[20]

Sittler anticipated the theological and moral dimensions of the environmental crisis many years in advance of others, but Sittler was not the only voice calling for the development of a biblical and practical theology of nature. Theologian Bernard Anderson, a contemporary of Sittler, addressed the ecologic crisis from a theological perspective in 1962, five years before the publication of "Historical Roots," in his essay, "Biblical Perspectives on the Doctrine of Creation." As Sittler's expertise lay in New Testament scholarship, Anderson was an expert on the Old Testament, and argued persuasively that it was the entire created order, not just human history, that is an expression of God's goodness. In the same way, all of creation, asserted Anderson, not just human beings, were to be the instruments of praise to God. The dominion of human beings over nature was to be understood as an expression of worship to God. As Anderson put it, "Human beings are to exercise sovereignty within God's sovereignty, so that all earthly creatures may be related to God through them and thus join the creation's symphony of praise to the Creation."[21] By 1964, the U.S. National Council of Churches, spurred both by the writings of Sitler and Anderson and the growing concern over environmental problems, formed the Faith-Man-Nature Group. Designed to create connections among theologians, church leaders, environmental activists, and scientists, the members included theologians and religious leaders H. Paul Santmire, Philip Joranson, Richard Baer, Jr., and Frederick Elder, all of whom would, in later years, make significant theological contributions to the theology of nature debate. The group was disbanded in 1974, largely a victim of its own success, for its objective of making environmental concerns and the care of creation a matter of concern in mainline Protestant churches was being largely realized. The growing awareness of environmental problems in the church was, however, not only, or even primarily, the outcome of prescient thinking like Sittler's or proactive efforts like the Faith-Man-Nature Group, but the fruit of a response to specific criticisms and charges leveled against the church as the cause of the ecologic crisis.

A CRITICAL CATALYST: LYNN WHITE, JR. AND "THE HISTORICAL ROOTS OF OUR ECOLOGIC CRISIS"

The beginnings of a contemporary theology of stewardship were still small efforts by the late 1960s, but they were not absent, and they drew on historic theological and biblical principles as grounds for expressing concern for the environment in theological terms. Historical analysis ought to take account of such matters. But Lynn White Jr.'s remarkable essay, "The Historical Roots of Our Ecologic Crisis" (1967)[22] did not. White either did not know or did not care about the contemporary efforts or the historical teaching within the church which addressed the problem. We have already examined White's thesis, and its flaws, in attributing the ecologic crisis to the Judeo-Christian tradition. But when a message, however poorly supported, reaches an audience that wants to believe it, its popularity is assured. The scientific and academic community gave "Historical Roots" instant fame, acclaim, and distribution, all with widespread and mostly unreflective application in every discipline from ecology to history to architecture to literary criticism.

The charges contained in the short, four-page essay "Historical Roots," specious as they were, had to be answered. So it was that much of the efforts of Christian theological and historical scholarship of the late 1960s and early 1970s were written as direct rebuttals to White. Among the first to answer was Gordon College professor Richard Wright in "Responsibility for the Ecologic Crisis," published in 1968 in *BioScience* (*Science* refused to accept this counterpoint response). Wright argued that, first, western cultures were not unique in their destructive tendencies toward nature, but that the environment had been equally ravaged by eastern cultures. This was a critical point since, if White's hypothesis was true, it would predict the absence of an exploitive attitude toward nature in cultures where Judeo-Christian teaching was also absent. But this was not the case. Wright further noted that science, as practiced today, is also a product of Christian views of man and nature. He called out the double standard employed by the scientific community in accepting White's thesis of environmental responsibility based on mere historical associations long since weakened, if not severed, while giving no weight to present scientific achievement based on the same sorts of historical associations. "Present-day scientists," noted Wright, "would consider it absurd to attribute the basic credit for their activity and discoveries to Christianity. I submit that it is just as absurd to hold Christianity responsible for crises that have arisen from the present-day applications of science just because several hundred years earlier science began within a Christian framework. Why not hold scientists responsible for their own activities?"[23] Why not, indeed? Not to put too fine a point on it, Wright asserted that, in fact, historians need not search the past for a historical common denominator when the causes of environmental destruction were present in our contemporary world. "The explanation reveals itself every day," wrote Wright, "if we care to look for it, because it is present in all of us—human greed, carelessness, and ignorance. To solve the ecological crisis, we must come to grips with these very evident and very basic aspects of human nature."[24]

Evangelical social critic and popular author Francis Schaeffer's short but widely read book *Pollution and the Death of Man* (1970) took on not only White but other writers who implicated Christianity as the cause of the ecologic crisis. Schaeffer argued that God and creation are categorically different, and therefore pantheism, which destroys these categories, is no answer. Rather, because God treats his creation with integrity, caring for it by meeting its needs, forming a covenant with it (Genesis 9:8–17), and making it part of his redemptive plan and purpose, so human beings, particularly Christians who love God, should also love the creation which he made. While not sparing the church for its failings to speak out against the abuses done to nature, Schaeffer nevertheless asserted that Christianity

offers the hope here and now of substantial healing in nature of some of the results of the Fall, arising from the truth of redemption in Christ. In each of the alienations arising from the Fall, the Christians, individually and corporately, should consciously in practice be a healing redemptive factor—in the separation of man from God, of man from himself, of man from man, of man from nature, and of nature from nature. A Christian-based science should consciously try to see nature substantially healed, while waiting for the future complete healing at Christ's return.[25]

These publications are but two of the earliest among many that, during the next 10 years, would become a literary flood of scholarship addressing the human relationship to nature. Joseph Sittler's scholarship in theology, which had been accumulating throughout the 1960s, was drawn together in a single book, *Essays on Nature and Grace* (1972).[26] From the eastern Orthodox tradition, Paulos Gregorios produced *The Human Presence: An Orthodox View of Nature* (1978).[27] In the Christian Reformed Church, scholars of Calvin College published *Earthkeeping: Christian Stewardship of Natural Resources* (1980).[28] And a lone but eloquent voice of the agrarian tradition, Wendell Berry, produced perhaps the most penetrating response of all in his book *The Gift of Good Land* (1982).[29] Berry's work is especially notable because he eschewed theoretical and theological abstraction and went directly to the practical nature of the problem:

> The divine mandate to use the world justly and charitably, then, defines every person's moral predicament as that of a steward. But this predicament is hopeless and meaningless unless it produces an appropriate discipline: stewardship. And stewardship is hopeless and meaningless unless it involves long-term courage, perseverance, devotion, and skill. This skill is not to be confused with any accomplishment or grace of spirit or of intellect. It has to do with everyday proprieties in the practical use and care of created things....[30]

These examples are only illustrations of the large body of scholarship that emerged from the Christian community beginning in the late 1960s and continued with increasing force and frequency into the 1970s. Armed with more sophisticated and detailed theological resources in contemporary formats, most major denominations had formed or were forming official statements on environmental stewardship from the 1970s onward. As early as 1966, a year before the publication of "Historical Roots," the U.S. National Council of Churches issued its first policy statement on the environment. Denomination statements began in 1969 with a resolution on the environment by the Lutheran Church—Missouri Synod, resolutions on the environment by the National Association of Evangelicals in 1970 and 1971, official statements and resolutions by the Baptist World Alliance, and the World Alliance of Reformed Churches in 1970. In the same year, the American Lutheran Church issued an official statement of its General Convention, "The Environmental Crisis," detailing the most pressing current environmental problems of that time, declaring that every Christian was responsible to act as a steward of God's creation, and offering concrete suggestions on how to do so. Within a year of the Lutheran statement, in 1971, the General Assembly of the Presbyterian Church began urging action toward "environmental renewal."[31]

In the same year, the Roman Catholic Church issued the papal epistle *Octogesima Adveniens*, an apostolic letter of Pope Paul VI. The epistle devoted one section to the environment, declaring:

> Man is suddenly becoming aware that by an ill-considered exploitation of nature he risks destroying it and becoming in his turn the victim of this degradation. Not only is the material environment becoming a permanent menace—pollution and refuse, new illness and absolute destructive capacity—but the human framework is no longer under man's control, thus creating an environment for tomorrow which may well be intolerable. This is a wide-ranging social problem which concerns the entire human family. The Christian must turn to these new perceptions in order to take on responsibility, together with the rest of men, for a destiny which from now on is shared by all.[32]

From early writings that were at first only direct responses to Lynn White, Jr., the Christian community progressively developed a comprehensive biblical and theological understanding of the human relationship to nature in a contemporary context. But the problems that the church addressed, including and especially the need for moral authority and guidance in addressing environmental problems, also were beginning to make themselves felt in environmental policy and conservation science.

THE NEED FOR MORAL AUTHORITY–THE SCIENTIFIC COMMUNITY REACHES OUT

If White had been wrong in his accusations about the historical implications of Christian faith in fostering the ecologic crisis, he had been right in one clearly stated prediction, "More science and more technology are not going to get us out of our present ecologic crisis ... "[33] White concludes this sentence with "until we find a new religion, or rethink our old one."[34] But many begged to differ. Some scientists thought that more technology and more science would be just the thing, with no need of religion, new or old. An example manifested itself in Los Angeles.

In 1972, the city of Los Angeles decided to install 900 plastic trees and shrubs in concrete planters along the median strip of a major boulevard because the construction of a new box culvert along the strip had left insufficient soil to support real trees. The artificial replicas were to be constructed of factory-made leaves and branches that were wired to plumbing pipes, covered with plastic, and then "planted" in aggregate rock covered with epoxy.

The advocates for this plan could marshal a rationale of coldly frightening logic. Only plastic trees, they argued, would survive in Los Angeles's smog-laden inner-city environment. And a plastic tree, however synthetic, would be much more attractive than a dead and rotting real one. Urban planner Martin Krieger, commenting in *Science*, defended the decision in terms of economic costs and benefits. He wrote, "the demand for rare environments is a learned one," and "conscious public choice can manipulate this learning so that the environments which people learn to use and want reflect environments that are likely to be available at low cost . . ."[35] An environment composed of plastic trees would certainly meet this criterion, inexpensive to install and practically costless to maintain.

Not everyone agreed with Kriegar. Legal ethicist Lawrence Tribe responded in what would become a classic work on environmental law and policy, "Ways Not to Think About Plastic Trees." Tribe argued that plastic trees stripped nature of its reality and value and rendered only "nature abstracted to pure categories of human need."[36] They possessed no true value of their own, or any need (much less right) to even exist. Rightly discerning the dangers inherent in Krieger's views, as well as in the older traditions of the Resource Conservation Ethic, Tribe commented,

> Policy analysts typically operate within a social, political, and intellectual tradition that regards the satisfaction of human wants as the only defensible measure of the good, a tradition that perceives the only legitimate task of reason to be that of consistently identifying and then serving individual appetite, preference, or desire. This tradition is echoed as well in environmental legislation which protects nature not for its own sake but in order to preserve its potential value for man.[37]

When human needs and preferences are treated as the ultimate frame of reference, and when human goals and ends must be taken as externally given, rather than generated by reason, Tribe argued, then

> environmental policy makes a value judgment of enormous significance. And, once that judgment has been made, any claim for the continued existence of threatened wilderness areas or endangered species must rest on the identification of human wants and needs which would be jeopardized by a disputed development. As our capacity increases to satisfy those needs and wants artificially, the claim becomes tenuous indeed.[38]

With this judgment, the true identity and value of the created object is destroyed.

Tribe's essay was not an isolated voice, but an articulate expression of a growing concern that was beginning to alter the very way in which science itself perceived the natural world and its role in preserving it. Only a few years after the publication of "Plastic Trees," in 1978, well-known biologist Michael Soulé made an impassioned plea to fellow academic scientists, zookeepers, and wildlife conservationists at the First International Conference on Conservation Biology in San Diego, California. The scientific community, Soulé argued, could no longer enjoy the leisure of dispassionate professional advocacy that had characterized it since the Enlightenment. The world was facing a crisis of species extinction. Environmental scientists and conservationists must change their posture from passive recorders to impassioned advocates for the preservation of biodiversity. They must join forces with others, including nonscientists, to save threatened and endangered species from imminent extinction. They must affirm the value of global biodiversity and rise up to save it.

Soulé's remarks sparked controversy, but not inaction. The world of science, at least in conservation, was changing. A new scientific organization, the Society for Conservation Biology (SCB), and a new discipline, conservation biology, would ultimately emerge from this vision.

Today Soulé is regarded as one of the founders of modern conservation biology, which he defined as a crisis discipline. The crisis was biodiversity, and the imminent threat was of irreplaceable loss of life and species.[39] Conservation biology, said Soulé, is to biology and ecology "what surgery is to physiology or war to political science."[40] The scientific community was confronting an emergency situation with only incomplete information, but it would have to respond. In Soulé's vision, conservation biology would become a discipline deliberately and intentionally stressing *intrinsic values* of biodiversity and entire communities, not simply economic or utilitarian values.[41] Although conservation biology had legitimate scientific interest in understanding the nature, extent, and causes of biodiversity, the discipline was defined by its *commitment* to the *value* of biodiversity.

As we saw in Chapter 1, the current members and leadership in conservation biology, in practice and professional society, are engaged in controversy and struggle. Should the society continue to emphasize a commitment to being a mission-driven, value-laden discipline seeking to actively *protect and preserve* biodiversity, or should it advocate that conservation biology become a regulatory science whose goal is to provide value-free information to environmental policy analysts and decision makers? The emergence of conservation biology as a mission-driven, value-laden enterprise within the scientific community in the early 1980s revealed the growing dissatisfaction of scientists themselves with traditional secular, morally vacuous approaches to doing science. In forming the SCB, the founding members, as well as many subsequent ones, affirmed White's prediction. More science and more technology, by themselves, were inadequate answers to conservation problems. The moral mission of conservation had to be recovered.

Although *Historical Roots* would receive continued attention, and even some qualified affirmation, through the late 1980s, the tensions and divisions that it had attempted to create between Judeo-Christian faith and the ecologic crisis were breaking down more rapidly than expected. The urgency of environmental problems, and the increasing realization of many in the scientific community that these problems were fundamentally moral in nature, began to form unlikely but effective alliances to attempt their solution.

UNLIKELY ALLIES: COALITIONS OF FAITH AND SCIENCE IN THE CARE OF THE EARTH

In July 1990, the late astronomer and spokesman of science, Carl Sagan, published a letter in the *American Journal of Physics* entitled, "Preserving and Cherishing the Earth—An Appeal for Joint Commitment in Science and Religion." Sagan wrote, "We are close to committing—many would argue we are already committing—what in religious language is sometimes called Crimes against Creation."[42] Sagan affirmed White's assertion that more science and more technology alone were not the answer, that environmental problems required "radical changes not only in public policy, but also in individual behavior. The historical record makes clear that religious teaching, example, and leadership are powerfully able to influence personal conduct and commitment."[43] Speaking on behalf of the scientific community to the religious community, Sagan noted that, as scientists, "we understand that what is regarded as sacred is more likely to be treated with care and respect. Our planetary home should be so regarded." [44]

This letter was not the first such appeal from Sagan, nor was it entirely his own work. Rather, the appeal had been framed out of a major world conference, The Global Forum of Spiritual and Parliamentary Leaders on Human Survival, which had convened in Moscow six months earlier in January 1990. Sagan's letter, drafted with help from two religious leaders, James P. Morton and Paul Gorman, developed out of the context of this conference and in conjunction with a number of major statements that had issued from it. These statements included both the Moscow Declaration, which called for a new planetary perspective and a "spiritual and ethical basis for human activities on earth," and the Forum's Plan of Action, which included many measures to raise public awareness as well as specific steps to reverse actual environmental degradation.[45] The signatories included 32 distinguished scientists and policy makers and 270 religious leaders. In the latter category were 37 heads of national and religious organizations, 50 Cardinals, Lamas, Archbishops, Head Rabbis, Patriarchs, and Mullas, 17 religious leaders of indigenous peoples, and 55 professors of theology, seminary presidents, cathedral deans and heads of religious orders from around the world.[46]

Sagan's wording to these religious leaders, including those of Jewish and Christian faith, sometimes carried a tone of condescension and a thinly cloaked hope for using religion as a behavior modification device for cleaning up the planet, without engaging or taking seriously its central claims, and some were not shy in pointing this out. Religious leader John Haught noted:

> The well-intended effort by the skeptics to co-opt the moral enthusiasm of the religious for the sake of ecology is especially puzzling, in view of the fact that it is only because believers take their religious symbols and ideas to be disclosive of truth of reality that they are aroused to moral passion in the first place.

If devotees thought that their religions were not representative of the way things really are, then the religions would be ethically impotent . . . It is hard to imagine how any thorough transformation of the habits of humans will occur without a corporate human confidence in the ultimate worthwhileness of our moral endeavors . . . [47]

Despite the fact that the appeal may have been interpreted by some as manipulative, the effort was affirmed, and its support well coordinated, in many parts of the religious community. Only a month before the Moscow Forum, on December 8, 1989, Pope John Paul II delivered his papal address, "Peace with God the Creator, Peace with All of Creation," from The Vatican. This was done in advance and in celebration of the World Day of Peace to be observed on January 1, 1990. It was the first papal address to be devoted exclusively to environmental concerns within a theological context. After a thorough review of the scriptural basis for the care of creation, and an equally thorough review of the biblical record of the rebellion of human beings against their Creator's plan for that care, John Paul II stated, "When man turns his back on the Creator's plan, he provokes a disorder which has inevitable repercussions on the rest of the created order. If man is not at peace with God, the earth itself cannot be at peace."[48] John Paul II was explicit in naming Christians as those particularly called to address the environmental problem, closing his address saying,

> Even men and women without any particular religious conviction, but with an acute sense of their responsibilities for the common good, recognize their obligation to contribute to the restoration of a healthy environment. All the more should men and women who believe in God the Creator, and who are thus convinced that there is a well-defined unity and order in the world, feel called to address the problem. Christians, in particular, realize that their responsibility within creation and their duty towards nature and the Creator are an essential part of their faith.[49]

If appeals to the religious community from science, like that of Carl Sagan, contained some elements that were condescending or disingenuous toward believers, other environmental ethicists and activists began to adopt a more humble stance, expressing regret and offering apologies for their former identification of Christian faith as the cause of the environmental crisis. In *Caring for Creation: An Ecumenical Approach to the Environmental Crisis* (1996), Yale philosopher Max Oelschlaeger wrote, "For most of my adult life I believed, as many environmentalists do, that religion was the primary cause of the ecologic crisis. I also assumed that various experts had the solution to the environmental malaise. I was a true believer . . . I lost that faith by bits and pieces . . . by discovering the roots of my prejudice against religion. That bias grew out of my reading of Lynn White's famous essay blaming Judeo-Christianity for the environmental crisis."[50] Oelschlaeger goes on to describe how his viewpoint radically changed, until, he admits, "The church may be, in fact, our last best chance. My conjecture is this: there are no solutions for the systemic causes of ecocrisis, at least in democratic societies, apart from religious narrative."

The church's theological response to the ecologic crisis not only changed its relationship to the scientific and environmental communities but also created a breadth and depth of intellectual resources that Christians engaged in teaching and practicing environmental conservation began to use to inform, at first, traditional teaching in Christian colleges and universities, and, subsequently, entire curricula and degree programs around environmental study and creation stewardship. If belief structures are the rails on which life runs, the church had, by this point, constructed a new intellectual railroad that would deliver its students to destinations of direct engagement with environmental problems, creating the opportunity for a new level of activism in environmental conservation in the contemporary Christian community.

NOTES

1. Wendell Berry, "The Gift of Good Land." In *The Gift of Good Land: Further Essays Cultural and Agricultural by Wendell Berry* (New York: North Point Press, 1982), p. 267.

2. Mark Stoll, *Protestantism, Capitalism, and Nature in America* (Albuquerque: University of New Mexico Press, 1997), pp. 152, 153.

3. Quoted in Stoll, p. 154.

4. Aldo Leopold, "The Land Ethic," *A Sand County Almanac with Essays on Conservation from Round River* (New York: Ballantine, 1970), pp. 243, 244.

5. Ibid., p. 246.

6. Ibid., p. 240.

7. Liberty Hyde Bailey, *The Holy Earth* (New York: MacMillan, 1923), p. 33.

8. Ibid., p. 5.

9. Ibid., p. 6.

10. Quoted in Roderick F. Nash, *The Rights of Nature: A History of Environmental Ethics* (Madison: University of Wisconsin Press, 1989), p. 97.

11. V. A. Demant, "Christian Strategy." In *Malvern 1941: The Life of the Church and the Order of Society* (London: Longmans, Green and Company, 1941), pp. 121–149, 145, 146.

12. Daniel Day Williams, *God's Grace and Man's Hope* (New York: Harper and Brothers, 1949), p. 164.

13. Leopold, p. 239.

14. Ibid., pp. 246, 247.

15. Ibid., pp. 102, 103.

16. Martin Marty, "Foreword." In Joseph Sittler, *Evocations of Grace: Writings on Ecology, Theology, and Ethics*, eds. Steven Bouma-Prediger and Peter Bakken (Grand Rapids, MI: Eerdmans, 2000), p. vii.

17. Joseph Sittler, "God, Man and Nature," *The Pulpit* 24, no. 3 (August 1953): p. 16. Cited in Bouma-Prediger and Bakken, p. 3.

18. Sittler, "A Theology for Earth," *The Christian Scholar* 37 (September 1954): pp. 367–374. Cited in Bouma-Prediger and Bakken, p. 25.

19. Psalm 104:14, NASB.

20. Sittler, "Called to Unity," *The Ecumenical Review* 14 (January 1962): pp. 177–187, 178, 179.

21. Bernard Anderson, "Biblical Perspectives on the Doctrine of Creation." In *From Creation to New Creation* (Minneapolis: Fortress, 1994), p. 33. Although the book listed in this note was published in 1994, the specific essay from which the quote comes was published in 1962.

22. Lynn White, Jr., "The Historical Roots of Our Ecologic Crisis," *Science* 155(1967): pp. 1203–1207.

23. Richard T. Wright, "Responsibility for the Ecologic Crisis," *BioScience* 20 (1970): pp. 851–853, 852.

24. Ibid.

25. Francis Schaeffer, *Pollution and the Death of Man* (Wheaton, IL: Tyndale House, 1970), p. 81.

26. Joseph Sittler, *Essays on Nature and Grace* (Philadelphia: Fortress, 1972).

27. Paulos Gregorios, *The Human Presence: An Orthodox View of Nature* (Geneva: World Council of Churches, 1978).

28. Loren Wilkinson, ed., *Earthkeeping: Christian Stewardship of Natural Resources* (Grand Rapids, MI: Eerdmans, 1980).

29. Berry, op. cit.

30. Berry, p. 275.

31. A summary of major denomination statements on the environment during this period can be found in Robert Booth Fowler, *The Greening of*

Protestant Thought (Chapel Hill: University of North Carolina Press, 1995), pp. 15–16

32. Pope Paul VI, *Octogesima Adveniens*, Apostolic Letter of Pope Paul VI, available from http://www.vatican.va/holy_father/paul_vi/apost_letters/documents/hf_p-vi_apl_19710514_octogesima-adveniens_en.html. Accessed 7 October 2009.

33. White, p. 1206.

34. Ibid.

35. Martin H. Krieger, "What's Wrong with Plastic Trees?" *Science* 179 (1973): pp. 446–455, 451.

36. Lawrence H. Tribe, "Ways Not to Think About Plastic Trees: New Foundations for Environmental Law," *The Yale Law Review* 83 (1974): pp. 1315–1348, 1347.

37. Ibid., p. 1325.

38. Ibid., p. 1326.

39. Michael Soulé, "What is Conservation Biology?" *BioScience* 35 (1985): 727–734.

40. Quoted in Fred Van Dyke, *Conservation Biology: Foundations, Concepts, Applications* (Dordrecht, The Netherlands: Springer, 2008), p. 3.

41. Ibid.

42. Carl Sagan, "Preserving and Cherishing the Earth: An Appeal for Joint Commitment in Science and Religion," *American Journal of Physics* 58 (1990): pp. 615–617, 615.

43. Ibid.

44. Ibid.

45. Summarized in Fred Van Dyke, David C. Mahan, Joseph K. Sheldon, and Raymond H. Brand, *Redeeming Creation: The Biblical Basis for Environmental Stewardship* (Downers Grove, IL: InterVarsity Press, 1996), p. 163.

46. Sagan, p. 616.

47. Cited in Herman E. Daly, *Ecological Economics and the Ecology of Economics: Essays in Criticism* (Cheltenham, U.K.: Edward Elgar, 1999), p. 182.

48. Pope John Paul II, *Peace with God, Peace with All of Creation*. Message of His Holiness John Paul II in celebration of the World Day of Peace, 1 January 1990. Available at http://www.vatican.va/holy_father/john_paul_ii/messages/peace/documents/hf_jp-ii_mes_19891208_xxiii-world-day-for-peace_en.html. Accessed 7 October 2009.

49. Max Oelschlaeger, *Caring for Creation: An Ecumenical Approach to the Environmental Crisis* (New Haven: Yale University Press, 1996), p. 1.

50. Ibid., p. 5.

CHAPTER 7

The Beginnings of Christian Environmental Activism

He presented another parable to them saying, "The kingdom of
heaven is like a mustard seed, which a man took and sowed in
his field; and this is smaller than all seeds, but when it is full
grown, it is larger than the garden plants and becomes a tree, so
that the birds of the air come and nest in its branches."

Matthew 13:31–32

ACTIVISTS AND ACTIVISM: A DISTINCTION WITH A DIFFERENCE

In examining the history of environmental stewardship in the
Christian church, we need not begin in the last half of the twentieth
century if we want to find environmental activists inspired by Christian vision. Francis of Assisi wrote canticles of worship inviting created things to praise God with him. In response to the excesses of
the industrial revolution, Gilbert White urged his readers to turn
from the "unpleasing, tasteless, impotent expense" offered by urban
wealth to the beauty and riches of nature, and John Ruskin proposed
an early version of a land conservancy to stop the destruction of
natural environments simply to produce a railway system whose fruit
was that "every fool in Buxton can be at Bakewell in half-an-hour;
and every fool in Bakewell at Buxton."[1] Francis Orpen Morris and
his fellow clergymen formed the first organization, The Association
for the Protection of Sea Birds, dedicated specifically to saving

species, and the eminent British physicist and devout Christian Michael Farraday led the first scientific inquiries into the environmental reasons for mining disasters and water pollution. In the United States, John Muir proclaimed his mission of saving the Sierras and, eventually, of forming an entire system of national parks, through biblical imagery, and Gifford Pinchot, the first chief of the U.S. Forest Service, was also one of the first to understand and express his work in creating sustainable timber harvests from the nation's forest in terms of stewardship for the welfare of future generations.

It is wise to review this small sampling of the many examples already presented to guard us from the falsehood of thinking that the presence of Christian environmental activists, as they would be called today, is a recent development. It is not. However, in remembering the work of Christians who were activists toward the environment, it is also wise for us to distinguish the difference between *activists* and *activism*. The former refers to individuals whose Christian faith inspired them to specific actions for the good of God's creation and the good of others in relation to it. The latter is a broader concept and is better used of groups and organizational responses than of individuals. *Activism* in things environmental is characterized by a strong stance toward the development of appropriate practices, laws, and regulations that affect *everyone*, a goal of bringing about not merely *compliance to law*, but *transformation of values* in society, and a specific agenda of *goal-oriented objectives* that are intended to change society and its future.

Political scientist and environmental ethicist Corrado Poli has noted that when an environmental problem exists, attempting to solve it can generate one of two responses in those who address it. The solution-seekers can (1) try to find the answer in the existing social structure and its philosophical underpinnings or (2) consider alternative social and ethical structures. The first approach implicitly approves of existing structures and ethics as they are. The second approach explicitly questions, or even states its disapproval of, the same structures, and looks to a different path for answers.[2] In the work of environmental conservation, Christians and their organizations consistently find themselves in the latter category. What does environmental activism look like when it is organized around an attempt to change one's values and bring the participants into a new framework of ethical and social relations?

A GARDEN OF MUSTARD SEEDS

When Jesus tried to explain to his followers what the Kingdom of God looked like, and how it worked, he did not offer long arguments based on concepts, premises, and conclusions. Rather, he did something much more insightful, entertaining, and effective. He told stories. He knew that the Kingdom of God was richly multidimensional and many-faceted, so much so that didactic arguments could never capture its life and purpose. Thus, he told parables to explain it, each one focusing on a distinct but important kingdom characteristic. One was that of a mustard seed. A tiny seed, Jesus noted, not much to look at, but, when planted, a seed that can grow into the largest of all the garden plants, and a blessing (place of rest) for others, which, in his parable, are called "the birds of the air."

The details of parables should not be pressed too hard, but neither should the main point be missed. In this parable Jesus is saying, "Don't expect things that are part of the Kingdom of God to have impressive beginnings. They start small. They seem insignificant. But they grow up to create effects so powerful that everything around them is changed." As we look at the beginnings of Christian environmental activism, a phenomenon that is primarily one of the last 30 years, we will see these kind of beginnings in works and organizations so small you couldn't find them with a microscope, much less an organizational directory. But these are works which, in time, transform their environments. Here it is wise to look at the last phrase of the parable, "the birds of the air come and nest in its branches."

In these last words we find a parable within a parable, for the phrase "the birds of the air come and nest in its branches" is used in other scriptural stories to indicate a wider range and scope of blessing than what human beings originally can intend or conceive. The exiled Jewish prophet Daniel brought this understanding to the Babylonian King Nebuchadnezzar when he was told of the king's dream and asked to give an interpretation. Nebuchadnezzar told Daniel that he saw a great tree grow up, "Its foliage beautiful and its fruit abundant, and in it food for all. The beasts of the field found shade under it, and the birds of the sky dwelt in its branches."[3] Daniel replied, "The tree you saw, which became large and grew strong, whose height reached to the sky and was visible to all the earth and whose foliage was beautiful and its fruit abundant, and in which was food for all, under which the beasts of the field dwelt and in whose branches the birds of the sky lodged—it is you, O king, for you have become great and grown strong, and your majesty has become great and reached to the sky and your dominion to the end of the earth."[4] Daniel would complete the interpretation of Nebuchadnezzar's dream with bad news that the king did not want to hear: Nebuchadnezzar would be cut down and driven from his throne until he acknowledged that "the Most High," Daniel's own God, was ruler over all the Earth.

The prophetic image of the tree, branches, and birds is also used to reveal the work of God himself that will bring blessing and healing to all the nations, even the godless Gentiles, those the Jews were prone to despise. Speaking of Israel's restoration after its captivity in Babylon, God says, through his prophet Ezekiel, "On a high mountain of Israel I will plant it [God's "new Israel"], that it may bring forth boughs and bear fruit and become a stately cedar. And birds of every kind will nest under it; they will nest in the shade of its branches. All the trees of the field will know that I am the Lord; I bring down the high tree, exalt the low tree, dry up the green tree and make the dry tree flourish. I am the Lord; I have spoken, and I will perform it."[5]

Guided, then, by the Bible's interpretation of itself, we can understand Jesus' parable of the mustard seed to mean that God's work in the world will begin in small and insignificant ways, but that same work will, in time, grow to be something not only large, but a blessing to all the Earth. The examples we now trace in Christian environmental activism in this chapter and the next will show that pattern.

THE EDUCATION OF ACTIVISTS

In 1956, three young men, John Olmstead, Harold Snyder, and Eldon Whiteman, friends and fellow graduate students in the Department of Fisheries and Wildlife at Michigan State University who loved the outdoors, began to dream of a summer camp for Christian youth, somewhere in rural, northern Michigan. Their vision was original, if still embryonic. They hoped to develop a camp curriculum that would integrate conservation science with Christian faith, seeing the first as an application of the second. They explained their ideas to their supervising professor, Dr. Gib Mouser, who supported and encouraged their aspirations. Their resources were meager, but Mouser knew of a landowner, Louie Kleinschmidt, who was offering some land for sale near Big Twin Lake in the upper Au Sable River region. Harold Snyder's father, a successful orthopedic surgeon in

Grand Rapids, loaned them the money to buy it, and the deal was done. John, Harold, and Eldon began repaying their debt to Dr. Snyder from their own earnings at the prodigious rate of $25 per month, and at the same time began building accommodations for campers on their new property. Progress was slow, but by 1958 the camp was running, although in that year it served only a single church, Calvary Church of Grand Rapids. But Harold, now a local high school science teacher, began to dream of bigger things. He spoke with friends about expanding the current work, which had been christened the Au Sable Trails camp for boys, into a full summer program that could serve more churches. He still didn't have much money, but he made up for small funds with great persuasion. From 1959 to 1961, the summer program at Au Sable Trails expanded its curriculum and slowly enlarged its audience.

In autumn of 1962, Snyder joined the faculty of Taylor University, a Christian school in Indiana, and began to see the value of using Au Sable Trails to give Taylor students training in camping and re-creation, elements that were already part of the curriculum in Taylor's education department, Snyder also began to involve Taylor students as counselors and program assistants in the youth program of Au Sable Trails. Snyder's vision expanded to the idea of offering college courses in biology, and he persuaded not only Taylor students to take them but students from Spring Arbor College in Michigan and Greenville College in Illinois. By 1963, the curriculum and students were in place and being served by a full time staff.

The original Au Sable property was only 65 acres but the seller, Louie Kleinschmidt, owned other nearby lands. Kleinschmidt was known to his neighbors as somewhat cantankerous and fiercely inde-pendent, but Snyder and his family befriended Kleinschmidt through all the years of Au Sable's early development. Over time, they came to be among the few who were on good terms with him and whom he considered friends. One winter, when Kleinschmidt had not been seen by anyone for several days, a neighbor went to check on him and found him dead in his home. In the ensuing settlement of his estate, his heirs discovered that Kleinschmidt had left another 80 acres of his property to the camp. At the time, the gift was received with gratitude as a kind, if surprising, gesture, but without any particular excitement. There was little on the new holding but small red pine and spruce trees, and its value as real estate was, at that time, perhaps $100 an acre. But the land held a secret beneath it that would radically transform the work of Au Sable Trails.

In 1975, Amoco Oil contacted the board of trustees of Au Sable Trails, seeking a lease to explore for oil on the new 80 acres. The letter triggered further investigation by the board, which eventually negotiated a much more favorable lease and royalties agreement with the Peninsular Oil Company of Michigan. Their exploration discovered an oil reef that would prove to be perhaps the richest deposit ever found in that region. The windfall of royalties, which began to bring in hundreds of thousands of dollars, moved the trustees to restructure Au Sable Trails, already a not-for-profit organization, into a more comprehensive educational institution, a reorganization that would make it easier for the organization to use its newfound oil money directly in pursuit of its own programs and maintain full compliance with U.S. Internal Revenue Service regulations. Its name was changed to the Au Sable Institute of Environmental Studies, and under the leadership of its first CEO, Cal DeWitt, Professor of Environmental Studies at the University of Wisconsin-Madison, the Institute changed its mission to "the integration of knowledge of the Creation with biblical principles for the purpose of bringing the Christian community and the general public to a better understanding of the Creator and the stewardship of God's creation."[6]

The Institute, true to its promise, completely revised its offerings and appealed to a new target audience. The new curriculum began in 1979 and featured advanced courses in ecology, geology, botany and zoology, as well as courses in practical skills and technologies in land use planning and policy. Over time, Au Sable expanded its offerings to serve more than 80 colleges, developed new campuses in the state of Washington and in Kenya, and organized a cooperative curriculum with Bishop Heber College in India. Under DeWitt's leadership, the Institute also began to host annual symposia on various aspects of environmental stewardship, many of which were instrumental in refining a theological understanding of stewardship practice and policy implications. Such meetings produced notable books including *Tending the Garden: Essays on the Gospel and the Earth*, *Missionary Earthkeeping*, and *Evangelicals and the Environment: Theological Foundations for Christian Environmental Stewardship*.[7] These and other works formed out of the Au Sable symposia contributed to the growing theological and ethical foundation for conservation already established by Christian scholars and continued to add support to the design of environmental curriculum at Christian colleges throughout the United States and Canada.

Au Sable was exemplary in educational activism in its environmental curricula, but it was not alone. Increasingly, member colleges of the Coalition of Christian Colleges and Universities (CCCU) began making small but creative institutional initiatives to connect a growing theological understanding of environmental care with actual curricular offerings. By 1981, the faculty of Dordt College in Iowa had established an Agricultural Stewardship Center to train students in how to practice environmental conservation as a normal part of farm operations and management. The primary facility of the Center was an on-campus farm run by faculty and students that demonstrated the practicability of conservation and sustainable agriculture embedded in traditional farming practices and animal husbandry, organic farming techniques, nontraditional crops (including prairie grasses and wildflowers), and integrated wetland and wildlife management. Only 10 miles away, neighboring Northwestern College had, beginning in the 1990s, established a cooperative partnership between its own environmental science program and the U.S. Fish and Wildlife Service to investigate the effects of prescribed burning and mowing on restoring native prairies on former farmlands in Iowa and Missouri,[8] and had enrolled some of its own college-owned land, including a college farm, in the U.S. Natural Resource Conservation Service's Conservation Reserve Program (CRP).[9]

By 1998, Greenville College had established the Zahniser Institute of Environmental Studies, named after one of its own alumni, Howard Zahniser, who had been a lifelong and nationally known advocate for wilderness and one of the principal architects of the Wilderness Act of 1964. The mission of the institute that bore his name was "to promote the preservation of unique and wild places; to facilitate the integration of an ethic of environmental stewardship into the conservative moral constructs of our society; and to use muscle, sinew, will, and spirit to restore Nature." With the Zahniser Institute, the college also established its own environmental consulting firm run by Greenville faculty and students. The business began with local work involving wetland restoration in Illinois, but subsequently expanded to other states, as well as other kinds of efforts, including restoration and consultation projects on abandoned mine land, prairies, and forests. More broadly based programs such as the Global Stewardship Initiative, established and funded by the Pew Charitable Trusts in the early 1990s, helped initiate and strengthen fledgling efforts in environmental and conservation programs at Christian colleges, especially by providing equipment and new technology, such as Geographic Information System devices and software. During the same period, Taylor University developed the first graduate program in environmental science at a CCCU school. More systemically, Christian colleges during this period, in both Protestant and Catholic traditions, were beginning to develop entire majors devoted to environmental study and steward-ship. The work that was transforming the educational landscape of Christian colleges and universities was now poised to fuel significant efforts in political activism.

POLITICAL ACTIVISM–THE CHRISTIAN COMMUNITY CHANGES THE SHAPE OF POLITICAL CONSTITUENCIES

In 1995, the U. S. Republican Party and its Speaker of the House Newt Gingrich, fresh from a resounding victory in the 1994 con-gressional elections, were poised to initiate an agenda for sweeping legislative change. One of the most visible targets of the Republican Revolution was the U.S. Endangered Species Act (ESA), targeted by Republicans as one of the top ten worst regulations in federal law. The now-majority Republicans were prepared to dismantle the ESA in total, and there seemed to be little to stand in their way. But that autumn, about 70 evangelical Christian clergy and lay leaders gathered at the Bear Trap Ranch in the mountains of Colorado. This was one of the first meetings of the newly formed Christian Environmental Council (CEC), and it had been convened to rescue the ESA. During and sub-sequent to the Bear Trap meetings, the CEC began to develop a strategy to take their message directly to Washington and the U.S. Congress.

At about the same time, Target Earth, a Christian environmental organization working to protect endangered species and promote environmental activism among college students, began a massive effort to bring hundreds of students from Christian colleges to Washington, D.C. for the same purpose. Cal DeWitt and other CEC leaders went to Capitol Hill, and there DeWitt proved himself an academician who could master the sound bite and manage the press. Showing up at one publicity event with a live (leashed) mountain lion, DeWitt delivered the line that stuck to the airwaves, "The Endangered Species Act is the Noah's Ark of our day [and] Congress and special interests are trying to sink it."[10]

Other Christian environmental organizations joined the fray, many working cooperatively through the Evangelical Environmental

Network (EEN), and congressional Republicans found themselves under fire from a constituency, evangelical Christians, whom they had always found (and usually taken for granted) as being enthusiastically supportive. Faced with withering and increasingly harsh criticism of their efforts, the proposal collapsed. In the end, the Republican's ESA Reauthorization Act never reached the floor of the House. Moderate Republicans, alarmed by the groundswell of religious opposition that was turning the ESA Reauthorization bill into a political suicide mission, withdrew their support. The press was astonished and at a loss to explain why the act had failed. But for those close to the events, the reason was obvious. As political scientist David Johns noted years later, "It was the Evangelical Environmental Network, not conservation biologists of the Sierra Club that stopped Newt Gingrich's attempt to dismantle the U.S. Endangered Species Act."[11]

Opposition to the ESA Reauthorization Act had come primarily from Protestant, especially evangelical, groups. But the U.S. Conference of Catholic Bishops, spurred particularly by bishops in the state of Washington, also began, during the same decade, a determined effort to stop the construction of dams and other environmentally damaging developments along the Columbia River. Beginning with the formation of a steering committee in 1997, the bishops planned and hosted multiple listening sessions through the Columbia River watershed to hear from people affected by the condition and potential further development of the river. Following the completion of these sessions and other venues of information gathering, the bishops published, on January 8, 2001, a Pastoral Letter entitled, "The Columbia River Watershed: Caring for Creation and the Common Good." Their letter began, "The Columbia River stands as one of the most beautiful places on God's earth. Its mountains and valleys, forests and meadows, rivers and plains reflect the presence of their Creator. . . . We, the Catholic bishops in the international watershed region of the United States and Canada, write this pastoral letter because we have become concerned about regional economic and ecological conditions and the conflicts over them in the watershed. We address this letter to the Catholic community and to all people of good will."[12]

The bishops, after detailed descriptions of the problems facing the river and the people in its watershed, made 10 specific policy recommendations associated with its management. Among these were to conserve the watershed as a common good, protect its wildlife, respect the dignity of indigenous peoples, promote social and ecological responsibilities in extractive and agricultural industries in the watershed, conserve energy and establish alternative energy sources, integrate transportation and recreation needs with the requirements for a sustainable ecosystem, and promote community resolution of economic and ecological issues (that is, favor local resolution over higher level regulation). Although the letter did not address or advocate specific legislative initiatives, it has become an important document in debates on legislation and policy that are now affecting the watershed.

Outside the United States, NASSA-Caritas, a Catholic relief and development organization active in the Philippines that serves as the social and development arm of the Catholic Bishop's Conference of the Philippines, developed a comprehensive set of plans and programs to address rural poverty. The Catholic Church had learned much from its involvement in the politically charged and often physically dangerous conflicts over land reform in South America during the 1980s and 1990s and increasingly understood that alleviation of rural poverty was embedded in political, economic, and environmental issues that had to be simultaneously addressed.[13] Thus, the NASSA-Caritas program included detailed provision for the development of sustainable agriculture and "ecology protection and promotion of the integrity of creation," which was defined as that which "seeks to mitigate environmental deterioration, and to secure and preserve the sustainability of life and the whole of creation ... "[14] The NASSA-Caritas plan also included programs of political education designed to "hone political consciousness and maturity of the people through education, community building and advocacy [and] facilitates people empowerment projects that ensure the participation of the people in democratic processes."[15]

More recent initiatives like these by the Christian community attest to a broad-based level of engagement in environmental issues and environmental law. By the early 1990s, evangelical Christians concerned with environmental issues began exploring ways to address them systemically within the evangelical community. The Evangelical Environmental Network (EEN), noted previously for its role in resisting the dismantling of the Endangered Species Act by the Republican-dominated congress of 1995, was one such effort. The EEN describes itself as a nonprofit organization "that seeks to educate, inspire, and mobilize Christians in their effort to care for God's creation, to be faithful stewards of God's provision, and to advocate for actions and policies that honor God and protect the environment."[16] This was a noble aspiration, but a difficult task. The first challenge facing the

EEN was to bring a variety of evangelical groups and interests to points of basic agreement on a Christian understanding of and response to the environmental crisis.

STAKING ITS CLAIMS–CHRISTIANS DEFINE AND DEFEND ENVIRONMENTAL "STEWARDSHIP"

EEN's first meeting took place in the summer 1993 at the Au Sable Institute in Michigan, and the work of producing a statement on the environment that could be affirmed with widespread support throughout the evangelical community was the first problem the fledgling organization tackled. Loren Wilkinson, the principal author of the book *Earthkeeping: Christian Stewardship of Natural Resources*,[17] an early and seminal work on the biblical basis of environmental ethics and practical creation care, was asked to write the first draft of the statement, ambitiously called *An Evangelical Declaration on the Care of Creation*. Working with DeWitt and Susan Drake Emmerich, a senior environmental officer and environmental treaty negotiator with the U.S. Department of State, Wilkinson penned a "Declaration" that opened with these words:

> As followers of Jesus Christ, committed to the full authority of the Scriptures, and aware of the ways we have degraded creation, we believe that biblical faith is essential to the solution of our ecological problems.[18]

This statement expressed the first of five major affirmations of the "Declaration." It was followed by an affirmation of the reality of the problem, a summary of appropriate biblical responses, a call to followers of Christ to affirm and live out the principles of creation care, and the claim that Jesus Christ was the only ultimate hope for men, women, children, and the rest of creation suffering the consequences of human sin.[19] The "Declaration" was published the following year in *Christianity Today*, the most widely read and respected evangelical magazine in the United States, and widely circulated elsewhere. At the time of its original publication, it bore the names of nearly 300 signers, all identifying themselves as Christians, including Christian college and seminary presidents, professors, authors, denominational leaders, scientists, and other individuals both knowledgeable and concerned about the environmental crisis and the church's response.

As with any widely publicized statement, there was no shortage of critics. Many came from within the Christian community itself. One pastor wrote to Wilkinson saying, "Christ's redemption is always in purchasing the chosen or elect from their trespasses ... The redemption of the earth from its groaning will be vaporization and replacement. Its value is in providing our habitation; it is a variable, we are the constant with God."[20]

If the "Evangelical Declaration" drew private criticism quickly, it was not much longer before it drew more targeted public attack in "The Cornwall Declaration on Environmental Stewardship." Produced by the Cornwall Alliance in 2000, a self-described coalition of "clergy, theologians, religious leaders, scientists, academics, policy experts and others,"[21] "The Cornwall Declaration," like its evangelical counterpart, affirmed that the environmental crisis was first and foremost a moral one. "The moral necessity of ecological stewardship," it declared, "has become increasingly clear."[22] Unlike the "Evangelical Declaration," however, the "Cornwall Declaration" changed the purpose of such stewardship from its previous emphasis on preserving and protecting creation to that of promoting "growing affluence, technological innovation, and the application of human and material capital ... to environmental improvement."[23] Cornwall drew distinctions between environmental problems it judged to be of warranted concern, including issues of human health, inadequate sanitation, and, in its own words, "primitive agricultural, industrial and commercial practices,"[24] and those concerns it considered unfounded. These included species loss, overpopulation, and global warming.[25] Cornwall also stated its hope for a future world in which private property and private, market economies would be normative institutions and conditions.[26]

In this battle of "dueling declarations," the "Cornwall Declaration," unlike the "Evangelical Declaration," did not identify itself as a specifically Christian document, although it did claim to draw on Old Testament concepts as its source of moral insights. While never mentioning the "Evangelical Declaration" by name, Cornwall was clearly constructed to address and attempt to refute key affirmations in it. The most fundamental difference between the two was their respective understandings of the *purpose* of stewardship. In the evangelical version, that purpose was the care of creation itself, even if such care required Christians to remember Christ' words that "our lives do not consist in the abundance of our possessions" and therefore Christians are to "resist the allure of wastefulness and overconsumption by making personal lifestyle choices that express humility, forbearance, self-restraint and frugality."[27] Cornwall, in contrast, defined good human stewardship as that which "unlocks the potential in creation for all the earth's inhabitants . . . " and the purpose of such stewardship was to produce "more of the good and services responsible for the great improvement in the human condition."[28] In other words, in the eyes of the "Evangelical Declaration," the outcome of good stewardship was the flourishing of non-human creation through adjustment and reduction of human demands upon it. In Cornwall, good stewardship was essentially the same as what is usually called "development," whether economic, social, or cultural, that benefits the human condition and increases human affluence through the "better" use of nature.

If the controversy ignited by the claims of the "Evangelical Declaration" helped to define its positions, and their alternatives, with greater clarity, it also revealed the flaws in the stewardship model of understanding and expressing the human relationship to the non-human creation which had, to this point, been more or less uncritically accepted. The primary problem, one that we shall examine in more detail when we return to the questions of environmental ethics, is that the stewardship concept, on its own, defines neither the appropriate means nor the appropriate ends of its efforts, both of which can be redirected from the care of nature to an improvement in the human condition. As theologian and ethicist Norman Wirzba has noted, "Though it [stewardship] serves well as a titular designation, its programmatic neutrality with respect to means and ends. . . . makes it susceptible to misuse and distortion."[29]

Although the stewardship concept contained the seeds of serious problems in both thought and practice, it continued to serve as the model of choice for Christians engaged in environmental activism, especially when speaking to issues of environmental policy. In the following examples, we see how this model was effectively used to both address and resolve significant environmental issues and conflicts by Christian organizations and individuals.

THE SANDY COVE COVENANT: CHRISTIANS ADDRESS CLIMATE CHANGE

By June 2004, Jim Ball, then Director of EEN, had successfully organized a gathering of evangelical Christian leaders in Sandy Cove, Maryland. From that meeting emerged "The Sandy Cove Covenant," a document calling for evangelicals to begin to take the problem of climate change seriously and work constructively toward its solution. Signatories of Sandy Cove included Ted Haggard, president of the National Association of Evangelicals; David Neff, editor of *Christianity Today*; Ron Sider, president of Evangelicals for Social Action; Sir John Houghton, chairman of the John Ray Initiative and one of the world's leading authorities on global climate change; Bruce Wilkinson, vice president of International Programs of World Vision; and 26 other evangelical leaders, all of whom affirmed that, "We covenant together to make creation-care a permanent dimension of our Christian discipleship and to deepen our theological and biblical understanding of the issues involved ... Our continuing goal is to motivate the evangelical community to fully engage environmental issues in a biblically faithful and humble manner, collaborating with those who share these concerns, that we might take our appropriate place in the healing of God's creation, and thus the advance of God's reign."[30]

What was significant about the Sandy Cove gathering was, first, its expansion of participants to include not only theologians and church leaders but also Christians on the forefront of environmental activism, advocacy, and policy. Its second distinction was the increasingly explicit references activists made to christian faith in expressing their understanding of and commitment to their own missions in conservation. A classic example came in the keynote address. Here the speaker, Larry Schweiger, president and CEO of the National Wildlife Federation, one of the largest conservation NGOs in the United States, reflected on the linkage between his own conversion to Christ and his career of activism in environmental conservation. First Schweiger told his audience of his childhood struggles with dyslexia, of the death of his infant brother, and of his childhood memories of a dismal and disappointing vacation on a polluted Lake Erie shore, where the beach and shoreline waters were covered with dead pike embedded in rotting mats of vegetation. Collecting these memories together, Schweiger recalled,

> I remember making a decision for Christ, I knew I had something out of whack, and I made a decision for Christ through that experience of my younger brother dying. But I was on that beach and I remember making a promise to God. I remember the promise: 'God, I don't know how I'm going to do this, but if you open doors, I will spend my life working on this stuff.' And you know something, God has demonstrated that in my life

in ways I couldn't even imagine, that that boy on the beach, with dyslexia, would be standing here, President of the National Wildlife Federation.[31]

Following Schweiger's example, the Sandy Cove signers pledged themselves to a more active role in environmental care, and did so, in part, by inserting in their "Declaration" specific recommendations regarding environmental policy at the federal level. Affirming the importance of the effort, Jim Ball wrote, "Communicating the contents of this statement through a variety of political and media channels, we hope the (US) administration will make common cause with the Christian faithful who recognize that conservatives and conservation are natural allies."[32] Additional and more widely publicized actions grew from the Sandy Cove effort. These included the "Evangelical Climate Initiative" (ECI), a document in which the 86 signatories called for policy makers to take steps to reduce the threat of global climate change. It included many of the most prominent leaders in the North American evangelical community, who acted together to speak against the threat of global climate change and its implications for biodiversity,[33] a stand that drew praise from the scientific community, as well as a congenial welcome to the signatories.[34]

As Christian political activists have begun to take on larger problems related to the environment, Christian organizations have also become more specific in their approaches to environmental problems, with even relatively small organizations taking on significant legal and regulatory issues. For example, in 1999, the Christian environmental organization Caring for Creation teamed with the Center for Biological Diversity, a secular environmental institution, to sue the U.S. Fish and Wildlife Service in order to secure a larger area of land for the protection of two locally endemic species, the Alameda whipsnake and the arroyo toad. Although the actual amount of land designated as critical habitat for these species continues to be a point of contention and negotiation in California, the lawsuit drew attention to the conditions and needs of these species and the threats posed to them by housing developers.

Some secular critics of the church in the 1970s and 80s had dismissed its scholarly and educational work on the environment as no more than pious platitudes. By the 1990s, however, that was a charge that would no longer stand scrutiny. The Christian church was becoming increasingly engaged, specific, and sophisticated in its political engagement on the environment, and the reality of environmental concern had begun to permeate even its most traditional organizations and activities. Nowhere was this more evident than in the area of Christian missions.

MISSIONS, MISSIONARIES, AND ECOSYSTEMS: NEW DIRECTIONS IN ORGANIZATIONS AND INDIVIDUALS

While some Christian organizations like Caring for Creation became exclusively devoted to environmental concerns, other traditional, more established Christian mission and development organizations were beginning to retool their internal organizational structures to address environmental issues themselves and, in doing so, increasingly became part of the new presence of Christian environmental activism, particularly in the developing world. World Vision (WV), the development arm of the Billy Graham Evangelistic Association, considered by many to be the world's largest nongovernmental organization (NGO) in development, began to create a comprehensive battery of environmental programs to complement its more traditional development efforts. Its reorganization to allocate resources more directly to environmental needs was quiet but systemic, and the fruits of such change are becoming increasingly apparent.

For example, WV celebrated World Environment Day on June 5, 2009, with, among other things, a celebration at the Humbo Farmers Managed Natural Regeneration Project in Ethiopia. Before the project was initiated by WV in 2006, the lands around the Humbo people had been severely degraded. Soil erosion was extensive, landslides were common, and food production was inadequate for the needs of the growing human population. WV worked with the community to rehabilitate the area, closed large portions of it to grazing, and gained community acceptance of land use practices that promoted natural revegetation and reforestation. In only three years, significant improvements in revegetation and production were evident.[35] Similarly, in Kenya, World Relief, another major Christian development organization, has worked among the Masai to improve livestock husbandry, cultivation techniques, environmental preservation, water access, shelter, and health and educational opportunities.

Although Christian organizations have been actively reforming and remaking themselves to better address environmental concerns, especially in the last two decades, their understanding and models for addressing such concerns were very different from their secular organizational counterparts. Christians believe that the entire created order is included in God's plan and purpose of redemption, expressed eloquently in the previously examined doxology of Colossians that the apostle Paul wrote in praise of Jesus Christ: "For it was the Father's good pleasure," wrote Paul, "for all the fullness to dwell in Him, and through Him to reconcile all things to Himself, having made peace through the blood of his cross."[36] Thus, the Christian view of environmental conservation, from the earliest days of the church, did not see the problem as a polemic of human needs versus nature preservation, nor did they see the human community as a destructive cancer on an otherwise perfect natural world.

The biblical view sees both the human and non-human community living in the same desperate need of redemption. Therefore, the solution to the problem is not to preserve the one (nature) from the other (human), but to first reconcile human beings and nature to one another, and to God. Thus, the theology of Christian environmental stewardship, as it began to be worked out in specific applications, approached the problem as one of fundamental alienation among humans, nature, and God and not simply a problem of (human) over-population or technological misapplication and industrial pollution. The solution was not preservation, but reconciliation.

Existing organizations necessarily had to move slowly to begin to incorporate their theological understanding of creation into long-standing organizational structures. Individual efforts, in contrast, could move much more rapidly. One of the best examples of an individual initiative to apply a reconciliation-oriented approach to environmental conflict has been embodied in the work of Christian environmentalist Susan Drake Emmerich. As noted earlier, Emmerich, one of the original drafters of the "Evangelical Declaration on the Care of Creation," had served in the U.S. State Department as a senior environmental officer and a delegate to the United Nations Environmental Programme. Leaving that position to earn her Ph.D. at the University of Wisconsin-Madison in the early 1990s, Emmerich, who had worked extensively in environmental treaty development and negotiation, desired to investigate the problem of environmental conflict resolution at the community level.

Frustrated with traditional "objective" methodologies that separated the researcher from direct involvement in both the problem to be studied and the community in which it was located, Emmerich chose to work with a relatively new paradigm of investigation called "action research." In this approach, the investigator herself takes an active role in the community and its struggle to solve its own environmental conflicts. A thoughtful Christian who believed that biblical principles, rightly applied, could lead to significant progress in conflict resolution and reconciliation between a human community and its environment, Emmerich had observed, from her experience as an environmental activist and environmental treaty negotiator, that the long-standing frustration of many conservation organizations with uncooperative local communities was rooted in a wrong-headed approach to the fundamental problem. Specifically, Emmerich perceived that conservation organizations too often saw such conflicts as about some "thing" that was wrong with the environment, and not as a more basic issue of the way people related to that environment.

Emmerich herself expressed her thesis simply. "I believed," said Emmerich, "that environmental problems in faith-based communities require faith-based solutions."[37] But where to find such a faith-based community that was also experiencing a significant environmental conflict? A test case presented itself in Tangier Island, Virginia. The people of the Tangier community had, for centuries, earned their living as watermen, fishing the waters of Chesapeake Bay for oysters, sea bass, blue crab, and other species. But by the 1980s, increased pollution and deteriorating environmental conditions in the Chesapeake had all but eliminated oysters and substantially reduced sea bass and other fisheries. Only the blue crab, a species relatively tolerant of pollution, persisted in sufficient numbers to support the economic life of Tangier. Concurrent with this, a Christian revival had swept the island in the early 1990s, making what had been a nominal Christian community into one that was now enthusiastically committed to Christian faith. Religious conversion, however, even among watermen themselves, did not solve the problem of declining harvests and increasingly restrictive government regulations. The region's largest environmental NGO, the Chesapeake Bay Foundation (CBF), was lobbying aggressively for even more restrictions on the crab harvest. CBF's advocacy for restricting harvests, and their increasing political success in achieving it, was infuriating local watermen, resulting in conflict that was moving beyond verbal disagreement into property damage, arson, and death threats.

Consistent with her commitment to the paradigm of action research, Emmerich began living on the island as part of the Tangier community and engaging its members in conversations about the nature of the current conflict. Over time, Emmerich came to understand that the conflict was rooted in fundamental estrangements in both person-to-person relationships (watermen to CBF staff and supporters) and human-to-non-human relationships (watermen to Chesapeake Bay). Her approach to resolving the conflict involved not only the perception of the problem as primarily relational and worldview-oriented, but also recognized that the community's primary decision-making institutions were the local churches, and therefore these institutions had to become involved to legitimate any proposed solution. Working through the churches, Emmerich, through both pulpit messages she was invited to give and meetings of the watermen she was asked to lead, helped watermen to identify and articulate a faith-based environmental ethic founded on the teachings of scripture, particularly Genesis 2:15 and its admonition to serve and protect the Earth. The new ethic, in turn, led watermen to develop the "Waterman's Covenant," a self-imposed pledge written by watermen to respect existing conservation laws as an expression of obedience to biblical commands and principles of stewardship and of loving their neighbor.[38]

THE OUTCOMES OF ACTIVISM

Deep in a tropical forest in Papua New Guinea, the Evangelical Alliance, a Christian missionary organization, constructed a new center for its work in 2001. This would hardly seem to be newsworthy. Christian organizations build centers for their own work all over the world all the time. What is significant about this construction, however, is that the center is not primarily a center for evangelism, theological education, or organizational management. The new site, called the Hogave Conservation and Retreat Center, is dedicated to training Christian pastors and laity alike in the principles and practices of forest management. The Hogave Center is located in the middle of an important nature reserve, one which was established by three clans of indigenous people, all Christians, who united their holdings in order to form the reserve and protect the forest that had always been their home.

Papua New Guinea is one of the world's major centers of biodiversity. Part of the East Melanesian Islands biodiversity hotspot, as demarcated by Conservation International, it is one of the most geographically complex and biologically unique areas on Earth. The region contains 8,000 known species of plants and animals. Of these, more than one-third of its plants, 40 percent of its birds, reptiles, and mammals, and 90 percent of its amphibians are endemic species found nowhere else on Earth. The persistence of this biodiversity, however, extensive as it is, is uncertain. More than 70 percent of the region's original vegetation has been destroyed, and deforestation is continuing in the name of development.

Papua New Guinea is also, coincidentally, an area in which Christians make up the vast majority of the population. Of 5.1 million human residents, 4.9 million (96%) are active Christians. Their construction of the Hogave Conservation and Retreat Center and their pledge to use it to further forest conservation make perfect sense, both theologically and practically. Like the watermen of Tangier Island, the most pressing concern on the minds of these indigenous people is the threat to their traditional way of life, what the "Cornwall Declaration" might have had in mind in its reference to "primitive agricultural, industrial and commercial practices."[39] The sustainable management and conservation of the forest is the first and most foundational issue that must be addressed if such cultures, including their expression of Christian faith, are continue for succeeding generations.

Christians active in conservation, as well as many active conservationists who are not Christians, are becoming increasingly cognizant of the repeated coincidence between the locations of biodiversity hotspots and the locations of human populations that are predominantly Christian. Whether one looks at Papua New Guinea, the Philippines, the Cape Floristic Region of South Africa, or any number of other examples, the pattern, although having many exceptions, is globally pervasive. Worldwide, Christians are concentrated in some of Earth's most biologically diverse regions. Their understanding of their relationship to that biodiversity, and their interaction with it, will have significant effects on the success or failure of the global conservation effort. The world is entering a period in history in which traditional Christian missionary organizations like the Evangelical Alliance of Papua New Guinea and others active in the developing world are uniquely positioned to affect the preservation of species and their habitats, just as the Christians who live in these regions also are uniquely in need of a right understanding of their relationship to nature in order to maintain their traditional cultures and ways of life. The needs and opportunities occasioned by such an overlap of Christian presence and endemic regional biodiversity is, today, not only becoming the concern of traditional missionary organizations but of an entirely new kind of organization, the conservation faith-based organization, whose missions are concentrated in the work of environmental and biodiversity protection. In the next chapter, we examine the history, characteristics, and work of these organizations and the difference they can and do make in the world conservation effort.

NOTES

1. John Ruskin, *The Genius of John Ruskin*, ed. John D. Rosenberg (New York: George Braziller, 1963), p. 369.
2. Corrado Poli, "The Political Consequences of an Environmental Question." In *Environmental Ethics and Policy: Theory Meets Practice*, eds. Frederick Ferré and Peter Hartzel (Athens: University of Georgia Press, 1994), pp. 125–141.
3. Daniel 4:12, NASB.
4. Daniel 4:21–22. NASB.
5. Ezekiel 17:23–24. NASB.
6. Au Sable Institute, *Au Sable Institute of Environmental Studies 2010 Official Bulletin* (Mancelona, MI: Au Sable Institute, 2010), p. 3.
7. Wesley Grandberg-Michaelson, ed., *Tending the Garden: Essays on the Gospel and the Care of the Earth* (Grand Rapids, MI: Eerdmans, 1987). Calvin B. DeWitt and Ghillean T. Prance, eds., *Missionary Earthkeeping* (Macon, GA: Mercer University Press, 1992). J. M. Thomas, ed., *Evangelicals and the Environment: Theological Foundations for Christian Environmental Stewardship* (Cambridge, UK: Paternoster Periodicals, 1993).
8. A variety of research efforts in this program were funded by the Fish and Wildlife Services Cooperative Cost-Share Program and Nongame Bird Program, and generated new knowledge for managers and scientists engaged in grassland conservation published in such journals as *Restoration Ecology* (2004), *Biodiversity and Conservation* (2007), and in the book, *Vertebrate Conservation and Biodiversity* (2007).
9. The enrollment of the Northwestern College farm and the restoration of a native tallgrass prairie on part of this property is told in Fred Van Dyke, *Conservation Biology: Foundations, Concepts, Applications* (Dordrecht, The Netherlands: Springer, 2008), pp. 421–422.
10. Quoted in Bruce Barcott, "For God So Loved the World," *Outside* 26 (2001): 3:84–126.
11. David M. Johns, "Orr and Armageddon: Building a Coalition," *Conservation Biology* 19 (2005): pp. 1685–1686, 1685.
12. Catholic Bishops Conference, *The Columbia River Watershed: Caring for Creation and the Common Good.* 2001. Available at http://www.columbiariver.org/files/pastoral-english.pdf. Accessed 30 October 2009.
13. The conflicts over rural poverty in South America, particularly Brazil, often found the Catholic Church pitted against government officials and wealthy landowners in defense of poor farmers who were often evicted from

lands they had traditionally used in the course of agricultural "development."
Although these conflicts were not primarily about ecological issues, environmental pollution and land degradation associated with large, corporate farming practices in Brazil increasingly posed threats to the rural poor, making it
a growing concern of the church. For a more detailed account of the nature
of these conflicts, see Madeleine Cousineau Adriance, *Promised Land: Base
Christian Communities and the Struggle for the Amazon* (Albany: State University of New York Press, 1995).

14. NASSA-Caritas Philippines, *Responding to the Needs of the Filipino Poor.*
Available at www.rc.net/rome/afprs/mallillin1.doc. Accessed 30 October 2009.

15. Ibid.

16. Evangelical Environmental Network Web site, www.creationcare.org.
Accessed 4 December 2009.

17. Loren Wilkinson, ed., *Earthkeeping: Christian Stewardship of Natural
Resources* (Grand Rapids, MI: Eerdmans, 1980).

18. R. J. Berry, ed., "An Evangelical Declaration on the Care of Creation:
The text," pp. 17–22, p. 18.

19. Ibid., pp. 19–22.

20. Quoted in Loren Wilkinson, "The Making of the Declaration." In
The Care of Creation: Focusing Concern and Action, ed. R. J. Berry (Downers
Grove, IL: InterVarsity Press, 2000), p. 54.

21. Anonymous, "About the Cornwall Alliance: Dominion. Stewardship.
Conservation." Available at http://www.cornwallalliance.org/about/.
Accessed 5 December 2009.

22. Anonymous, "The Cornwall Declaration on Environmental
Stewardship." Available at http://www.cornwallalliance.org/articles/read/
the-cornwall-declaration-on-environmental-stewardship/. Accessed
5 December 2009.

23. Ibid.

24. Ibid.

25. Ibid.

26. Ibid.

27. Berry, p. 21.

28. Cornwall Declaration, op. cit.

29. Norman Wirzba, *The Paradise of God: Renewing Religion in an Ecological
Age* (Oxford, UK: Oxford University Press, 2003), p. 132.

30. Anonymous, "The Sandy Cove Covenant," *Creation Care Magazine* 26
(2004, Fall): pp. 10–11, 10.

31. Larry Schweiger, "From Gurdy's Run to Global Leadership, Part I,"
Creation Care Magazine 26 (2004, Fall): pp. 12–15. Available at http://www
.creationcare.org/magazine/fall04.php. Accessed 5 December 2009.

32. E. Kintisch, "Evangelicals, Scientists Reach Common Ground on
Climate Change," *Science* (2006): pp. 311:1188–1192.

33. A. Haag, "Church Joins Crusade Over Global Climate Change," *Nature* (2006): pp. 440:136–137.

34. Editors of *Nature*, "A Warm Welcome: Scientists Should Embrace a Move by Evangelicals to Join the Debate on Climate Change," *Nature* 44 (2006): p. 128.

35. Anonymous, "Ethiopia: Marking Environment Day by Celebrating a Success Story," 2009. Available at http://www.wvi.org/wvi/wviweb.nsf/updates/6F10AD2E962FF7B4882575CB00731E32?opendocument. Accessed 30 October 2009.

36. Colossians 1:19–20, NASB.

37. Quoted in Jeffrey Pohorski, producer. *Between Heaven and Earth: The Plight of the Chesapeake Bay Watermen.* Skunkfilms Inc. 2001.

38. Susan D.Emmerich, "The Declaration in Practice: Missionary Earth-keeping." In *The Care of Creation: Focusing Concern and Action* (Downers Grove, IL: InterVarsity Press, 2000), p. 147–154.

39. Cornwall Declaration, op. cit.

CHAPTER 8

The Rise of the Christian Faith-Based Organization in Conservation

Ninety per cent of conservation work is with people. . . . What, then, changes people?

Achim Steiner[1]

WHITHER THE CONSERVATION FBO? THE ROOTS OF FAITH-BASED ACTIVISM

The Stockholm Conference of 1972 is considered one of the watershed events in the development of global environmental conservation. At Stockholm, the United Nations became involved in conservation in an entirely new way, for it was here that the UN created its first environmental agency, the United Nations Environmental Programme (UNEP), an agency charged with creating new environmental conventions (that is, treaties) to foster conservation and environmental protection. Today, nearly four decades later, the work of UNEP forms the basis of much international law and policy that protects the environment on the global scale. UNEP's role in creating the Convention on International Trade in Endangered Species (CITES), the UN Conference on the Law of the Sea (UNCLOS), the Man and Biosphere Reserve Program, and innumerable other efforts have made important contributions to environmental protection. But the long-term effect was not the same as the short-term response.

At Stockholm, many scientists made dramatic presentations of how countries throughout the developing world were selling their rainforests for cash, only to find themselves left with an aftermath of eroded and impoverished soil and, as years passed, the need to import from other countries timber they had once had in abundant supply within their own borders. The intent of such presentations was to move the delegates to return to their countries and stop such rampant deforestation. That is not what happened. Many business people and politicians returned with their eyes opened to prospects they had not seen before. They learned that their countries' tropical forests were valuable resources and that there were plenty of multinational companies willing to pay good money to log them. The rate of tropical rainforest destruction did not decline after Stockholm. It increased, rising perceptibly after the conference and for several years thereafter. As Martin Palmer of the World Bank explains, "Both politicians and environmentalists had the same data. But they had different assumptions, different values, and different frameworks."[2] Never underestimate the power of a worldview.

The Stockholm example could be dismissed as a case of good worldview versus bad worldview, or environmental worldview versus economic worldview, which many conservationists would consider the same thing. But it is not that simple. Conservationists can, when limited by their own presumptions and perspectives, make mistakes as damaging to the environment as the rainforest destruction that arose from the Stockholm delegates seeing their national forests as so many board feet of profit.

In the previous chapter we examined the case of Susan Emmerich and the Tangier Watermen, one in which Emmerich's work of developing a community-based Christian environmental ethic was the key to resolving environmental conflict. Part of Emmerich's motivation to achieve this kind of solution arose from her frustration with traditional conservation approaches, such as those employed by the region's dominant conservation non-governmental organization (NGO), the Chesapeake Bay Foundation. Her frustration can be expressed in the words of Michael Shellenberger and Ted Nordhaus in their classic essay "The Death of Environmentalism." Speaking of the myopia of most environmentalists to the underlying dimensions of environmental problems, Shellenberger and Nordhaus note, "What the environmental movement needs more than anything else right now is to take a collective step back to re-think everything. We will never be able to turn things around as long as we understand our failures as essentially tactical and make proposals that are essentially technical."[3]

Such short-sightedness is, in many cases, not merely ineffective but stupid. Martin Palmer of the World Bank relates an example that shows just how stupid.

> I was recently shown a copy of a proposal, drawn up by a very respectable international environmental group. It was a plan based on the knowledge that the gases emitted by cattle can contribute quite considerably to global warming. The proposal was to persuade nomadic people in the Central Asian steppes to agree to have their herds of cattle killed. And in return for having their traditional way of life trashed in the name of preventing global warming, the nomads were to be offered solar-powered TV sets by the environmental group.[4]

Someone in this organization must have thought there was no problem with treating other people, in this case pastoral nomads, as the means to a desired environmental end. But these were not just any people. They were poor people who, in their poverty, might be particularly vulnerable to such shameless bribery and manipulation. For the sake of fewer carbon emissions, the nomad's worldview, a worldview that, whatever its faults, certainly made people aware of their close connection to the Earth and the local environment, would be replaced with a western, television-informed worldview in which there was no environment except the fictitious one created on a television screen. Palmer perceptively identifies this proposal's more serious faults by reflecting on those whom the environmental organization did *not* try to bride. The environmentalists didn't offer TV sets in exchange for lower carbon emissions to "the huge multinationals—automobile manufactures creating car exhaust, for example, or the dairies and burger chains with their vast cattle production—that contribute so massively to global warming, but have stronger lobbying groups than the nomads."[5] To the credit of the World Bank, the proposal was not funded.

The philosopher Immanuel Kant wrote, "In the realm of ends everything has either a *price* or a *dignity*. Whatever has a price can be replaced by something else as its equivalent: on the other hand, whatever is above all price and therefore admits no equivalent, has dignity."[6] Through such moral logic Kant arrived at one of his most important ethical principles: rational human beings, as individuals, have no equivalent. Therefore, they are never to be treated as a means to an end, but always as *ends in themselves*.

Not only have secular conservation organizations focused over-much on the technical and tactical dimensions of the conservation problem, they have often treated people outside their own circle simply as means to an end, rather than as individuals who were ends in themselves. It was this means-ends confusion that prevented the Chesapeake Bay Foundation from effective interaction with the Tangier Watermen. This is a problem that plagues conservation efforts throughout the world. One solution might be to have the executives of all conservation NGOs read Kant. But let us consider a more seri-ous proposal, an alternative perception of the nature of the conserva-tion problem and what to do about it.

AN ALTERNATIVE UNDERSTANDING: CONSERVATION AS RECONCILIATION

In the early 1980s, a young British pastor, Peter Harris, and his wife, Miranda, were leading a small, struggling church in England's Merseyside District of Liverpool. Peter Harris, formally educated and trained as a minister, was also an avid amateur ornithologist. He spent most of his days off watching and photographing birds on the nearby River Mersey and other local natural areas. His attention to birds in the midst of his pastoral duties sometimes produced comic conflicts. Recalling a pastoral call to encourage a lonely, homebound lady who was part of his church, Harris explains,

> We were deep in conversation when my eyes strayed to the lawn that was visible over her left shoulder and I noticed a Brambling feeding among the customary flock of Chaffinches. Very few had been seen in the area that winter, but I suspected that she wouldn't feel it was quite the consolation she was looking for. "Cheer up, there's a Brambling on your lawn" wasn't one of the recognized punch lines in the counseling manuals we had been given at theological college.[7]

No, it wasn't. But increasingly, through events in their lives and encouragement from friends and colleagues, the Harris's began to envision the possibility of a Christian field study center dedicated to the care of God's creation and, in that work, a proclamation and manifestation of the gospel of Jesus Christ. Improbable as the idea appeared, it gained the support of The Bible Churchman's Missionary

Society (today CrossLinks), and in 1982, a small trust fund was established to support the Harris's idea to begin work on the coast of Portugal. Here they began a small conservation field station. Driving the development of the vision was the Harris's desire to create a community of Christians empowered to be actively engaged in conservation *and* committed to being uniquely Christian neighbors to a surrounding culture that was losing touch with the beauty and value of its own environment. The Harris's worked diligently for the preservation of the unique wetlands in that vicinity and their associated wetland-dependent species. But the Harris's were missionaries, in the fullest sense, laboring to establish a transformed human community, one marked by the reconciliation of human beings to one another and to their surrounding creation. In both efforts, they achieved remarkable success.

Today the Harris's initial effort in Portugal has grown to an international organization, A Rocha (a Portuguese phrase meaning "the rock"), with chapters in 19 countries. Emphasis on human community and cultural transformation are integral features of A Rocha efforts, exemplified in, among other examples, the work of A Rocha Lebanon. In the politically unstable climate of Lebanon, A Rocha has succeeded in preserving the last major marsh area in the land bridge between Europe and Asia, the Ammiq Wetland. A major stopover for hundreds of species migrating between Eurasia and Africa, A Rocha's efforts have combined scientific study, an environmental education program for local schools, a community arts program for women, and a science club for local students.

Conservation in Lebanon is not for sissies. Peter Harris describes his first tour of the area with Chris Walley, one of the leaders of the then still unofficial chapter of A Rocha Lebanon, "Leaning out of the window of his old Renault at the frequent check-points to greet the baffling variety of military and para-military groups with what we (and perhaps they) felt was unnecessarily high humour, he was clearly doing his best to prepare us for the glory, despair and sheer hard grind of the next A Rocha national incarnation."[8] The end of the first day brought sober reflection in difficult circumstances.

> As we lay awake listening to the unfamiliar sound of shelling, far to the south around the border, we wondered if this time the difficulties of the place would be too great for A Rocha to bring any hope at all. But as soon as we went down to the marsh at dawn the next morning, we knew why everyone there felt that

we had to try ... Millions of birds of prey, storks, wildfowl and waders make their way along the valley between their wintering quarters in Africa and the breeding ground of Europe and western Asia. The disappearance of the marsh would mean the loss of a vital rung in the ladder of habitats that sustain all these migrants. ...[9]

Ultimately A Rocha Lebanon was established, and the Ammiq Wetland was preserved. A Rocha Lebanon leaders were able to introduce local farmers to improved management techniques that reduced pumping of water from the wetland for irrigation, along with a shift to less moisture-dependent crops. The effects of these changes were dramatic, and the wetland began to recover from its long abuse more rapidly than anyone expected. In the meantime, floral and faunal surveys conducted by A Rocha Lebanon members, documenting the enormous biodiversity of the wetland as well as the presence of rare species of birds, mammals, reptiles, and amphibians, brought national and international attention to the need for conserving the Ammiq. By 1999, the wetland had been declared a Ramsar Site, giving it official status and protection under the terms of the 1971 Convention on Wetlands of International Importance. In 2005, the Ammiq Wetland, with the adjoining Al Shouf Cedar Nature Reserve, was designated an official Biosphere Reserve by the United Nations Educational, Scientific and Cultural Organization.

Today A Rocha is actively and cooperatively involved in the study, management, and conservation of many species of plants, invertebrates, reptiles, amphibians, fish, birds, and mammals throughout the world. That its work is taken seriously by the conservation community is evident in the fact that A Rocha is the only faith-based organization to enjoy member status in the International Union for the Conservation of Nature (IUCN).

The IUCN is the world's largest nongovernmental conservation organization, and its research, management, and conservation activities are of global influence. Comparatively, the efforts of A Rocha are small, because A Rocha lacks the financial, technical, and organizational capacities typical of major international and national conservation NGOs. What distinguishes A Rocha from other conservation NGOs, however, is not the size of its budget or the number of its nature reserves, but that A Rocha and other Christian conservation organizations have been able to make two unique contributions to conservation's credibility and legitimacy.

First is their ability and confidence, rooted in the teachings of the Judeo-Christian tradition, to state the basis for the intrinsic value of nature with clarity. "God saw all that he had made, and behold, it was very good" (Genesis 1:31). The second is their perception that the underlying problem of conservation is not one of tactical management error or inadequate technological expertise, but rather of reconciliation in relationship. That is, A Rocha and other Christian conservation organizations perceive the conservation problem to be rooted in a fundamental antagonism between the human community and its natural surroundings, an antagonism arising from a more fundamental estrangement from God, and, as a result of that estrangement, a loss of knowledge and a lack of desire to advance God's intentions for the care of his creation. Both human and non-human creation stand in need of reconciliation to one another and to God. This reconciliation must be manifested in practices that demonstrate reconciliation between people and God, people with one another, and people with the non-human environment. Thus, all A Rocha initiatives emphasize the condition of the human community and its attitude toward its non-human neighbors. The goal is never to exclude human beings from the non-human world, or to exclude appropriate human benefit from it, but to end the kinds of exploitation that reflect an alienation between humans and nature. The ultimate objective is that local residents take personal responsibility for the welfare of their environment and their non-human neighbors who depend on it.

THE NEW RELATIONSHIP BETWEEN CONSERVATION, SCIENCE, AND RELIGION

During the last 30 years, principles embodied by the work of the Harris's and others in A Rocha have become the basis for the development of an entirely new kind of organizational animal in the conservation community, the faith-based organization (FBO). Christianity is not unique among world religions in having faith-based conservation organizations. There are conservation FBOs in Islam, Judaism, Buddhism, Hinduism, and other religions. All are of fairly recent origin. Where did they come from?

The environmental crisis of the 1960s did not improve with age. It got worse. The response of the scientific community was passionate but not always effective. Its ineffectiveness arose from the fact that, at first, it was disorganized, as different scientists and scientific societies perceived the problems in different ways. Second, the scientific response was often unpersuasive to the public. To a conservation biologist, the fact that a species has become endangered is sufficient basis for promoting action to save it. To the nonscientific public, the need for such action is not self-evident. Their response may just as likely be an apathetic "so what?" Conservation biologist and ethicist Kyle Van Houtan captures the problem clearly when he notes that the scientific community often fails to inspire "enthusiasm, allegiance, and personal sacrifice—in other words, actual changes in human behavior."[10]

Scientific and political leaders recognized this failing. And if they did not have a ready solution in hand, they knew where to look. They turned to the religious community. As a result, the 1980s and early 1990s became a period of intense interaction between science and religion on the problem of the environment. Many mark the Conference of Assisi in 1986 as beginning of that engagement. The Assisi gathering was sparked by the initiative of His Royal Highness Prince Philip of Great Britain, who, in that year, was serving as president of the World Wide Fund for Nature (WWF). Prince Philip asked leaders of the world's five major religions—Buddhism, Christianity, Hinduism, Islam and Judaism—to gather with him and with representatives of the conservation community at Assisi, Italy, the birthplace of Saint Francis. The question to be answered was, how can your faith community save the world? From the conference came five statements, one from each faith, which outlined the distinctive features of that tradition's approach to the care of nature.

Meetings that brought together leaders of the world's major faith communities and conservationists multiplied. The Global Forum of Spiritual and Parliamentary Leaders, first held in 1988, and then repeated in 1990, 1992, and 1993, assembled thousands of representatives from more than 80 nations, including representatives from all of the world's major religions. In 1995, the Summit on Religion and Environment in Windsor, England, assembled leaders from nine world religions with secular leaders and conservationists and led to the development of plans for religion-based conservation efforts. This was also the beginning of the Alliance of Religion and Conservation (ARC). Although a secular organization, ARC was formed to help the major religions of the world develop their own environmental programs, each unique to its own perspective and tradition.

As part of its mission, ARC continued to hold gatherings similar to the 1986 Assisi Conference. An ARC-sponsored conference in 1997 led to linkages between the world's major religions and The World Bank in developing programs for sustainable development and conservation. By 2000, ARC had expanded to 11 world religions, coupled with partnerships from The World Bank, the World Wildlife Fund, and other conservation organizations. With these relationships and resources in place, ARC initiated the Sacred Gifts for a Living Planet Program in which various religious leaders and their constituencies designated 26 "sacred gifts" of land and resources to conservation and environmental protection. The gifts included a garbage dump converted to a public park in Egypt, a "sacred forest" in India, and, from the Christian church, a coastal forest in Lebanon. In 2007 the Faith and Forestry initiative was convened in Sweden and created a Religious Forestry Standard that led to millions of acres of forests being protected by religious organizations and constituencies. The following year UNEP and ARC developed a plan to involve major religions of the world in creating the Seven and Eight Year Generational Plans to embed practices and teachings in all major faiths that would explicitly address issues of environmental conservation. During the same period, major development and conservation organizations, including Conservation International, World Wildlife Fund, the World Bank, UNEP, and others began to dedicate specific organizational programs and personnel to working with religious organizations.[11]

The work supported by these initiatives was not confined to Christianity, but it created the opportunity for faith-based organizations to succeed within the Christian community and to have significant effects on global conservation. What, then, are the distinctive characteristics of Christian environmental FBOs and what do they offer to world conservation efforts?

THE CONSERVATION FBO: ORGANIZATION-BASED ACTIVISM IN THE CHRISTIAN COMMUNITY

Environmental scholar Alethea Abuyuan, in her comprehensive study of environmental organizations, noted a basic difference between secular NGOs and religious, including Christian, environmental FBOs. Religious FBOs, noted Abuyuan, emphasize a *value-rational* approach compared to the traditional *goal-rational* approach of secular NGOs. Although FBOs pursue measurable goals in conservation, their underlying aim is to transform human character and human relationships to the environment through an altered set of values which their members embrace as part of a larger belief structure. As Abuyuan puts it, the difference between traditional conservation NGOs and conservation FBOs is one of "technical competency versus moral endeavor."[12] Abuyuan notes that FBOs are not equally effective in every part of the world, but are especially influential where

> a sense of cynicism and distrust toward the government prevail . . . Such places have come to see the Church, and the various faith-based initiatives connected with it, assume a leadership role that entails not only guiding the citizenry toward peace and order, but also in providing them with the social services they need. In the midst of all this, the Church and faith-based NGOs have managed to maintain their credibility and independence—valuable traits especially in places where government institutions are wrought with corruption, mismanagement, and bureaucracy.[13]

Most secular NGOs perceive problems in conservation as problems of costs and benefits to be solved by welfare maximization strategies. In contrast, Christian FBOs see the same problems as conflicts between consumption and conscience. That is, the problem can only be solved by making people distinguish between different kinds of desires, the desires we have (for goods or wealth from the environment) and the desires *we ought to have* (for the proper treatment of the environment, its creatures, and our neighbors). This is a problem—the problem of the freedom of the will—we have explored earlier because of its fundamental and profound implications for the development of an environmental ethic. This perspective also changes an FBO's perception of conservation priorities. Secular NGOs are more likely to define priority conservation targets as those places most immediately threatened, or those with the greatest density of biodiversity, or both. Christian FBOs, like A Rocha, will consider not only the threats to the biological diversity of a natural environment but also the condition of the people in it. As A Rocha's founder, Peter Harris, put it, "The fractured relationship between people and places has often been the most significant factor in their degradation."[14] Susan Emmerich's explanation of the Chesapeake Bay Foundation's failure to achieve a solution to the conservation problems associated with the Tangier watermen is similar, but even more pointed. "The most pressing concern on the minds of watermen," noted Emmerich, "was the threat to their existing way of life."[15] No proposed solution to

the environmental degradation of the Chesapeake could hope to earn
the watermen's support if it did not address that threat. Many conservation initiatives throughout the world have failed for similar reasons.
To understand the reasons for these failures, let us return to the
example of one of the contributions to ARC's Sacred Gifts initiative,
the ancient cedar forests of Lebanon.

WHY DIFFERENCES MATTER

During the last 30 years, the coastline of Lebanon has experienced
rapid development. Its shorelines and hills have been converted from
natural areas to roads, homes, and urban business centers. Yet it was
these shorelines and hillsides that were the home of the famed cedars
of Lebanon, forests of massive and ancient trees unique in the Mediterranean world. Their height was so great that the Bible uses it as
the standard for everything else. Speaking of his destruction of an
enemy of Israel, the Amorites, God says, through the prophet Amos,
"Yet it was I who destroyed the Amorite before them, though his
height was like the height of the cedars. . . ."[16]
Most of these forests had been destroyed by the time the
international conservation community realized the gravity of the situation. UNEP and other conservation NGOs identified these
Mediterranean forests as a conservation priority, ranking them among
the 200 most important world ecosystems to be protected. But were
any left? Upon investigation, the answer turned out to be yes. A siz-
able ancient forest covering three hills, locally known as the Forest
of Harissa, was located north of Beirut. But who owned it? The owner
turned out to be a church, the Maronite Church of Lebanon, which
had held title to the land for many centuries. To the Maronite Church,
this forest was not the Forest of Harissa, but the Holy Forest of Our
Lady of Lebanon. In the center of the forest was the Cathedral of
Our Lady and an enormous outdoor statue of the Virgin Mary.
UNEP and other conservation organizations prepared a 48-page
proposal and delivered it to the church. The proposal demanded a
promise from the church to abide by national and international laws
to ensure protection of the forest. As the authors of the proposal put
it, "The area's custodians must have protection of biodiversity as a
first order management objective. If other objectives take precedence
over biodiversity protection, then the area as a whole, or those parts
of the area where other objectives take precedence, should not be

classified as a protected area."[17] Presented with the idea that protecting biodiversity was an ultimatum from outside interests who possessed neither sympathy nor understanding of the church's work and mission, the Maronite Church declined to enroll the forest as an area of protected status.

Given the failure of this effort, ARC and WWF tried a different tact. Working with more locally based forest conservation groups, they met directly with the patriarch of the Maronite Church, and almost immediately gained a commitment from the patriarch to protect the forest. The reasons for that protection were framed in a new statement, written mainly by the patriarch, who expressed the new proposal in different words for a different purpose:

> For centuries the Church has defended the natural beauty and Godliness of the forests and hills of Harissa, as well as many other holy places in Lebanon. . . . In so doing, we observe that the land and the flora and fauna on it, do not ultimately belong to us. We are simply the guardians of what belongs to God. . . . In protecting this area, the Church will continue to ensure that the diversity of plants, trees, animals and birds given by God, nurtured by the Church, will be maintained. . . .[18]

The contrasts of these two approaches reveal some of the reasons why Christian FBOs in conservation can succeed where secular conservation NGOs fail. No one in UNEP initially bothered to learn about the history of the church or its founder, Saint Maron, a Syrian Christian monk of the fifth century. Maron, in his early years of ministry, was an active missionary and drew many followers who were attracted by his preaching and the miraculous healings that accompanied it. In his later years, Maron, believing that the contemplation of God alone was his highest calling, became a hermit, living in a forest on a mountain in Syria called Ol-Yambos. Many of his followers, imitating the saint's example, devoted themselves to monastic life and built cathedrals and shrines within forests as their centers of worship and ministry.

UNEP felt that the presence of unique biodiversity within the Forest of Harissa was sufficient motive for preserving it. The Maronite Church did not. They had preserved the forest for centuries as a sacred trust to God, long before UNEP even existed. Subsequent to making a formal declaration to protect the forest and its biodiversity, the Maronite Church created an ecology center for young people,

formally protected two other woodland sites, and developed a program of environmental education and activism in 77 Lebanese villages
and towns, making the church one of the largest and most effective
environmental organizations in Lebanon and one of the most influential advocates in the country for environmental protection. As Martin
Palmer of the World Bank observed in retrospect, "By insisting that
people adopt their view of the world, many campaigning groups cut
themselves off from natural allies, who may see things differently,
but no less compassionately."[19]

THE FUTURE OF THE CHRISTIAN
CONSERVATION FBO

What Abuyuan called the "culture of rationality" within secular
conservation organizations motivates their need to develop solutions
rooted in technical expertise and measurable indices. What Abuyuan
described as the "culture of hope" intrinsic to Christian environmental organizations supports a faith that believes that their actions will,
in the end, really matter, an attitude that preserves their members
from the cynicism and despair so commonplace in the secular conservation community.[20]

Because they provide opportunity for people to transform faith
commitments into meaningful action, Christian FBOs engaged in
conservation inspire high levels of loyalty and commitment among
their staff, volunteers, and constituency. They create meaningful
connection with local communities and generate profound ethical
motivation for their conservation work. They are capable of effective,
productive partnerships with secular organizations, and their influence
is widespread and growing. For example, A Rocha France now works
with a number of French government agencies and conservation
NGOs, including Conservatoire des Espaces Naturels de Provence,
Agences des Alpilles, and the Tour du Valat, as well as with churches
and other Christian organizations.[21] Regarding more intentional,
active engagement of Christian organizations with world conservation
efforts, Tony Whitten, leader of the Faith and Environment Program
at The World Bank, recently remarked, "I ask them [skeptics] why on
Earth they wouldn't [engage FBOs]? Why would they avoid working
with these NGOs when they're available? When they reach people so
easily, when their agendas coincide—what on Earth could be the
reason for not doing it?"[22]

Christian conservation organizations are credible to the public because they are able to tie their immediate goals to a larger mission and an inspirational moral message. They also are more holistic in their approaches to conservation problems because they do not view conservation issues in isolation from the human condition. This kind of credibility and holism is not something the conservation community can do without. Both are essential elements in every conservation effort, but they become active components of conservation strategy only when Christian and other FBOs become active participants in conservation.

JOINING, SUPPORTING, AND WORKING IN A CHRISTIAN CONSERVATION FBO

THE ROLE OF THE FBO IN THE CHRISTIAN COMMUNITY

In a 2008 Barna Institute poll in the United States, 78 percent of Christians indicated that they wanted to see Christians take a more active role in caring for creation. Among evangelicals, the proportion was 90 percent.[23] Tom Rowley, Director of A Rocha USA, took these results a step further, asking A Rocha USA members, "What keeps you from becoming more involved in creation care?" The largest group of respondents, 37 percent, cited a lack of opportunity, and the second largest group (30 percent) indicated a lack of knowledge of appropriate actions to take.[24]

Rowley's current plan is to establish a summer training institute in the United States to help Christians build increased understanding and conviction related to environmental problems, create opportunities for engagement in solving such problems, and apply the theological, scientific, and practical expertise in A Rocha's membership to make such opportunities meaningful to the participants and in a way that solves the problems addressed. But there are other means, already at hand, that provide opportunities for engagement with Christian FBOs active in conservation.

THE FBO HYBRID—CONSERVATION AND MISSION IN THE CHRISTIAN COMMUNITY

If the secular conservation community sometimes has trouble seeing the work, or even the existence, of Christian conservation

FBOs, it is not entirely their fault. Some Christian conservation organizations are unusual and novel hybrids of conservation concern and missionary effort, but these strange organizational animals offer unique opportunities for those who take the time to participate in their efforts. In the early 1970s, an Indiana businessman, Richard Duggar, led groups of high school students on repeated visits to Haiti. The trips moved Duggar and the students to consider what might be done to help the poor in developing countries. Out of this concern, Duggar and others formed the Educational Concerns for Haiti Organization (ECHO), which focused on agricultural and development projects specific to Haiti. In 1981, Martin Price, a former university professor with a Ph.D. in biochemistry and experience in agricultural research, became head of ECHO and began focusing the organization's efforts on wider spheres of need and influence. The work in Haiti was closed, the name Haiti was replaced with the word Hunger in the organization's name, and the new ECHO began to re-direct its resources to supporting missionaries around the world, and particularly in the Caribbean, through the encouragement of sustainable agriculture. Price began to develop a model international farm at the ECHO headquarters in North Fort Myers, Florida, in which plants adapted to the climatic and environmental conditions on every continent were segregated into region-specific gardens in order to study what sorts of crops and agricultural techniques were uniquely suited to individual regions. At the same time, Price began to build what would become ECHO's most important and distinctive resource, the ECHO seed bank, a collection of seeds from around the world, with a catalog and database describing the nutritional, structural, and medicinal values of the plants that produced them.

Despite running the operation on mostly volunteer labor, Price eventually built ECHO into one of the world's leading centers of tropical agricultural knowledge, practical and technical understanding of sustainable crop production, and seed banks. Under Price, ECHO developed a wide range of practical and technical services, including dissemination of technical publications (the "ECHO Development Notes") and many kinds of plant propagation materials from ECHO's seed bank. Expanding into formal education efforts, ECHO developed training programs, courses, and seminars with Christian colleges and environmental organizations like the Au Sable Institute (see Chapter Seven), as well as development organizations to teach both college students and missionaries how to develop sustainable, environmentally sensitive agricultural practices in association with more traditional missionary efforts that could provide food and medicine to poor, rural populations that would combine low cost, easy mainte-nance, and high accessibility.

Price retired from ECHO in 2006, but the work of ECHO has continued to expand. Today people engage in ECHO's ministries of creation care by attending courses and workshops sponsored by the institute or working as volunteers or interns in ECHO's agricultural training program. These individuals may work at one of the indoor jobs at ECHO, processing information about useful agricultural crop plants or adding information to ECHO's already prodigious seed bank database. Outdoor workers may apply their efforts on ECHO's global farm on its main campus or in ECHO projects abroad. Another ECHO program, the ECHO Ambassadors, enlists people throughout the United States and Canada to give presentations about ECHO to churches and other organizations to encourage support and involve-ment in ongoing work.[25]

Similarly, Floresta, a Christian mission organization active in the Caribbean, is committed to reversing poverty and deforestation through intensive reforestation and agroforestry programs. Floresta's founder, Thomas Wodard, explained the organization's history and development in light of his own experience. "After serving as a relief volunteer in the Dominican Republic," said Wodard, "I realized that true development should not force people to rely on handouts and an unceasing flow of donations. People want an opportunity to provide for themselves and their families. Agroforestry and reforestation help accomplish this goal while restoring the productivity of the land."[26] Floresta fosters community development through low-interest loans and credit programs to local entrepreneurs who can establish sustain-able, community-based businesses to alleviate poverty. Floresta cou-ples this work with a program of Christian discipleship designed to not only lead people to understand and embrace Christian faith but to be effective Christian leaders in their communities.

Floresta's approach combines community development projects, innovative and sustainable agriculture and forestry programs, and eco-nomic stimulus through credit for micro-enterprises in a context of evangelism and discipleship. Like ECHO, one can find opportunities to work with Floresta by serving with them as a volunteer, by hosting an event in a local community to tell others about Florista's work and engender support, and by traveling with Floresta workers on any of a number of planned trips to sites where Floresta is actively working. The last avenue is one in which Floresta adopts a more ecotourism approach to generate income for its efforts, with trip participants paying a fee for their excursions but receiving in return the opportunity to see Floresta's efforts in action in local ecological context and to interact with Floresta leaders and board members.

GENERATION-SPECIFIC CHRISTIAN CONSERVATION FBOs—MOBILIZING ACTIVISM BY AGE GROUP

Some Christian FBOs active in conservation, while fully committed to a broad environmental agenda, nevertheless tailor their activities to specific age groups, especially college students. Three noteworthy efforts are Target Earth, Restoring Eden, and Renewal.

Target Earth summarizes its mission as "Serving the Earth, Serving the Poor." One of the most comprehensive of all conservation FBOs, Target Earth engages environmental problems on multiple levels. At the forefront, it develops original conservation programs specifically designed to protect endangered species and their habitats. As we saw in Chapter 7, Target Earth connects these efforts in the field with what have become increasingly sophisticated engagements in the legislative process, sponsoring, among other things, events that bring Christians to Washington, D.C. for direct contact with their congressional representatives. In the developing world, Target Earth creates service projects and internships designed to simultaneously reduce environmental degradation and alleviate poverty at the community level.

Target Earth has placed increasing emphasis on building conservation coalitions with all types of environmental organizations, brought together in its Eden Conservancy (EC) program, begun in 1993. EC was established to counter the problems of deforestation by acquiring, through direct purchase, the world's endangered lands. EC has targeted a number of sites for acquisition, including, among others, 8,000 acres of rainforest in Belize adjacent to the Blue Hole National Park.

Working with the Belize Audubon Society, the acquisition of these lands by Target Earth was closely integrated with development of its Jaguar Creek program in environmental education and its Global Stewardship Study Program (GSSP), both of which permit students to study at the organization's Jaguar Creek property in courses that explore scientific, theological, ethical, sociological, cultural, and economic dimensions of environmental problems. The credits earned are counted toward the student's degree requirements at their college and become part of each student's college education, albeit completed in Belize.[27] Although Target Earth makes its appeals generic and accessible to the public at large, much of its on-site work is done by college-age individuals, especially through its internships programs. Similarly, its ministry emphasis in education, as manifested in Jaguar Creek and GSSP, targets the needs, interests and aspirations of college students. Other Christian FBOs follow a similar model. One of these is Restoring Eden.

Restoring Eden identifies itself as a Christian ministry dedicated to being an advocate for wild species, natural habitats, and indigenous subsistence cultures. It describes its own work in the categories of nature appreciation, environmental stewardship, and public advocacy. In the first, Restoring Eden encourages the appreciation of nature as a normative spiritual discipline and experience within the Christian church. To this end, Restoring Eden compiles and provides theological and liturgical resources in the form of Bible studies, denominational statements, sermons and other materials that frame the care of creation within the context of ordinary church life and activity.

In its work of environmental stewardship, Restoring Eden provides information on practical ways to reduce consumption through various lifestyle changes, including recycling, alternative transportation, and reducing home energy consumption. It complements efforts like these with service projects in which participants learn how to practice conservation in everyday life.

Of all its initiatives, Restoring Eden has been most effective, and sometimes most controversial, in its work of environmental advocacy. It has made definitive stands and public statements on climate change, the treatment and rights of indigenous cultures, and strengthening the U.S. Endangered Species Act. Its workshops have included instruction in how to write a letter to your congressman, how to organize a letter-writing campaign, and how to lobby a congressional representative. These efforts are logical complements to its JUSTPower events that bring college students to Washington, D.C., to speak with their congressional delegations. Restoring Eden's most recent efforts have been centered on its Appalachian Tour events, which have focused on the environmental and cultural degradation associated with a form of coal mining called mountaintop removal. Restoring Eden Appalachian Tour events take participants to view both degraded and pristine areas. These visits are combined with meetings with local people affected by mountaintop removal practices, including times for discussion, prayer, and reflection by tour participants.

Like Target Earth, Restoring Eden is an FBO with a comprehensive environmental mission, and consequently frames its message to reach all age groups, socioeconomic levels, and cultural backgrounds. But, also like Target Earth, much of its efforts are designed to be particularly appealing and accessible to college students, and many of the foot soldiers in its frontline activities are drawn from this constituency. Likewise, many of its speaking tour events, such as its recent Ankle Deep in Reality tour, have been targeted to college campuses. Ankle Deep in Reality, for example, called attention to local and personal effects of climate change in Africa and the South Pacific. On this tour, speakers from affected regions brought personal testimonies of how global warming had changed their countries, their cultures, and their personal lives.[28]

If Target Earth and Restoring Eden could be described as FBOs with comprehensive strategies but concentrated focus in their appeals to younger generations, Renewal is even more explicit in the age-specificity of its mission. Like Target Earth and Restoring Eden, Renewal's organizational self-description is generic, affirming simply that it is "a Christ-centered creation care network that focuses on living in right relationship with God."[29] But Renewal is much more specific in identifying its primary target audience. Its self-described task is to "build the student creation care movement,"[30] a work it pursues through enabling and encouraging students on campuses throughout the United States and Canada to take leadership roles and personal initiative in changing their local campuses and communities. In addition to providing resources and training workshops for leadership in environmental initiatives on college campuses, Renewal, like Target Earth and Restoring Eden, also facilitates student involvement in congressional lobbying that includes face-to-face meetings with lawmakers. Additionally, Renewal provides directories and connections to students for employment and internships in environmental service and advocacy and supports opportunities for students in the United States and Canada to participate in environmental study abroad.

Collectively, the descriptions of these three organizations, Target Earth, Restoring Eden, and Renewal, should be received as illustrations, not exhaustive listings or even necessarily normative models of all Christian FBOs in conservation. They do reflect, however, the growing capacity, activity, and engagement of such FBOs in the scientific, educational, social, and political dimensions of environmental conservation, especially in the current generation of college-age young people. But whether such FBOs are generic or generation specific, what stands out are the ways in which they are consistently similar to one another and the ways in which they are consistently different from traditional conservation organizations.

WHY PEOPLE MATTER IN CONSERVATION

Regardless of tactical strategy, targeted mission, or age-specific audience, all Christian conservation FBOs show remarkable unanimity on the importance and dignity of human beings in their environmental context. None focus exclusively on the non-human world. All believe that, at heart, environmental problems are problems of alienation of human beings from God and creation, not simply environmental disfunction associated with specific human activities. Although Christian environmental FBOs accurately perceive such disfunctions, such as mountain top removal in Appalachia, as important elements of the environmental dilemma, they work with equal effort to preserve the local culture and its supporting community, rather than to simply establish a preserve that protects nature from people.

This agreement of emphasis is a manifestation of a shared belief system. Christian FBOs believe that human beings are made in the image of God and from this derive dignity and respect, even if current human practices are causing the environmental problem. The solutions adopted also reflect a fundamental Christian precept that the basic problem with the human condition is its sinful state, not its ignorance of environmental conservation. In order to protect the environment, humans must not merely *change* behavior by adopting a more appropriate and less environmentally harmful technology but actively *repent* of attitudes previously held toward God, others, and nature and adopt new postures of reconciliation toward all three.

Christian conservation FBOs often can be more effective than their secular counterparts in local communities because they can work through already established networks of organization, relationships, and tangible assets present in local churches. They possess inherent credibility because of their faith-based tradition, and that credibility translates into higher levels of trust from local residents. Finally, they focus on *cognitive* and *relational* factors as solutions to conservation problems, rather than focusing overmuch on the *environmental* factors that create such problems. Doug McAdam and his colleagues differentiate these effectively. "*Cognitive* [mechanisms]" notes McAdam, "alter how actors perceive their identities, interests, and possibilities for change; *relational* mechanisms affect the connections among actors and their networks in ways that enable them to cause change; and finally, *environmental* mechanisms are external factors that affect actors' capacities to engage in change."[31]

Christian FBOs change the *cognition* of human beings toward their environment because they replace the concept of ruling nature through domination by the model of ruling by service.[32] They also change the perception of possibilities for change by teaching people to see themselves as authorized and empowered agents of God who are responsible for the state of the creation around them. Christian FBOs also can change *relational structures* of people with one another and with their environment. Human opponents of one position or another, even if identified as "enemies" of the interests of the FBO, are to be treated with love, concern, and respect (Matthew 5:43–48). Disagreements may be real, but the goal is not to *dominate* others through political, social, or economic power but to *reconcile* interests with others through deliberation and mutual respect. Conservation success is not to be pursued as the spoils due the political victors who have outvoted, outwitted, or outspent the opposition. It is to be pursued as the fruit of humble and persistent efforts to love one's neighbor while serving and protecting the creation, realizing that the neighbors, as residents and stakeholders in the system, must be considered in developing the best path of interaction with the form of nature that surrounds them.

If this description seems hopelessly inadequate to deal with real-world relations, the only response that can be offered is that, somehow, against all odds, Christian FBOs like A Rocha, Floresta, Restoring Eden, Target Earth, and others are getting the job done, and sometimes in areas and circumstances where no one else has. It was not UNEP that succeeded in preserving the Ammiq Wetland in war-torn southern Lebanon through a list of international regulations and dictates. It was A Rocha Lebanon that succeeded through building trust and involvement within the local community.

Hopelessly idyllic as the Christian FBO approach appears in theory, it has a growing record of success. On this point, objection to the strategies of Christian FBOs parallel objections to Christian faith and practice in general. In the calculus of conventional worldly wisdom, one cannot survive by loving one's enemies, working for reconciliation instead of controlling domination, and expecting big returns from small investments by simply buttressing them with faith and prayer. But that description of the Christian FBO's strategy in conservation is, at its best, merely a particular illustration of the history of Christian faith in the world. That faith also, illogical as it might seem in argument, provides proof of its effect from the witness of history. It has shown itself to be an approach that can change the world and the people in it, and it has. In the next chapter, we return to the great questions of environmental ethics and examine more specifically how particular elements of Christian faith, including those manifested in the practices of Christian environmental FBOs, can lead to the construction of a Christian environmental ethic, inform the construction of environmental policy, and change the human relationship to nature.

NOTES

1. Quoted in Peter Harris, *Kingfisher's Fire: A Story of Hope for God's Earth* (Oxford, UK: Monarch Books, 2008), p. 154.

2. Martin Palmer with Victoria Findlay, *Faith in Conservation: New Approaches to Religion and the Environment* (Washington, D.C.: World Bank, 2003), p. xv.

3. Michael Shellenberger, and Ted Nordhaus, "The death of environmentalism: global warming politics in a post-environmental world." Available at http:www.thebreakthrough.org. Accessed 20 May 2010.

4. Palmer, p. 16.

5. Ibid.

6. Immanuel Kant, *Foundations of the Metaphysics of Morals*, Second edition. Trans. by Lewis W. Beck (Upper Saddle River, NJ: Prentice Hall, 1997), p. 51.

7. Peter Harris, *Under the Bright Wings* (Vancouver, British Columbia: Regent College Publishing, 1993), pp. 2–3.

8. Peter Harris, *Kingfisher's Fire* (Oxford, UK: Monarch, 2008), p. 81.

9. Ibid., p. 84.

10. Kyle Van Houtan, "Conservation as Virtue: A Scientific and Social Process for Conservation Ethics," *Conservation Biology* 20 (2006): pp. 1367–1372, 1371.

11. The history of the efforts and conferences summarized here is a synthesis of material available from the Alliance of Religion and Conservation Web site at http://www.arcworld.org (accessed 3 November 2009) and from the work of Alethea T. Abuyuan, *Faith-based Organizations, International Development Agencies, and Environmental Management*. Ph.D. Dissertation. (Los Angeles, University of Southern California, 2006).

12. Alethea T. Abuyuan, *Faith-based Organizations, International Development Agencies, and Environmental Management*. Ph.D. Dissertation (Los Angeles, University of Southern California, 2006), p. 9.

13. Ibid., p. 61.

14. Cited in Abuyuan, p. 185.

15. Susan D. Emmerich, "The Declaration in Practice: Missionary Earth Keeping." In *The Care of Creation: Focusing Concern and Action* (owners Grove, IL: Intervarsity Press, 2000), p. 150.

16. Amos 2:9, NASB.

17. From the document endorsed by the WWF Core Forest Advisory Group, 1999. Cited in Palmer, p. 8.

18. Palmer, p. 9.

19. Ibid.

20. Abuyuan, p. 18.

21. Ibid., p. 120.

22. Ibid., p. 221.

23. Barna Group. 2008. "Evangelicals Go Green with Caution." Available at http://www.barna.org/barna-update/article/13-culture/23-evangelicals -go-qgreenq-with-caution. Accessed 3 December 2009.

24. Tom Rowley, personal communication.

25. For a comprehensive view of ECHO's mission and strategies, as well as opportunities for engagement with ECHO's work, visit the organization's Web site at www.echonet.org.

26. Thomas Wodard, *Floresta Mission Statement*. 2009. Available at http://www.floresta.org/mission.htm. Accessed 30 October 2009.

27. A complete description of Target Earth's mission, resources and programs can be viewed at their Web site, www.targetearth.org. Accessed 3 December 2009.

28. A complete description of Restoring Eden's mission, resources and programs can be viewed at their Web site, www.restoringeden.org. Accessed 3 December 2009.

29. Renewal web page. Available at http://www.renewingcreation.org. Accessed 3 December 2009.

30. Ibid.

31. Doug McAdam, S. Tarrow, et al., *Dynamics of Contention* (New York: Cambridge University Press, 2001). Quoted in Abuyuan, pp. 121–122.

32. This concept of ruling through service will be more fully developed in Chapter 9, but it is an explicit instruction for Israel's kings in the Old Testament (Deuteronomy 17:16–20), and becomes more sharply focused in the teaching of Jesus in all of the Synoptic gospels (Matthew 20:25–28, Mark 10:42–45, Luke 22:25–27) and in Jesus' example to his disciples in the gospel of John (John 13:5–15).

CHAPTER 9

A Comprehensive Christian Environmental Ethic

What if thou make us able to make like thee—
To light with moons, to clothe with greenery,
To hang gold sunsets o'er a rose and purple sea!

George MacDonald[1]

THE GREAT QUESTIONS REVISITED—IS THERE A GENUINELY CHRISTIAN ETHIC OF THE ENVIRONMENT?

Any ethic of the environment must answer the great questions of environmental ethics with which we began. A comprehensive environmental ethic should be able to explain the basis of the environment's value and our appropriate response. It must be able to explain what gives humans the authority to care for, manage, or use nature differently than other kinds of creatures. All non-human creatures use nature for their own interests. Humans have the power to self-consciously advance the interests of other species, but should they? Further, an effective environmental ethic must answer the question of whether non-human entities can be treated as moral subjects. This is a question related to but distinct from the value of these entities, for it raises the issue of whether or not they can be the subjects of protective contract, covenant, or law, and whether they can, in any meaningful sense, be imbued with rights that humans can recognize and respect. Finally, a comprehensive environmental ethic must address nature's future. Specifically, what is that future, and do present actions toward the environment make sense in light of it? Altogether, the moral theory that underlies the ethic must, in the words of Willis Jenkins, "show how nature's moral status can bear upon a variety of environmental issues" and "link nature's moral standing with practical obligations and motivations for human agents."[2]

THE WORLD IS A GOOD CREATION

THE INTRINSIC VALUE OF NATURE

A Christian ethic of the environment begins with the affirmation of nature's value: "God saw that it was good." The six-times repeated phrase of Genesis 1:1–25 should be understood in its context to affirm that all things God created are good in and of themselves. We can know this to be a correct interpretation of the statement because God needs nothing and thus can have no instrumental use for anything that he has made, and because human beings, at the time the valuation is declared, do not exist, nor will they be asked for their assessment of the creation after God creates them. This intrinsic value is located in the object itself. There it can be perceived by humans, but it exists whether humans perceive it or not. When they do not, they are burdened with an anthropocentric worldview that distorts their understanding of God, nature, and themselves. "Behold now, Behemoth," God says to Job, "which I made as well as you. He eats grass like an ox. Behold now, his strength in his loins and his power in the muscles of his belly. . . . His bones are tubes of bronze; his limbs are like bars of iron. He is the first of the ways of God. . . ."[3]

In answer to Job's repeated complaint that God has treated him unjustly, God's repeated response is to make Job understand that his own view of the world and God's work in it is too self-centered to understand the truth about God or nature. Speaking of the great beast Leviathan, God taunts Job by exposing his ignorance about how to value the world and its creatures as God does. He does so by contrasting Job's market-based valuations with God's estimation of worth. "Can you draw out Leviathan with a hook?" asks God. "Can you put a rope in his nose or pierce his jaw with a hook? . . . Will you play with him as with a bird, or will you bind him for your maidens? Will the traders bargain over him? Will they divide him among the merchants? . . . Lay your hand on him; you will not do it again! Behold, your expectation is false . . . No one is so fierce that he dares arouse him; Who then is he that can stand before Me?"[4] In the end, Job learns his lesson: The creation is to be viewed theocentrically, not anthropocentrically. "Therefore, I retract," says Job of his past statements and viewpoints, "and I repent in dust and ashes."[5]

THE AESTHETIC VALUE OF NATURE

In current strategies of environmental ethics, many ethicists stress the importance of intrinsic value over all others. The goal, as previously noted, is to "protect" creation from a one-dimensional instrumental analysis that can easily turn into an anthropocentric assessment of human welfare maximization. This strategy is well-intentioned, but a Christian environmental ethic cannot fully endorse it. In contrast, a Christian environmental ethic requires a more multi-dimensional valuation of nature that begins with intrinsic value but does not end there.

It is significant that the text of Genesis 1 does not say of any created thing that "It was good," but rather "God *saw* that it was good." The divine Valuer possesses an appreciation of *aesthetic* as well as *intrinsic* value. An appreciation of nature's aesthetic value is aroused by *seeing* the beauty of God's creatures and the created world. That appreciation grows through in-depth study of non-human creatures and their environments. For example, Saint Basil expresses the joy he finds in his study of the behavior of cranes when he speaks to his congregation in Homily 8 on the works of God in creation:

> How could I possibly make an accurate review of the peculiarities in the lives of birds? How the cranes in turn accept the responsibility of outposts at night, and while some sleep, others, making the rounds, provide every safety for those asleep . . . [how] in their flight, a different one takes up the task of guiding at different times and, having led the flight for a certain appointed time, goes round to the rear, transferring the leadership of the journey to the one behind him.[6]

The cognitive appreciation of the harmonious functioning of creatures in nature deepens an understanding of nature's aesthetic value still further. Aquinas captures an understanding of this dimension of aesthetic value well in words we have read before:

> For God brought things into being in order to communicate the divine goodness to creatures and this be represented by them.

And because God's goodness could not be represented by any single creature, God produced many and diverse creatures, that what one lacked in representing divine goodness might be supplied in another. For goodness, which exists in God simply and uniformly, exists in creatures multiply and distributively.[7]

Appreciation of aesthetic value also emerges from the contemplation of the nature of the universe, even when such contemplation is beyond human cognition and understanding. "When I consider your heavens," wrote David, "the work of your fingers, the moon and the stars which you have ordained, what is man that you take thought of him, and the son of man that you care for him?"[8] The world is to be understood as intrinsically valuable, but it is also to be enjoyed, studied, and contemplated to better apprehend its aesthetic value, an experience uniquely available to the human being as a way of sharing God's own pleasure in what he has made.[9]

THE INSTRUMENTAL VALUE OF NATURE

The goodness of the world is not only intrinsic and aesthetic, but instrumental, for each part of the created order serves the needs of others, including humans. Human need, however, is never to usurp the needs of other elements of creation. All species on Earth are not here to serve just one species. Rather the reverse. The one is to serve all, working, as only it can, to understand and nurture the proper function of all creation in its entirety. God finds pleasure in how his creation sustains the needs of every creature, and humans are to do the same. Aquinas' understanding of this instrumental value is summarized by Catholic ethicist Jame Schaefer:

God values the entire universe most as a functioning whole of intrinsically valuable beings that achieve their purposes for existing by acting or being acted upon according to their natures. Concurrently, God values all types of entities as instruments of others progressively up the hierarchical chain by which the universe maintains itself. For Aquinas, the universe is God's instrument for achieving God's purposes for it.[10]

A Christian environmental ethic affirms and celebrates nature's instrumental value. But instrumental value must not be limited by an anthropocentric perspective. The needs of all creatures are met instrumentally through the right functioning of the good creation, and humans are not unique in finding their needs met by God in this way. Again the point is clarified in God's discourse with Job. "Can you hunt the prey for the lion, or satisfy the appetite of the young lions, when they crouch in their dens and lie in wait in their lair? Who prepares for the raven its nourishment when its young cry to God and wander about without food?"[11] God's answer to his rhetorical question is, "I do." Human beings are particularly important objects of God's care and provision, but they are not the only objects of God's care and provision.

When value is understood within the context of an ethic that affirms its multi-dimensional nature, and asserts that such value, in every dimension, is manifested only in the full and complete functioning of the natural world, we have an ethical position that at once establishes the primacy of intrinsic value of the non-human world, provides motivation for humans to devote themselves to the study and contemplation of that world (aesthetic value), and affirms the goodness of the provision that world creates for every living creature (instrumental value). We are spared from, and can categorically reject, the false dichotomy of "us or them" in our ethical decisions about the environment. We are to learn to celebrate the good gifts we receive from nature, but to all the more study and appreciate what other creatures receive from nature and how we might help provide it. Because we are now in an ethical position that rejects the premise that our good cannot be met without nature's loss, we are committed to finding a way forward to understand and provide for the instrumental needs of all creation, neither excluding humans from nature nor destroying nature's functioning capacities for other creatures. This *position* of valuing is the first step on the path of reconciliation between humans and nature. In a Christian environmental ethic, we believe that path must exist, for we believe that this is the very essence of the way the world has been made.

HUMANITY'S FIRST ENVIRONMENTAL RESPONSIBILITY IS TO SERVE AND PROTECT THE GOOD CREATION

Critics of the "strategy of nature's moral standing" have had much to say on the failure of this approach to identify or imagine proper human *behaviors* toward nature, whatever they may think of its value. Some, as we have seen, dismiss the strategy altogether as useless in real

debates about real choices. Recall the sarcastic assessment of environmentalist Lynn McGuire and philosopher James Justus. "Although
intrinsic value may get conservationists out of bed in the morning
and into the field or up to the bargaining table, it does not serve them
well once they get there. Conservation requires decision-making, and
here intrinsic value falls short."[12] Yes, left to itself, it does. A Christian
environmental ethic, however, is not guided solely, or even primarily,
by its recognition of nature's intrinsic, aesthetic, and instrumental
value. It is directed by specific instruction regarding the human task
toward nature: "Then the Lord God took the man and put him into
the Garden of Eden to cultivate it and keep it."[13]

We have noted earlier that the Hebrew verbs used here are better
and, in other contexts, more often translated as "serve and protect."
They are consistent with the injunction to "rule over the fish of the
sea, and the birds of the air, and over every living creature that moves
on the face of the earth"[14] when viewed in the Christian understanding
of rulers as servants of God and of those they govern. "For it [the ruling
authority]," wrote Paul, "is a minister of God to you for good. . . . For
because of this you also pay taxes, for rulers are servants of God,
devoting themselves to this very thing [governing]."[15] If Paul teaches
clearly that rulers are servants of God, Jesus is even more plainspoken
that those who rule must see themselves as servants of their subjects,
and he is explicit in contrasting this understanding with the world's
perspective on ruling. "You know that the rulers of the Gentiles lord
it over them, and their great men exercise authority over them. It is
not this way among you, but whoever wishes to become great among
you shall be your servant, and whoever wishes to be first among you
shall be your slave."[16]

Here we must make the point, and sharply, that in a Christian ethic of
the environment, the proper model and metaphor is that of humans as
servants of creation, not *stewards* of creation. The concept of *creation
stewardship* has been the most popular and widely used image of the
human relationship to nature in Christian teaching on the environment
for the last 30 years, and, to this point, we have used it repeatedly. It has
not been without good effect in communicating the importance of the
human responsibility to care for creation. The image is understandably
appealing as a picture of one given authority over the household, possessions, and resources of another. However, the image is rarely used
biblically or historically in the church's teachings. When it is, it is
almost always employed in the context of safeguarding a truth, teaching, or spiritual gift (for example, Matthew 13:52, I Corinthians 4:1–2,

I Peter 4:10), not a physical resource or environment. Further, the Bible typically uses the function or image of a steward and his steward-ship to describe a situation where the real landlord is *absent* (for example, Matthew 25:14–30, Luke 12:42). This is not an accurate way of describing God's relationship to creation.

The stewardship metaphor also becomes problematic because it emphasizes human control *over* creation rather human service *toward* creation. The former is a dangerous and potentially idolatrous illusion. The latter is an accurate and practical posture toward developing a humble and other-centered way for humans to act with the non-human world. Although a stewardship motif captures the concept of human accountability toward God, it is deficient in representing the equally important concept of humans being "other-directed" in giving primary attention to meeting needs other than their own, in this case, the needs of nature. As theologian Norman Wirzba notes, "Servant-hood . . . shifts the orientation of our action away from ourselves to the well-being of others. . . ."[17] In creating, God "makes room," in the homely words of John of Damascus, for life that is other than himself.[18] God, in his act of creation, performs a service to that which he creates by "giving it a place" without which it could not exist. So, humans, made in the image of God and designed to carry out his intentions toward creation, are to direct their activities first and foremost to "making room" for non-human life. It is this strong concept of *service* toward creation that enables the creation of parks and wilderness areas to make sense as part of the human vocation toward nature, just as it is this same concept of service that validates the work of saving species, even those whom we have no instrumental motive to "steward." This was the case when Francis Orpen Morris and his fellow pastors established the Association for the Protection of Sea Birds (see Chapter 5). A model of "serving" the interests of these seabirds makes much better sense of Morris's actions than a model of "stewardship." In fact, it does so in most examples of genuine and effective conservation effort.

If, according to Genesis 2:15, human beings are created to serve and protect creation, then humanity's prime concern must be to understand the needs of others, including others that represent non-human species. The provision of the U.S. Endangered Species Act that mandates the designation of critical habitat is a first, if still relatively weak, attempt to manifest this principle in practice. Similarly, the requirement of the U.S. National Environmental Policy Act to identify, through the mechanism of an Environmental Impact Statement, the potentially irrevocable consequences of a planned action by humans also expresses this principle in the opposite way, by identifying in advance the effects of human actions that create *adverse impacts* upon other creatures.

Unquestionably, modern human culture destroys the natural world. Holmes Rolston III explained our present condition eloquently:

> It is a sad truth that life preys on life, that culture does have to eat nature, but that is not the only truth; there is a glad truth that culture can be satisfied, can only be satisfactory, if its destiny is entwined with nature. I do not say that there is no further cultural development needed, only that we do not need further cultural development that sacrifices nature for culture, that enlarges the sphere of culture at the price of diminishing the sphere of nature. Nor will culture be harmed if we do not get it.[19]

It was not so long ago that humans believed that they could not power cars without gasoline, make electricity without mining coal or building dams, or construct a factory that did not produce solid or chemical waste. Today we have cars that do not need gas. We can make electricity without building dams or mining coal. We have designed factories with a closed-loop waste production stream such that everything used in the production process, even what was once considered waste, can now be transformed to re-enter that process at various stages (that is, recycled) or sold to another buyer who sees one market's waste as another market's good. And it was not so long ago that people believed that they could not burn lamps without killing whales, farm without using pesticides, and or cut timber without destroying forests. But history, recent and otherwise, has shown these assertions to be false.

Are we smart enough to see the trend? Perhaps our problem was not that we lacked the *ability* to serve and care for the Earth, but that we lacked the *intention* to do so. No human technology is without environmental effect. But is it possible that a defined and, dare we say, relentless intention to serve and protect the Earth in all human activity could be the greatest spark to technological innovation history has ever seen? And could such a determined intention also be the stimulus for the most effective effort yet made to curb the sins of affluence, materialism, and greed that are consuming the western world? Again it is Rolston who puts it well, "Few persons would need to go without 'enough' if we could use, justly and charitably, the produce of the already domesticated landscape. If such redistribution does not take place, people will be hurt. But it is better to try to fix this problem where it arises, within society, than to try to enlarge the sphere of society by the sacrifice of remnant natural values."[20] Who is willing to find out if these things could be?

A Christian ethic of the environment insists that right rewards are the fruit of right objectives. The right objective for humans in their interaction with nature is that they should learn and practice how to serve and care for it. Similarly, there are wrong rewards that are nothing but bribes because they are not the normal or "natural" fruit of right behavior. Affluence, an unending increase in material goods and economic production, and ever-increasing disconnection from the natural world in order to increase human levels of ease and comfort are the wrong objectives, and they will always generate the wrong rewards. Wisdom consists of choosing the right goal, desiring the rewards that are the natural fruit of that goal, and living in a manner consistent with obtaining it.

Jesus spells out this strategy as the fundamental cure for anxiety, for anxiety is invariably produced by trying to satisfy legitimate needs and wants in inappropriate and ineffective ways. Therefore, "Seek first the kingdom of God, and all these things will be added to you."[21] Jesus never disregarded the human desire for reward and significance. Nurturing a creation that glorifies God is one of the deepest of human desires, and its attainment is one of humanity's most satisfying rewards. But the glory of God is the thing to be pursued, and the service and care of his creation is an act of obedience to that pursuit.

HUMANS POSSESS UNIQUE ABILITY AND AUTHORITY TO SERVE AND PROTECT NATURE

Recently, in preparing a new textbook on conservation biology,[22] my editor allowed me to select the cover photo. I chose a picture showing three individuals, Betty, Sirius, and Wiwik, engaged in a common task related to a particular conservation study, the problem of extracting termites from a termite mound. All three individuals are Indonesian, but from there differences emerge. Betty and Sirius are much like one another. Wiwik is different from both. You see, Betty and Sirius are three- to four-year-old female orangutans. Wiwik is an Indonesian woman who works with them and other orangutans at an orangutan orphanage. The orphanage was created to address the growing problem of orangutan orphans, infant orangs whose mothers are killed by hunters so that the infants can be captured and sold as pets. This practice is against the law in Indonesia but nevertheless is widespread. If the perpetrator is caught, he might pay a fine or go to jail, but that does not solve the orangutan's side of the problem. The orphaned infant cannot survive in the forest without training. Orangutan orphanages, sponsored by various conservation organizations, attempt to provide that training.

What makes the picture of Wiwik, Betty, and Sirius enlightening to a discussion of a Christian environmental ethic is the fundamental differences it reveals among the three individuals. All are working on the same problem (getting the termites out of the termite mound), and all are employing considerable dexterity, determination, and intelligence to solve it. The difference is that, in engaging the problem and its solution, only Wiwik is taking the role of what a psychologist would call a *reflective interactant*. Betty and Sirius are approaching the problem from the perspective of orangutans. Ironically, so is Wiwik. In this effort, it is Wiwik who is serving as teacher. Betty and Sirius, although highly gifted and intelligent creatures, are her students.

This is an asymmetrical relationship. Betty and Sirius, for all their skill and intelligence, can only see the problem from their own viewpoint. Wiwik, on the other hand, can consciously choose to set aside her human perspective and intentionally place herself into their perspective. To accomplish this, Wiwik must see the world as an orangutan would see it. She must not consider her own needs in that world, but the needs perceived by an orangutan. And then Wiwik must determine not how she would meet those needs, but how those needs would be met *if she were an orangutan.*

Betty and Sirius are engaged in this exercise because they are hungry. Wiwik, on the other hand, is engaged in the problem because she thinks it is "the right thing to do." To make this work, Wiwik must consciously advance Betty's and Sirius's ends, rather than her own. Perhaps Wiwik would rather be home doing some gardening, reading a book, watching TV, or eating something that isn't trying to crawl off the plate. It is self-evident that Wiwik has the capacity to adopt the perspective and advance the interests of others, even if the others are not even members of her own species. The question is, where did Wiwik get this capacity, and what is its function in an environmental ethic?

Wiwik illustrates a premise that is fundamental to a Christian understanding of the human relationship to nature. Human beings, alone made in the image of God, possess unique qualities and capacities that equip them for their role as servants and protectors of nature. Humans alone possess the ability to consider themselves, to evaluate their own thoughts and their own desires. They can, in a real sense, separate themselves from themselves, not only having an awareness of their own thoughts and perspectives but a capacity to judge whether the thoughts they are thinking are the thoughts they *ought to be thinking*, whether the desires they are experiencing are the *right desires to pursue*, and whether those "others" they interact with have the same or different perspectives and needs in this world as they do. Only in so far as they are in possession of and aware of how to use these qualities can humans serve and protect creation.

When we understand these things, we see why humans, as rulers of creation, *must* approach their duties from the perspective of a servant, just as Jesus taught and as Wiwik is doing. Ruling over creation requires an other-centeredness that identifies and assesses the needs of non-human entities, judges their relative importance and urgency, and creates, from its own intellectual resources, a plan to meet them, to serve the needs of the other.

Ruling through service requires more than good intentions. Jesus makes clear it also requires a capacity for self-examination and self-correction. "Why do you look," he said, "at the speck which is in your brother's eye, but do not notice the log that is in your own eye? Or, how can you say to your brother, let me take the speck out of your eye, and behold, the log is in your own eye? You hypocrite! First, take the log out of your own eye, and then you will see clearly to take the speck out of your brother's eye."[23]

Humans not only have the capacity for self-reflection and critical self-evaluation, they must use it. God expects them to. Using this capacity is essential when dealing with environmental problems. As economist Peter J. Hill writes, "Every call to save the environment is predicated upon human action. We are asked to respond to stories of environmental disaster, to evidence that nature is being altered in unfortunate ways, and to appeals to reverse the damage that humans inflict upon the natural order. But every one of these is a call to change, and it is humans who are being asked to change."[24] In other words, humans cannot, if we may use the language of Saint Francis, criticize Brother Sun (or Brother Climate) by telling him that he is making the world too hot. They must begin every inquiry that touches their rule of nature with the question, "What have I done to contribute to this problem?" When the human ruler has answered this question honestly, then, says Jesus, he not only can see clearly to fix what may be wrong in the other (in this case, nature) but can do so with compassion instead of self-centeredness.

Finally, we must add that the service and protection of nature requires not only intention, but skill. It is a *task* which requires us to be able to *do* specific things. A Christian ethic, therefore, teaches that the practice of stewardship requires learning the skills of stewardship and taking responsibility to use those skills charitably for human and non-human neighbors alike. As Wendell Berry puts it, "How do you love your neighbor if you don't know how to build or mend a fence, how to keep your filth out of his water supply and your poison out of his air; or if you do not produce anything and so have nothing to offer, or do not take care of yourself and so become a burden? . . . How will you practice virtue without skill?"[25] For this reason, a Christian environmental ethic affirms that what institutions of higher education should teach about stewardship is not merely its *concepts* but its *skills*, just as such institutions should teach the value of what the Amish would call "merited occupations," work that is truly charitable to human and non-human neighbors alike because of what it produces for both, as well as for what it does not produce. Again to quote Berry, "You cannot affirm the powerplant and condemn the smokestack, or affirm the smoke and condemn the cough."[26] A Christian environmental ethic affirms that humans are, among all creatures, uniquely capable of making responsible choices and *must* do so through the application human skill and intellect that is directed to benefit the creation around them.

If we would affirm and practice a Christian environmental ethic, we must neither deny nor denigrate the uniqueness of being human. To deny human uniqueness is a lie, although one which modern culture is endlessly congratulating itself for having discovered as an important "truth." To denigrate the uniqueness of being human is a futile exercise in species' self-flagellation. When we spend our best energies imagining the world without us, which is what Eric Pianka and the producers of *After People* and *The Day the Earth Stood Still* are guilty of, we accomplish nothing for humanity or the non-human world. There is no empowerment in continually saying, "If only humans weren't here." We are here. We are here for a purpose. That purpose is to use for good the unique capacities that belong to us, as creatures made in the image of God. Aquinas clarified this critical perspective in his own teaching, that the natural dominion exercised by humans is based on their ability to know and to will good ends. In doing this, humans are subservient to God's dominion when exercising their dominion, which is never an absolute, but subordinate to the plans and purposes of God. Thus, the goal of human dominion is to cooperate with God in carrying out God's plan for his creation.[27] Informed by the careful study of nature and the regenerative work of the Holy Spirit in the experience of life, human beings can rule creation as God intended, by serving and protecting its interests and its functional integrity.

NON-HUMAN ENTITIES IN NATURE SHOULD BE TREATED AS MORAL SUBJECTS

At first, it might seem that focusing on the question of moral subjects is the same as addressing the question of nature's value. These questions are related but different. Establishing the basis of nature's value tells us what sorts of things ought to be given moral consideration, but it does not tell us precisely how such consideration should be expressed. A Christian environmental ethic can be more specific. Non-human entities are appropriate moral subjects. They are, in the language of ethics, "morally considerable." Further, Christian teaching shows that such entities, living and nonliving, can be the appropriate objects of law and covenant. They can receive and hold legal rights, and humans can and should be punished when those rights are abused.

Perhaps the closest we have in modern law to this concept is the U.S. Endangered Species Act (ESA). In this law, as environmental historian Joseph Petulla noted, "a listed non-human resident of the United States is guaranteed, in a special sense, life and liberty."[28] Therefore, it is not inappropriate for such listed species to have their interests represented in court, as was the case in *Palila v. Hawaii Department of Land and Natural Resources*, in which the Sierra Club Legal Defense Fund represented the palila, a bird that is an endangered species of Hawaiian honeycreeper, against the Hawaii Department of Land and Resources, charging the agency with violation of the Endangered Species Act by permitting the presence of feral goats and sheep within the palila's habitat, thereby contributing to the destruction of that habitat. The Ninth Circuit Court of Appeals found in favor of the palila, concluding that the state had indeed violated the ESA through these actions. A Christian environmental ethic would affirm that this kind of legal protection, as well as legal action on behalf of protected creatures, is ethically appropriate. Both have precedent in God's covenant with the creatures of the ark (Genesis 9:8–17), as well as in the inclusion of Sabbath rest for animals (Exodus 23:12) and the land (Exodus 23:10–11, Leviticus 25:1–22).

Further, the failure of humans to observe such laws is a prosecutable offense, and the punishment of the violator shall include relief that runs to the benefit of the injured party, even if the party is the land itself (II Chronicles 36:21).

A Christian environmental ethic, then, advocates the full development of environmental laws that recognize non-human creatures and other environmental entities as moral subjects and gives such entities legal standing in court, in effect, a "standing right to sue" if their interests are violated. Thus, the answer to Christopher Stone's famous rhetorical question, "Should trees have standing?"[29] is yes, if they are trees that have been deemed necessary to protect. A Christian environmental ethic affirms that, because these entities should be viewed as moral subjects, they also are appropriate objects of legal protection that recognizes rights and interests appropriate to them.

Although a Christian ethic affirms that interests and rights of non-human entities really exist, it also affirms that not every kind of right or interest is appropriate or attributable to non-human creatures or nonliving environmental entities. This is because, to repeat a point made earlier, there is a difference between moral consideration and moral significance. Although non-human creatures deserve moral consideration, humans possess greater moral significance, and this is a factor in making ethical decisions. This fact, however, is never to be used as a reason to abuse nature. One of the things that give humans added moral significance is that they have the capacity for reflective decision-making, and their decisions are morally significant because they can affect nature powerfully. Thus, the recognition of greater moral significance in human beings is not to be used as a warrant for humans to assert privileges over other kinds of life, but as a reason to recognize that all human actions must be carefully considered in light of their effects on such life, indeed on all of nature. Laws such as the U.S. National Environmental Policy Act are an expression, albeit still a relatively weak one, of the principle that, because human actions can have powerful effects on the environment, the significance of those actions and their effects must be considered in advance of the action itself. When humans affirm their own moral significance relative to other species, they begin to understand why their decisions are important to other species.

This realization guards against two errors. The first is treating all morally considerable entities as beings of equal moral significance. This position easily and naturally leads, in humans, to a kind of species-specific self-loathing, an "I wish my species had never evolved" attitude in those who hold it. If we are indeed no better than bacteria, then it's time to stop using disinfectants. This is a posture of environmental defeatism. It poses as ecological humility. It is really moral ignorance. Unless humans recognize that their own species is uniquely equipped to perceive, serve, and protect the interests of other creatures, they will never use that capacity for those purposes.

The second error is the opposite and equally dangerous mistake of assuming that greater moral significance equals greater license and privilege in things environmental and becomes a justification for irresponsible behavior toward nature. The human who recognizes her own moral significance toward God must at the same time recognize that one of the most basic expressions of that significance is the power of her actions on the natural world. Humans can never assume that any action of their own is without importance to the world in which they live. Therefore, no actions that humans propose toward nature can ever be exempted from moral scrutiny.

THE PRESENT CARE OF NATURE MUST CONSIDER ITS FUTURE DESTINY

Sustainability is one of the most commonly invoked principles for constructing environmental ethics. "Sustainable development" was defined in the Bruntland Report (*Our Common Future*) as "meeting the needs of the present generation without compromising the ability of future generations to meet their own needs."[30] But if sustainability simply refers to an endless iteration of things as they are now from one generation to the next, it hardly inspires enthusiasm. A concept of sustainability that naively sees the global human population always and forever living on a trajectory of ever-increasing wealth (with an attendant attitude of ever-increasing greed) is not a picture of heaven, but of hell. Sustainability, in its best clothes, is an admirable, if limited, concept, but it does not begin to encompass a transforming moral vision of redemption.

A Christian environmental ethic does not aim merely at maintaining the status quo or of offering unquestioned assent to every aspiration of modern material consumption. The Bible provides snapshots of redemption, brief and cryptic visions of what redeemed communities and people would look like, and they look very different from their counterparts in the modern world. A redeemed world is, first of all, one in which God is explicitly acknowledged as Creator and Sustainer of life. In a redeemed environment, this understanding permeates everything. Such knowledge is the foundational requisite to the prophecy of the lion and the lamb given in Isaiah 11. The lion and the lamb only lie down together where "They will neither hurt nor destroy in all my holy mountain, for the Earth will be full of the knowledge of the Lord as the waters cover the sea."[31]

It is a redemptive future that gives significance to present effort, no matter how small, if that effort is oriented to the same end as the future redemption. This is what Simon Stuart and his colleagues meant when they wrote, "Every time we celebrate a conservation success story such as the recovery of the white rhinoceros in southern Africa, we are strengthened in this present hope that God is working with us to redeem his creation; furthermore, these present successes are a very real foretaste of even greater things to come on that day when God will fully restore all that He has made."[32]

Redemption, more than any other ethical element, requires a change of *intent* and not merely a change of *technique*. The current wave of "going green" is a superficial example of a shift in cultural intention. The phrase is used to describe all kinds of efforts, radically diverse in their forms and applications, but united in their common effort to minimize harm to the Earth. This is a good trend, but a shallow one, and its shallowness is betrayed by its approach. Driving a more efficient car, building a more efficient power plant, and screwing in more efficient light bulbs can be beneficial changes, but they all address the problem of the environment as a problem of *technology*. The right (read "new") technology is good. The wrong (read "old") technology is bad. In some cases this is correct, as far as it goes. But technological innovation is not the same as moral redemption. Some cultures that have been most beneficent to the Earth and the land, like the Amish, achieve their effects not by improving on modern technology but by renouncing it. But such renunciation is only possible when there is a change of human *intention*, not merely a change in human *technique*.

Current culture treats technological innovation as an imperative. We *must* change to the newest technology because we *can*, and because, like Mount Everest, it is there. A redemptive approach *chooses* an appropriate technology because the user has already made a more fundamental choice. Instead of taking human appetite and desire as givens, a redeemed mind steps back and asks, "What should I *choose to want*? What should I *choose to value*?" In the end, these are the choices that determine what kind of people we shall be, as well as the kind of world in which we shall live.

This approach to an environmental ethic requires humility, a particularly unpopular trait in modern societies. A Christian environmental ethic declares that the right action is to sublimate desires based on personal welfare to choose ends that reflect God's purposes and intentions for his creation that will increase the manifestation of his own glory. In a culture whose food and drink is self-actualization and personal autonomy, the idea of redirecting human effort to glorify God doesn't find much support, but such a change in intention must be the beginning of a redemptive ethic and the plans that arise from it. To a watching world, the concept of redemption is certain to be the single most repulsive idea contained in a Christian environmental ethic. Redemption is by its very nature subversive. If we would purchase a man who is a slave in order to bring him out of slavery, we condemn the practice of slavery in setting him free. And if he has known no other condition but slavery all his life, we will also have to teach him to live as a free man. This will require more than a change in his condition. It will require a change in who he is, and in what he aspires to become.

The effort I describe in this example would today be considered heroic. In times past it would have been considered criminal. And one such act, though aiming at the right end, would not bring an end to the institution of slavery. In the United States, that required a civil war. Redemption is costly and painful and always brings with it an element of judgment. Some things in this present world can, with care and nurture, be made part of the redemptive world. Some things must be cast aside. Some things must be destroyed altogether.

A Christian environmental ethic looks to a redemptive future. Ironically, this is the element which humans have the least ability to self-initiate, not only because of the limits of their own resources, but because, at any given historical moment, they are immersed in current cultural attitudes that make it difficult to see anything differently. Thus, the Bible teaches that redemption must be God-initiated, because only God possesses the ultimate redemptive vision for the world. And such redemption will come, in the end, as a painful event that takes ordinary life by surprise. So Jesus explained to his disciples, "As it was in the days of Noah, so it will be at the coming of the Son of Man. For in the days before the flood, they were eating, they were drinking. They were marrying, and they were being given in marriage, until the day that Noah entered the ark, and they did not understand until the flood came and took them all away...."[33]

Redemptive living looks stupid until redemption arrives. Redemptive efforts appear futile. On their own, they are. But redemptive effort is like the mustard seed in Jesus' parable about the kingdom of heaven. It is not the size or scope of the effort that matters as much as its alignment with an ultimate end that God will bring to pass.

Because a Christian environmental ethic is ultimately an ethic of redemption, it necessarily evaluates the means we use in our dealings with the environment in light of the ends they will produce, not only in the environment, but in ourselves. Thus, a redemptive orientation declares that we must change our current thoughts, practices, and objectives, no matter how rational or successful they appear under present circumstances, to conform to a greater ultimate reality that is on the way, but not yet here. To do so requires not only hope, but faith, which is defined biblically as "the assurance of things hoped for, the conviction of things not seen."[34] In an age of sensuality, materialism, and empiricism, this word is blasphemy. Nevertheless, it is the final and definitive element of a Christian environmental ethic.

SERVING AND PROTECTING CREATION SHOULD BE A NORMATIVE EXPERIENCE OF CHRISTIAN LIFE

The gospel of Mark records that Jesus began his public ministry with a simple and direct message, "The time is fulfilled, and the kingdom of God is at hand; repent and believe in the gospel."[35] In more contemporary language, the best restatement of "The kingdom of God is at hand" is "Here's the kingdom of God." As Christian philosopher Dallas Willard makes clear in *The Divine Conspiracy*, Jesus is not announcing that the kingdom of God has just come into existence, for it has always existed. What has changed is that, through Jesus Christ, the kingdom has become *accessible* to human beings, even in this fallen world.[36] It is the confident trust in and use of this access that has given Christians through the ages the ability to do things that no one would have thought possible.

Today the kingdom of God remains "at hand" through Christ, and its access remains one of the greatest privileges of faith. Christians who understand and appropriate this privilege can expect redemptive effects over the entire array of broken relationships they face in a fallen world. They can redeem their relationship to God. They can redeem their relationship to one another. They can redeem their own relationship to themselves and their secret but debilitating inner conflicts. And they can redeem their relationship to creation.

It is a good idea to start practicing what you are going to be doing for a long time, and the care of the Earth is one of those things. As Willard puts it, "God himself loves the earth dearly and never takes his hands off it. And because he loves it and it is good, our care of it is also eternal work and part of our eternal life."[37] The practice of serving and protecting the Earth was humanity's first vocation. It will remain an eternal one, but, in a redeemed world, such work will be empowered by abilities now beyond the limits of human imagination. Christian poet and novelist George MacDonald painted the possibilities of this new life and work in one of his poems.

And in the perfect time, O perfect God,
When we are in our home, our natal home,
When joy shall carry every sacred load,
And from its life and peace no heart shall roam,
What if thou make us able to make like thee –
To light with moons, to clothe with greenery,
To hang gold sunsets o'er a rose and purple sea![38]

Today, in this fallen world, the church should teach the faithful that the practice of serving and protecting creation is both normative experience in and fundamental preparation for an eternal life in which the now broken relationship between humanity and nature will be restored. In other words, it can prepare people to practice a meaningful environmental ethic now and for eternity. The church can move toward this goal by its attention to three foundational principles.

First, the church should nurture an *accurate understanding* of nature and of the problems that face the environment today. Only when people possess a common, shared, and accurate vision of the natural world can they begin to cooperatively approach solutions to it. I do not mean that it is the task of the church to teach courses on ecology and environmental science. It is not. But it is the task of the church, when it addresses these concerns with its considerable theological and moral resources, to speak of them accurately.

Second, the church should provide and facilitate *deliberate contact* between people and nature. It can choose to do so in the images it displays in worship, the settings of the worship itself, the locations of its congregational retreats, and the places to which it directs it members for practicing the disciplines of solitude and silence, both of which are essential to growth in Christian discipleship. It can go further, and plan times for its members to *be in nature* and *learn from nature* by planning retreats, long or short in duration, in which nature is not merely the backdrop or setting for a gathering but the subject of it. I recently led a half-day retreat like this for members of my own congregation, using a forest preserve within a mile of our church building. Simple teachings about how to tell different kinds of trees, flowers, and grasses from each other, how to distinguish one bird's song from another's, and how to read the shape of a landscape and predict what you might find on hilltops, slopes, and depressions profoundly affect human perception of nature, and human enjoyment of it.

Recognizing that things have names, that they are different, and that their differences are important is best learned by experience. When the church shows its saints how to make real contact with God's creation and how to look at it with discernment, such contact becomes the channel through which an accurate understanding of nature develops, as well as an affection for nature that makes it something that would be missed if absent, something to be sought if present, and something to be healed if it has been hurt.

Finally, the church should teach its members how to practice the *sacrificial concern* required to serve and protect non-human creation. One can have concern without sacrifice, but the Bible condemns this kind of concern as hypocrisy. "If a brother or sister is without clothing and in need of daily food," wrote James, leader of the first-century Jerusalem church, "and one of you says to them, 'Go in peace, be warmed and be filled, and yet you do not give them what is necessary for their body, what use is that?' "[39] James's rhetorical question expects the answer, "None." In the same way, concern for non-human creation and non-human creatures that knows only sympathy and never sacrifice is of exactly the same value. A wistful attitude toward nature dominated by an abundance of "If only . . ." statements changes nothing. Setting aside a portion of a newly planned church site for a restored prairie or a grove of large, old trees manifests the work of God in creation to everyone who looks at the church, but it costs parking slots and building space. To "make room" for nature requires sacrifice. Conservation organizations need money to do their work. Changing local zoning ordinances to permit parks and open space takes time. Participating in an active restoration effort that requires planting native species takes physical exertion. These efforts, however, are illustrations of how inactive sympathy can be transformed into sacrificial concern, concern that changes things. It has always been the role of the church to teach people how to manifest faith in work. It is no different in teaching how to serve and protect creation.

Implementing these practices in a contemporary church culture which largely ignores them requires a redeemed imagination. But making disciples of Jesus Christ, the fundamental mission of the church, also requires the experience and practice of work and habits that will be the expected norm in a redeemed world. Better to get started now. In the final chapter, we examine the practical possibilities for new paths and new directions for both the church and the conservation community in their interaction with one another, and the effects such changes could bring in the years ahead.

NOTES

1. George MacDonald, *Diary of an Old Soul* (Minneapolis: Augsburg Fortress Press, 1994), p. 30.
2. Willis Jenkins, *Ecologies of Grace: Environmental Ethics and Christian Theology* (Oxford, UK: Oxford University Press, 2008), pp. 44–45.
3. Job 40:15–16, 18–19. NASB.
4. Job 41:1–2, 5–6, 8–10. NASB.
5. Job 42:6.
6. Saint Basil, *Exegetic Homilies*, translated by Sister Agnes Clare Way (Washington, DC: Catholic University of American Press, 1963), p. 125.
7. Quoted in Jenkins, p. 125.
8. Psalm 8:3–4, NASB.
9. For a well-framed discussion of the various dimensions of aesthetic value that can be understood within a Christian environmental ethic, see Jame Schaefer, *Theological Foundations for Environmental Ethics: Reconstructing Patristic and Medieval Concepts* (Washington, DC: Georgetown University Press, 2009), p. 44ff.
10. Schaefer, p. 25.
11. Job 38:39–41, NASB.
12. Lynn A. Macguire and James Justus, "Why intrinsic value is a poor basis for conservation decisions," *BioScience* 58 (2008): pp. 910–911.
13. Genesis 2:15, NASB.
14. Genesis 1:28, NASB.
15. Romans 13:4, 6, NASB.
16. Matthew 20:25–27, NASB.
17. Norman Wizba, *The Paradise of God: Renewing Religion in an Ecological Age* (Oxford, UK: Oxford University Press, 2003), p. 135.
18. The idea of John of Damascus about creation as being an act of God "making room" for life other than his own is captured in the paraphrase of John's ideas by Robert Jensen. "For God to create is for him to open a place in his triune life for others than the three whose mutual life he is." Quoted in Wizba, p. 19.

19. Holmes Rolston III, "Winning and Losing in Environmental Ethics," in *Ethics and Environmental Policy: Theory Meets Practice*, eds. Frederick Ferré and Peter Hartel (Athens: University of Georgia Press, 1994), p. 231.

20. Ibid., p. 233.

21. Matthew 6:33, NASB.

22. Fred Van Dyke, *Conservation Biology: Foundations, Concepts, Applications* (Dordrecht, The Netherlands, Springer: 2008).

23. Matthew 7:2–3, NASB.

24. Peter J. Hill, "Environmental Theology: A Judeo-Christian Defense," *Journal of Markets and Morality* 3(2000): pp. 158–172.

25. Wendell Berry, "The Gift of Good Land." In *The Gift of Good Land: Further Essays Cultural and Agricultural by Wendell Berry* (New York: North Point Press, 1982), p. 275.

26. Ibid., p. 281.

27. Summarized in Schaefer, p. 26.

28. Joseph Petulla, *American Environmental History* (San Francisco: Boyd and Fraser, 1977).

29. Christopher Stone, *Should Trees Have Standing? Towards Legal Rights for Natural Objects* (Los Altos, CA: Kaufman, 1974).

30. World Commission on Environment and Development, *Report of the World Commission on Environment and Development: Our Common Future* (New York: Oxford University Press, 1987).

31. Isaiah 11:9, NASB.

32. Simon Stuart and others, "Conservation Theology for Conservation Biologists—An Open Letter to David Orr," *Conservation Biology* 19 (2005): pp. 1689–1692, pp. 1690–1691.

33. Matthew 24:37–39, NASB.

34. Hebrews 11:1, NASB.

35. Mark 1:15, NASB.

36. Dallas Willard, *The Divine Conspiracy* (San Francisco: HarperCollins, 1997).

37. Ibid., p. 205.

38. MacDonald, p. 30.

39. James 2:15, 16.

CHAPTER 10

The Future Landscape

But that is what is wrong with the conservation movement. It has a clear conscience. The guilty are always other people, and the wrong is always somewhere else.

Wendell Berry[1]

THE STATE OF THE ARK—WHAT AILS THE ARK-KEEPERS?

As I write this final chapter, the latest issue of *Conservation Biology* (CB), the pre-eminent journal of my professional discipline, lies open on my desk. The lead article of its opening section, "Conservation in Context," is, as usual, written by environmentalist David Orr, making his last regularly scheduled contribution as associate editor after more than 20 years and 64 columns. His final thoughts are contained in "Retrospect and Prospect: the Unbearable Lightness of Conservation." The title is borrowed from the novel, *The Unbearable Lightness of Being* by Czech writer Milan Kundera. In Kundera's novel, the characters struggle with the problem of significance. If there is only one life to live, and if that life and all decisions comprising it make no difference in the real world, it would have been better not to have lived at all. In Kundera's world, the great suffering of life is not in its physical pain or deprivation of experience, but in its deprivation of significance.

The ecological equivalent of Kundera's lament is latent in the words of Aldo Leopold. "One of the penalties of an ecological education," he wrote, "is that one lives alone in a world of wounds."[2] Leopold recognizes that such knowledge is warrant for exceeding grief, but not necessarily despair. "An ecologist," he continues, "must either harden his shell and make believe that the consequences of science are none of his business, or he must be the doctor who sees the marks of death in a community that believes itself well and does not want to be told otherwise."[3] These are sobering statements, but Leopold seemed to think that it still mattered to be a doctor of the ecosystem.

David Orr is not so sure. Speaking of the conservation community, he notes, on one hand, there is no lack of science to address conservation problems. "We know enough right now," states Orr, "to make far better decisions than we do about wildlife, ecosystems, and landscapes. That is to say, we do not lack for science or data . . . to make better decisions about our 'management of nature' or any number of other things."[4] To paraphrase Leopold, we conservationists are well-informed doctors who know the real wounds of this world. The reasons for despair run deeper. "What ails us, rather," continues Orr, "is fundamentally political and is the result of a yawning chasm between the world of science (and intellect generally) and that of public affairs. The rickety bridge connecting these two worlds is a jerry-rigged, patchwork thing at best."[5]

According to Orr, none of this is fundamentally the fault of conservationists. The bridge is rickety because of public ignorance, a corrupt, money-driven political system, a trivially minded, distraction-oriented media, American militarism, and the maintenance of the American empire. Reasons, indeed, for absolutely absolute despair. Still, Orr does believe conservationists could have done better:

> I think we should have learned to be more adept, personable, and creative in talking to the public and the guys down at the truck stop and the women working two jobs to make ends meet. I think we might have gone to fewer scientific conferences in exotic places and to more Rotary meetings and tedious city council sessions. We should have talked less often to ourselves in a scientific jargon and more often to the public in the common tongue.[6]

In short, "We were right, but we were ineffective. If only we could have been better communicators."

Perhaps there is more to the problem than communication. Is it possible that something more fundamental is at fault, not only in the conservation *message*, but in the conservation *mission*? Is it possible that conservation efforts have not failed for lack of communication but from lack of appropriate *intention*? Conservation, as both a cause and a way of life, still seems not to have touched the roots of human behavior and motivation.

In the United States, a recent examination of patterns of giving to conservation organizations determined that stock market indices, such as the Dow Jones Industrial Average and the Standard & Poor's 500 Index, gross domestic product (GDP), and personal income (PI) explained as much as 99 percent of annual variation in total revenue (including contributions) to four large nongovernmental conservation organizations, World Wildlife Fund, Sierra Club, Environmental Defense Fund, and The Nature Conservancy. These economic indicators also explained as much as 96 percent of the annual number of university conservation programs, 83 percent of membership in professional conservation organizations, and 93 percent of national park visitation.[7] Commenting on these extraordinarily high correlations between economic growth and conservation funding, these investigators noted, "The conservation activity parameters we measured may exhibit positive trends even in the face of declining biodiversity, but biodiversity conservation will ultimately require the cessation of economic growth. The challenge to the conservation biology community is to retain a significant presence during and after the cessation of growth."[8]

Ironically, contributions to conservation go up in proportion to increases in many of the things the conservation movement is trying to restrain. If conservation contributions only grow in a growing economy, what will happen in a shrinking one? Will those who gave when they were well off still give when they are not, or when they have deliberately begun to renounce their own affluence to promote a better, cleaner, world? The data seems to say that even those who give significant sums of money to conservation don't, apparently, go about it with a sense of discipline and sacrifice, one that could weather economic variation with less vicissitude in charity. It appears that conservation's contributors are more like the Pharisees, who put large sums into the temple offering, but which Jesus astutely observed came from their surplus, not from their devotion.[9] The only one in the "giving line" who had been genuinely touched, and therefore felt genuine obligation, was a poor widow who put in "two small copper coins." Jesus recognized that this was all she possessed, "all that she had to live on."[10]

The problem we are describing is a dilemma conservationists have created themselves. Environmental ethicist Marc Sagoff describes its origins:

> After Earth Day 1970, a new kind of organization appeared, epitomized by the National Resources Defense Council and the Environmental Defense Fund, staffed by lawyers, economists, scientists, and other experts. These outfits defined the 'environment' or 'environmentalism' in terms of whatever interests they presumed to represent. They...attracted wealthy patrons and foundation support. They hired professionals to pursue a Washington-based 'inside-the-beltway' strategy of lobbying congressional committees, influencing regulatory agencies, and working the courts.[11]

Eager to catch up to this new and seemingly more effective strategy, older conservation organizations like the Sierra Club, the National Wildlife Federation, and the Audubon Society followed suit. Audubon, for example, hired a consulting agency to shake off its ties to bird watchers, closed its regional offices, and reduced support to local chapters. Remaking themselves, these conservation organizations abandoned their past and their legacies.[12]

When David Orr expresses concern that the public perceives conservationists as "effete, overly intellectual snobs more concerned about nature than people,"[13] he is simply describing what many conservationists have chosen to become. And in the process of becoming, conservation lost touch with its public base. Conservation and environmentalism today, says Sagoff, are

> [H]igh on rationality and low on redemption. It presents nature as a system for interdisciplinary scientists to model and administer for the collective good rather than as an object for moral instruction and aesthetic appreciation for every individual.... [It] embraces an authoritarian, secular, scientistic, collectivist, elitist, anti-democratic, cosmopolitan, querulous intellectualism.... The problem is not that environmentalism of this sort is dead. The problem is that it deserves to die.[14]

What would it take to change this perception, to make conservation something that did not "deserve to die" but that was as important as "all we had to live on"? And what would happen if people stopped thinking that their money could represent them in the work of conservation and started acting to represent themselves by direct engagement in conservation effort? How can conservation move from being a cause that is just one more luxury of the affluent and elite to being a work that is systemic to all aspects of human community and society? Something more is needed than a visit to the truck stop and the Rotary Club.

The "rickety bridge" Orr refers to is very rickety indeed. At the far end, among the great mass of conservation's unreached public, stands the church. Christianity is the world's largest and most global religion, and, as previous chapters have shown, it has had, contrary to the view of Lynn White, Jr., a consistent record of teaching and at its best, practicing an understanding of the human relationship to nature that, if consistently applied, brings healing and reconciliation between human and non-human creation. But, as evangelical writer Francis Schaeffer commented years ago, the problem is "not because Christianity does not have the answer, but because we have not acted on the answer..."[15]

The church's current relations with the conservation community are often tenuous at best and antagonistic at worst. Most of these problems arise from contemporary manifestations of old heresies, including modern versions of neo-Platonism, Gnosticism, Docetism, and Manichaeism. They are the legacy of unfortunate ideas that infected the church tradition from its very birth but have become especially problematic in contemporary culture in evangelical Protestantism in the United States, for reasons explained in Chapter Five. Forward progress and shared achievement in conservation require change at both ends of the bridge. Since, however, it is the church that has received clear instructions from its founder regarding the necessity of self-examination, it is the church that should be first to name its own sins and determine its proper path of repentance.

THE REPENTANCE OF THE CHURCH: TAKING CONSERVATION SERIOUSLY

Northwestern College, a small liberal arts college in Iowa, publishes its own college magazine, *The Classic*. In the 2009 summer issue, Christian environmental writer Matthew Sleeth, author of *Serve God, Save the Planet*, contributed an article on the role and responsibility of Christians to care for the Earth. In the fall issue, one reader responded,

"God does not want us to worship or adore the earth or any of his creations. He didn't even ask us to preserve the earth. In Genesis 1:28 God commanded man to 'subdue' the earth. That is, to understand it and gain mastery of it; to put it to work in our own best interests. Certainly there is also stewardship implied, but preserving a 'pristine' earth may not be in man's best interest. Focus on saving souls."[16]

With elegant brevity this correspondent captures much for which the church must repent, not only to effectively engage the conservation community but to fulfill its own primary mission of making disciples. For the church, repentance today consists of taking seriously what it has failed to take seriously for a long time. Three changes are crucial.

TAKE SCIENCE SERIOUSLY

Science is one way of gaining knowledge about the world. Properly applied, it is a reliable way to do so. Today, when scientists explain the nature of environmental pollution in Chesapeake Bay, the endangerment of endemic species in New Guinea, or the increasing loss of ice coverage in the Arctic Ocean, they are not promoting unsupported theories of what might happen according to a particular simulation model. They are documenting real events. When science speaks of such events, the church should listen. Without a common, shared, and accurate understanding of how the world works, no Christian can respond effectively to its condition.

Repentance for the church begins with adopting an appropriate respect for science. Taking science seriously permits the church to develop genuine reality-based theology, a pre-requisite for any theological study and application, especially in serving and protecting God's creation. Theologians must know the relevant facts and accurately understand them in order to apply biblical perspectives and solutions to the problem itself. To do this, a church must avoid any form of modern Manichaeism, a picture of the world as a black-and-white dichotomy between the "children of light" and the "children of darkness." Some elements of the church make the assumption that the church contains only truth, while all other communities, including science, contain only error. That's not how truth works, and the Bible, of all books, shows this plainly. The Christian church must recognize truth about the world provided by science and learn to respect it. But the church can go farther, and the path to a farther place requires learning from creation itself.

TAKE CREATION SERIOUSLY

The Bible, as we have seen earlier,[17] teaches, in the voice of the Psalmist, that "the heavens are telling the glory of God; and their expanse is declaring the work of his hands."[18] Similarly, Paul instructs first-century Christians in the church at Rome that ". . . since the creation of the world his [God's] invisible attributes, his eternal power and divine nature, have been clearly seen, being understood through what has been made . . ."[19] These are but two illustrations of a recurrent biblical theme, that the world around us, which we today commonly call nature, but which was to the biblical writers "creation," is not a passive backdrop for human existence, but an active witness of the glory of God. Nature is a source of truth that illuminates the glory of God. Science illuminates nature. What would be the consequence if Christians believed this?

The first consequence, explored in the previous chapter, would be that regular, repeated, and deliberate contact with nature would become a normative experience and regular discipline of Christian life. Christian pastors and teachers of past eras understood that nature offered an object of moral instruction and aesthetic appreciation for every person. But if creation would fulfill this role for believers individually, it must also fulfill it corporately. This means every church should plan regular activities that bring its members into direct contact with nature, and not simply as a backdrop for something else (the church picnic, softball game, or missions conference) but activities in which *nature is the subject of attention, study, and revelation*, just as it was for Christians of the past like Basil the Great, Francis of Assisi, and Jonathan Edwards. Here we address the first objection of our correspondent to Matthew Sleeth: "God does not want us to worship or adore the earth or any of his creations." No, he doesn't. What God wants is that people should give attention to his creation and his creatures, learn from them, consider them, and appreciate them for what they really are, both for their own sake and for what they reveal about the work, character, and purpose of God.

Jesus provides an example of how to look at nature and learn about God. "*Look* at the birds of the air," said Jesus (emphasis mine). "That they neither sow, nor reap, nor gather into barns, and your heavenly father feeds them. Are you not worth much more than they?"[20] Here Jesus uses ready at-hand observation and common knowledge of the non-human world to provide his listeners with a reason to trust God in daily life. Watching these birds, says Jesus, provides warrant for faith in God's abundant provision for all life in this world. Jesus does not arrive at this knowledge by gaining mastery of the birds or using them in his own best interests, to use the words of Sleeth's respondent. The revelation of God's character (that he is a generous, caring, and capable provider) occurs by letting birds be themselves, and the moral lesson that you are valued by God enough to be provided for in every-day need is learned by seeing *how much* God concerns himself with "less valuable" life. If God's attitude to such life is to make provision for it, why would any person want to thwart his purposes by removing its provision from the earth (by destroying its habitat and food sources) or, worse, by destroying the life itself? Such destruction is not just "bad management." It is an act of destruction of God's revelation of himself to human beings. To avoid such destruction is not only an act of knowing but an act of willing, an act of intentional and knowledge-able obedience rather than an act of ignorant and prideful rebellion.

Jesus' teaching about birds is an illustration, not a curriculum. But his example can be a guide to the church of how to develop its curriculum in preaching, teaching, and ministry for taking God's creation seriously. Specifically, taking creation seriously means creating activities that give people frequent contact with creation itself as the subject to be attended to, providing people with real (that is, scientific) knowledge of the way things really work in creation, and expecting them to learn, from such attentive study, about the work and character of God.

TAKE PEOPLE SERIOUSLY

The admonition of this heading might seem unnecessary. Isn't that what the church does better than anything? At its best, the answer is yes. At its worst, the answer is no, such as in those situations in which the work of the church is not about "real" people at all, but about "saving souls." The church's failure on this point is not confined to environmental issues. Its failure in this area is but one symptomatic example of a much more serious problem.

In their groundbreaking book *unChristian*, David Kinnamon and Gabe Lyons reveal, with searingly painful precision, that the current image of Christians in the United States is declining. The decline, upon investigation, turns out not to be the work of a media conspiracy or a religiously hostile press, but is a result of the behavior of Christians toward others and the experiences of those others in Christian churches.[21]

What did these people find so negative about Christians and their churches? One complaint overarching almost all others was that Christians saw them only as "souls to save." Christians, the respondents complained, consistently failed to address other aspects of their needs and personhood, and usually terminated relationships when they did not show interest in conversion. As Kinnamon and Lyons put it, "Intentionally or not, we promote the idea to outsiders that being a Christ follower is about the mere choice to convert. We do not portray it as an all-out, into-the-kingdom enlistment that dramatically influences all aspects of life. . . ."[22] To recall our analysis from Chapter Five, this behavior, in evangelical circles, is an unfortunate holdover of revivalism, and it not only creates negative impressions among non-Christians but is a serious impediment to becoming a disciple of Jesus Christ. Christian philosopher Dallas Willard makes the same point in *The Divine* Conspiracy. As Willard puts it, discipleship to Jesus Christ, the fundamental aim of the Christian life, is not about my "spiritual life." In discipleship, says Willard,

I am learning from Jesus how to lead *my* life, my *whole* life, my real life. Note please, I am not learning from him how to lead his life. His life on earth was a transcendently wonderful one. But it has now been led. Neither I nor anyone else, even himself, will every lead it again. And he is, in any case, interested in my life, that very existence that is me. There lies my need.[23]

Our present, whole, real life is lived in this world, a world the Bible declares is to be included in the redemptive work of God. How could a Christian, then, ever work to harm the Earth and its creatures in such a way that would deprive others of clean air, clean water, or healthy food? How could they think that bringing a message of the gospel without concern for a person's physical environment and condition could be in any way a meaningful message? Knowing that both people and the world are objects of God's redemptive intent, it makes sense that Christian organizations like World Vision would, as we saw earlier,[24] engage in efforts to stop soil erosion, reduce grazing, and practice reforestation and revegetation on the lands of the Humbo people in Ethiopia. How could they care for these people and not do so?

When Christians perceive other people merely as eternal souls trapped in evil and temporal physical bodies, desperate to be saved from this sinful material existence, they practice a form of neo-Platonism, the idea that matter is evil and low and that spiritual things are good and high, and there is no relation between the two. God, on the other hand, asserts the significance of relation between the material and the spiritual in the strongest terms possible. That assertion is called the incarnation: God with us, in human form. The physical world, although fallen, is good. The physical world, although in rebellion from God, is the object of God's redemptive effort. The physical life of physical people in a physical world is one of God's supreme concerns. But in addition to the heresy of neo-Platonism, the errors of the church's view of people and creation, particularly in the evangelical church, are also products of a syncretism of three other heresies—Manichaeism, Gnosticism, and Docetism—that the church in its early centuries substantially eliminated, but into which its modern practices and teachings have increasingly fallen. *Manichaeism*, the view of perceiving everything outside the church as darkness and error, is a falsehood previously addressed. *Gnosticism*, a heresy also covered earlier,[25] teaches that matter is evil and only the spiritual (non-material) is good. When Christians perceive other people merely as eternal souls trapped in physical bodies, they are practicing a form of Gnosticism and in that practice will ignore the real needs of the person physically present to their senses. *Docetism*, a more particular version of Gnosticism, claims that, because the material world is so filthy and polluted, there is no point in attending to its present condition or its future state. Day-to-day existence is only "apparently" real. The future doesn't matter, history doesn't matter, and matter doesn't matter.[26] Recognizing and renouncing these ideas for the heresies they are can help the church to begin taking real people seriously in the real world, knowing that both are objects of God's redemptive plan and purpose.

TAKE THE DANGERS OF CURRENT CULTURE SERIOUSLY

As the church moves forward through the twenty-first century, its relative health is regionally specific. In South America, sub-Saharan Africa, and many parts of Eastern Europe and South Asia, the church is experiencing unprecedented growth. That growth has been most dramatic among people and classes who are poor, politically oppressed, and socially disenfranchised. But in these difficult circumstances, the church is spared many of the temptations besetting Christians in the West.

In the United States, and increasingly elsewhere, modern life is becoming a chaos of personal conflict and environmental dismemberment. The average American now spends over 100 hours per year commuting. Such mobility contributes to the environmentally destructive patterns of urban and suburban sprawl, just as John Ruskin described its effects in England. With that sprawl comes a lack of meaningful community formation based on associations of place. The modern U.S. church, especially among evangelicals, has shown remarkable adaptiveness in exploiting these conditions, creating "big box religion" in the form of mega-churches that appeal to placeless, "commuter" Christians, even to the point of strategically placing new churches close to freeway exits. Such churches may, in their early years, see exponential growth in attendance, along with 60 to 80 percent annual turnover rates among attendees (one hesitates to call such migrant Christians "members"). This kind of growth, however, is not a sign of health but of cancer, and its end is death, not life.

To paraphrase the old Bill Clinton presidential campaign slogan, the church is the last institution on Earth that can still say to the modern worldling, "It's not the economy. It's your life, stupid." In the words of environmental writer Bill McKibben, "Only our religious institutions. . . . can say with any real conviction, and with any chance of an audience, that there is some point to life beyond accumulation."[27] The church has shown great marketing skill in responding to the whims of materialistic culture, but little moral courage in naming these whims as evil, much less making a determined effort to change them. To the extent that the church profits from thoughtless and unreflective emphasis on material accumulation and irresponsible placelessness, with its attendant destructiveness of community and creation, it is a partner in the evil thereof. The church's repentance will consist of changing these patterns, working to foster life and community in which people know where they live, care how they live, and make room for God's creation to live where they live.

THE REPENTANCE OF THE CONSERVATION COMMUNITY

Just as we find a church today, particularly in the West, that has been morally lax and tragically complicit in encouraging people to ignore, abuse, and despise the natural world, we find in the same culture a community of conservationists expressing dismay, frustration, and hopelessness toward their efforts to save global biodiversity. Indeed, conservation biologist Reed Noss writes, in the same CB issue and but a few pages from Orr's essay, that hope for success in averting the coming extinction crisis "has little to do with it. Hope is an unnecessary distraction."[28]

Really? Hope a distraction! With admirable neo-Kantian consistency, Noss follows his logic to its dismal but inevitable categorical imperative, asserting that, for true conservationists, "We do the right thing regardless of whether we think we might succeed. We keep working because defense of nature is the right thing to do, however hopeless, futile, and pathetic our efforts ultimately may prove."[29] Whatever one might think of Noss's dedication, no effort can generate enthusiastic participation in a cause everyone believes is doomed to defeat. Noss seems closer to the truth when speaking, earlier in his essay, of his experience with his own son. When he learned his son had not renewed his membership in the Society for Conservation Biology (SCB), Noss admits,

> I laid on the guilt trip, explaining why he has a moral duty to support his professional society and contribute to its mission. I also reminded him of the more selfish reasons for belonging, especially the enhanced opportunity to establish and maintain professional contacts who might be able to help him find jobs down the line . . . Somewhat shamefully, my son wrote out his check for 10 dollars.[30]

Is that what modern conservation boils down to, a burdensome duty performed with sorrow and reluctance for the twin but paltry prizes of fulfilling a moral obligation that will make no difference and getting a job in the field so that you can keep working at not making a difference? With tragic irony, we have returned to play out the theme with which this chapter began, the incredible lightness of being. The lightness of conservation is perceived, by conservationists, as their failure to achieve meaningful goals. The heaviness of their burden comes from realizing the insignificance of their efforts.

The SCB, in its early years, was an organization with prodigious growth in membership. Now its membership is declining, most rapidly among students. Noss offers a hypothesis that the organization's efforts to go global served only to neglect their disproportionately North American support base, leading, in the long run, to dissatisfaction, disaffection, and dis-membership. This strategy may have been a contributing factor, but I think the real reason runs deeper.

At its inception, the SCB was short on resources but long on ideals. It was not ashamed to be called a "mission-oriented discipline."[31] Its break with the traditional, value-neutral approach to science blew through the dusty catacombs of older professional organizations like a breath of fresh air, or, better expressed, like a strong spring breeze that carried the scent of life and hope. Scientists and academics flocked to the new organization in droves, and older professional organizations were forced to reexamine their traditional stances on mission, values, and advocacy.

In these early years, the SCB and its primary journal, *Conservation Biology*, were unabashedly normative and ethically overt in their expression of what conservation was. In the words of one early contributor, Bryan Norton, in 1988, conservation biology must not "hide behind a façade of value-free science."[32] But as years passed, it did begin to hide its normative and ethical judgments, as the lure and advantages of becoming a strictly "regulatory science," whose goal was not to save biodiversity but simply to inform policy makers of its condition, began to take hold. Increasingly slipping into the default posture of scientific positivism, many conservation biologists began to assume, in the words of conservation scientist Dennis Murphy, that the discipline itself "exists only because biological information is needed to guide policy decision making."[33] Within a decade philosophers of science with sympathies to conservation were beginning to sound a warning of these trends and their dangers. In 1996, Dwight Barry and Max Oelschlaeger wrote in the pages of *CB* that, "If the state of conservation biology is to be judged by the pages of this journal, our science is becoming an exercise in applied ecology or biology. In contrast to the often overtly normative papers. . . . that appeared in the early volumes, the research presented in the contributed papers of *Conservation Biology*. . . . increasingly lacks evaluative judgment—even implicitly."[34]

This pattern of disciplinary development is predictable. Young organizations are highly mission-driven. Indeed, young organizations often have few resources but their mission and the determination to fulfill it. As an organization, or an intellectual discipline, gains professional respectability, it acquires tangible resources which increase its influence, such as graduate programs, endowed chairs, and large student enrollments in its courses, not to mention growing favor with older, more established disciplines which begin (finally) to treat it with respect. As reputation and stature increase, the discipline and its organizations become more risk averse because there are now vested interests to protect. Following this pattern, conservation biology's commitment to its original normative values has declined in proportion to its increase in professional stature. Posturing oneself as a value-free, regulatory science is a prudent strategy for protecting careers of established professionals, but it does not attract the idealistic and the adventurous. Truly, a professional society that follows this strategy has its reward in full.

One of the "rewards" will inevitably be an increasing sense of hopelessness toward achieving the original mission. But that doesn't matter much anymore, because the organization will survive, even if the endangered species don't. The motivation for belonging to and participating in the organization shifts from the hope of accomplishing the goal to the hope of finding a good job. The hope of actually saving the world's biodiversity becomes "an unnecessary distraction."

The dilemmas of the Society for Conservation Biology are not unique to environmental and conservation communities. They are typical of aging organizations: declining membership, declining zeal, declining effectiveness, and declining hope. Does conservation need something that it cannot generate on its own? Is it willing not only to repair the rickety bridge to reach a larger circle, like the Christian church, but to walk across it and learn something from the other side?

TAKE THE CHURCH SERIOUSLY

To return to the old familiar question of conservation biologist and ethicist Kyle Van Houtan, "On what basis can conservation achieve widespread cultural legitimacy?"[35] Does that legitimacy come, as David Orr suggests, by spending more time at the truck stop and the Rotary Club? Not if the message is poorly framed, or if conservationists discover they aren't even speaking the right language. And language is the key, because language betrays belief structure. Comparing conservation's problems, and their potential solutions, to the struggle for civil rights in the United States in the 1960s, Van Houtan noted, "Smart, socially abstract maxims, such as those of then-prominent intellectuals John Dewey and Gunnar Myrdal, achieved nothing substantial for African American rights . . . To the contrary, segregation and disenfranchisement were overthrown dialectically—in the particular language, logic, and practices of a particular tradition. In this case, the dialectic was biblical . . ."[36]

If this was true in the past, is it true now? Some conservationists, like Harvard's E. O. Wilson, have attempted to improve communication, and in the process cross the bridge, by direct appeal. In his book *The Creation: An Appeal to Save Life on Earth*, Wilson writes an open letter to an unnamed "Southern Baptist pastor" to make the case for the value of life and the reasons for saving it. Considering what the church needs to repent of, this is an appropriate appeal, for the church is beset by many sins that prevent her from seeing and protecting the value of creation. Unfortunately, Wilson, although demonstrating characteristic brilliance in explaining the nature and functions of biodiversity, never grasps Van Houtan's critical insight. Aside from making the concession of referring to nature as "creation," he never attempts to frame his argument within biblical language or concepts that his imagined Southern Baptist pastor, or his congregation, would consider an essential part of the appeal. Thus, Wilson's effort begins with impressive moral flourish, but, absent this dialectical element, sputters to a faint-hearted conclusion that saving the Earth is "the earthborn, yet transcendental, obligation we are both morally bound to share."[37]

The conservation community has too often approached the church as a sorry, ignorant audience that needs to be enlightened or, in worst cases, manipulated to do "the right thing" for saving biodiversity and reducing global pollution. It never occurs to many conservationists that the church might have wisdom to provide about *the nature of the conservation effort itself*, that the very manner in which conservationists are pursuing the effort is part of the problem. That is the second element of needed repentance.

Take People Seriously

We have already seen this subheading as an important element of the church's repentance. On that side of the bridge, taking people seriously means seeing their whole life and personhood in a real world that displays the glory of God and, from the provision of that world, demonstrates God's care for them and all living creatures. The same admonition here means something different.

For conservationists, taking people seriously means seeing the potential of the human presence to be a redemptive one for all of nature, as well as seeing that valuing people and teaching them an appropriate relationship to nature must precede setting up the national park. As C. S. Lewis noted, "You can't get second things by putting them first; you can get second things only by putting first things first."[38] The environmental community's failure to recognize the distinction and dignity of the human presence in nature will continue to be an insurmountable problem in communicating its mission until it is repented of. The failure to provide a more positive account of and role for the human presence in nature will be viewed by all people of faith, including Christians, as the supreme blunder, because the attention to the non-human condition without attention to or concern for the human condition will not only neglect the importance of human need, but will lead to failure of the secondary objective as well. Biodiversity will not be saved.

TAKE THE WORK OF CHRISTIANS IN CONSERVATION SERIOUSLY

Recall the examples of recent Christian work in conservation, such as Susan Emmerich and the Tangier watermen, A Rocha Lebanon and the Ammiq Wetland, or the Evangelical Alliance's Hogave Conservation Center in Papua New Guinea. They bear a recurring theme. The role of and interaction of people with nature was addressed first, not to encourage greater aspirations of affluence or consumption but to restore a healthy and beneficent relationship to nature so that the needs of human and non-human life were seen in right relationship to one another. Despite these and many other kinds of effective efforts by Christians who are active in environmental conservation, most segments of the conservation community are ignorant of them, and some actively ridicule such work. A better way would be to recognize and respect such efforts and extend invitation to these activists to join in larger efforts in the broader conservation community.

Some of these invitations are being made, but not enough. Just as Christians can be guilty of a modern Manichaeism that sees the world as a dichotomy between the children of light and the children of darkness, conservationists often indulge their own Manichaean fantasies by seeing themselves as the children of light and everyone else, including the church, as the children of darkness.

In an essay published in *Conservation Biology* in 2005, "Armageddon Versus Extinction," David Orr attacked one segment of the Christian community, the evangelicals, as being a significant contributing factor toward contemporary environmental destruction in the United States. "... Right-wing evangelicals," wrote Orr, "... have been placed in positions of authority throughout the federal government, including

departments and agencies that administer federal lands and environmental laws, and they have not been shy in amending scientific reports
in ways more agreeable to doctrine. ... Conservative evangelicals,"
Orr continued, "are now complicit with the political forces sweeping
us toward more terrible violence and the unavoidable catastrophes of
climate change and ecological ruin."[39]

No one could accuse Orr of being too subtle. What is more trou-
bling than such rhetorical excesses is the fact that, in this issue of *Conservation Biology*, no serious challenge is made to Orr's assertions. The
two "responses" to Orr's essay in the same issue, one by conservation-
ist Rick Flood and the other by theologian John Cobb, do not manage to get very far beyond "Atta' boy!" Flood praises Orr for his
"inimitable, penetrating style" which "has neatly characterized an
important dynamic in contemporary American politics."[40] Cobb, for
his part, admits that he too must "share Orr's distress about what
has become the most visible voice of Protestant Christianity in this
country."[41]

The "neatness" of Orr's characterization could not, in the long run,
conceal its errors of fact and interpretation, and these were pointed
out by numerous contributors in a later issue.[42] What remains deeply
disturbing is that one of the most respected journals in conservation
was so predisposed to uncritically accept such charges and publish
them without serious examination. The fact that such an accusation
was possible and, initially, even applauded without reflection reveals
two structural flaws in the conservation community that must be
repaired.

First, many conservationists still cling to stereotypes of Christians,
which limits their perceptions of and responses to the Christian community in general and to Christian efforts in conservation in particular.
To repent of this error, conservationists must pay attention to the variety and diversity of Christian engagement in the conservation effort.
Christian engagement in conservation is global, diverse, multifaceted,
and increasingly effective. The fact that some of the best and, suppos-
edly, most well informed conservation biologists are unaware of this
means that remedial education is in order.

Second, the conservation community still has few functional ties
with Christians and Christian organizations active in conservation
efforts. The conservation and environmental communities need to
establish working, productive linkages to the Christian community
by taking their work seriously. This means inviting representatives of
Christian conservation organizations to partner in planning and

executing conservation projects of mutual concern, shared subjects, and overlapping agendas of influence. It would mean giving such representatives opportunity to explain their work at meetings of professional organizations and, where possible and appropriate, sharing resources with these organizations when they can be applied to common goals.

Some of these linkages already exist and are functioning well, like the work of ARC, the Sacred Gifts Program, A Rocha and its membership in the IUCN, and the World Bank's Faith and the Environment program. In the United States, the Environmental Protection Agency has invited Susan Emmerich to present the findings and applications of her work among Tangier watermen (see Chapter Seven) to many of their top regional supervisors in seminars and training sessions designed to develop improved skills in resolving environmental conflicts, including their annual conference and training meetings on community involvement.

Examples like these need to become more common if the conservation community is serious about building a better bridge to the public. Forming these linkages requires an accurate understanding of people in the "other" group, as well as respect for their collective abilities, insights, and influence. Such effort is essential for restoring conservation to a position of cultural relevancy and moral legitimacy.

BUILDING A BETTER BRIDGE

There have been commendable efforts in both the religious and conservation communities to aid one another in shared goals. The Ecumenical Patriarch of the Orthodox Church, Bartholomew I, created opportunity for such mutual aid by, beginning in the mid-1990s, setting up regular conferences, or "floating seminars," which brought together scientists, theologians, politicians, activists, and others to address issues of environmental concern, especially issues of water pollution. The floating seminar designation was a very literal label because these conferences were held on the great rivers and seas surrounding the heartland of the Eastern Orthodox Church, the Black Sea, the Aegean Sea, the Danube River, and others. Bartholomew did not do this to be relevant, as if he thought the creator of the universe needed such a consideration to properly spin his image. He did this because of his theological understanding that all created things, human and non-human, living and nonliving, play a part in praising the Creator and revealing his work.

Such theology, for all its depth, is captured simply and elegantly in an ancient Orthodox Christmas hymn:

What shall we offer Thee, O Christ,
Who for our sake was seen on Earth as man?
For every thing created by Thee offers Thee thanks.
The angels offer Thee their hymns;
The heavens, the star;
The Magi, their gifts;
The shepherds, their wonder;
The earth, the cave. . . .[43]

It was in such a conference, convened by Bartholomew I, that Carl Pope, executive director of the Sierra Club, offered the apology on behalf of the conservation community, noted in Chapter One. A few words of it bear repeating here: "We [environmentalists] sought to transform society, but ignored the fact that when Americans want to express something wiser and better than they are as individuals, by and large they gather to pray. We acted as if we could save life on Earth without the same institutions through which we save ourselves."[44]

Not every effort toward joint understanding and cooperation is so well considered as Pope's apology or Bartholomew's floating seminars. Peter Harris, founder of A Rocha, recalls the response of one CEO of a prominent conservation organization who, upon discovering that A Rocha was a Christian conservation organization, told him, "Good, we have always wanted to get to the Pope. Any chance you could organize it?"[45] But even such a crude inquiry can be forgiven, if those involved are willing to persevere in mutual respect and common purpose.

Such perseverance, however, requires a different way of looking at things on both sides. Christians have their own apologies to make. Their repentance will mean taking science, and its applications in conservation, seriously. For conservationists who are not Christians, repentance will mean taking people seriously. Again it is Harris who makes the point well through the work of A Rocha Kenya. In Kenya, the impending loss of the last remnant of East African coastal forest, the Arabuko-Sokoke forest, led A Rocha leaders to work with local residents to create the Arabuko-Sokoke Schools and Eco-tourism Scheme (ASSETS). Through a combination of conservation measures that preserved the area and its wildlife and the development of visitor-friendly facilities that tourists could use (for a price) to enhance their observations of the forest's wildlife, the ASSETS program developed a fund to address the local community's most pressing problem: the failure of most of its children to continue in school past primary education because of insufficient funds. Money from the eco-tourism effort is moved back to the local community in the form of "eco-bursaries," which are equivalent to scholarships for local students to continue their secondary education. As Harris puts it, "At the time of writing [2008] over a hundred and seventy children are in secondary school and an extensive reforestation education programme is going on in many of the villages around the forest. To visit them, as we did last month, is a revelation, and there was no doubting the force of their own convictions that the forest must remain in a healthy state."[46]

Christian conservation organizations like A Rocha are essential components of building a better bridge between the church and the conservation community. It is unrealistic to expect the Church to routinely make direct engagement in conservation efforts, although such engagement is sometimes warranted and appropriate, as in the case of the Forest of Harissa or the Hogave Conservation Center. In most cases, the church lacks the necessary resources and expertise to do the things that conservation scientists can and should do for conservation. The Christian conservation organization, however, can serve as a critical link between the church and the conservation community, in an arrangement something like this:

Church
↕
Conservation FBO
↕
Conservation Science and Activism

From the church, the conservation FBO is theologically informed of an appropriate understanding of the human relationship to nature needed to guide its priorities. From the FBO, the church is informed of the science and specifics of conservation problems, but in the kind of dialectical analysis that Van Houtan described earlier, so that the problem is placed in the context of the church's tradition and theological perspective. Further, the church gains, from the FBO, identifiable ways and means for its members to participate directly in specific conservation efforts. From the community of conservation scientists and activists, the FBO gains a wider perspective on global needs in conservation and, in the best cases, logistical resources and support that help it to participate in a solution. From the FBO, the conservation community gains needed insights about Christian and public perception of their work. If it is willing to listen, it also receives reasons for enduring purpose and hope in efforts that might otherwise appear, in the short term, to have little chance of success or significance.

Tom Rowley, director of A Rocha USA, captures some of these ideas in his expression of the A Rocha USA strategy, which is to build understanding and conviction among Christians toward creation care, create opportunities to directly engage in such care, and apply expertise to such engagement, both through scientists who are members of A Rocha and through those who work with A Rocha through other organizations.[47] The first prong of the strategy, as in the diagram, is reciprocal. As A Rocha USA works to build understanding and conviction, it receives from the church a theological perspective upon which such understanding and conviction should be based. As it creates opportunities for engagement, it leads "ordinary" Christians toward more direct contact with nature and more careful attention to the science necessary to protect it. As it applies expertise, it creates contacts between the Christian and conservation communities in shared effort toward a common purpose.

A TRADITION THAT PRACTICES CONSERVATION

To recall the words of conservation biologist and ethicist Kyle Van Houtan, and his penetrating analysis of why conservation has failed to make much impact on modern life, we must understand the right and wrong way to frame the question. "Asking why we should care about conservation is not the right question. The social tradition names it a virtue: those doing conservation are just practicing their tradition. 'Does the tradition regard conservation?' is a better question. The reason many Americans are thus not outraged at environmental destruction is that the tradition most determinative of their lives— individualism, consumerism, nationalism—does not practice a conservation ethic."[48] There is much in the modern western church, particularly the evangelical church in the United States, indistinguishable from its surrounding culture of individualism, consumerism, and nationalism. But we have already named these things, among others, as sins the church must repent of, and not simply for the sake of conservation but for the sake of fulfilling the commission of its founder to make disciples who obey his commands, and in their obedience they are rescued from these evils.

But these sins do not plague all of the church today to the same degree in every place, nor have they plagued it to the same degree in all times and places in its long history of the last two millennia. As we have traced through earlier chapters, the church and its saints, though imperfect and fallen, offered, at their best, radical and vibrant examples of right thinking, practice, and goals for human interaction with nature.

Knowing this does not remove the many examples of complacency, ignorance, and bad theology that have marred the church's witness, as well as its integrity, in explaining the human relationship to creation from the first to the twenty-first century. But the exemplars examined through these many generations could not have existed had they not been inspired by revelation and vision beyond themselves, beyond the imagination of their own time and cultures, and beyond the knowledge of their own day. Their transforming vision was a product of their Christian faith. The thesis of *Historical Roots* was not merely an error of scholarship. It was a lie. It is time to call it that.

The Bible, Christian theology, the teachings and traditions of historic Christian faith, and the words and deeds of its saints demonstrate that the church has possessed and yet retains abundant intellectual, theological, and practical resources for addressing the current ecologic crisis and, much more fundamentally, the human relationship to nature. In his classic study of the human relationship to the environment, *The Wealth of Nature*, historian Donald Worster concluded that if

> The environmental crisis is really the long-preparing consequence of this modern world-view of materialism, economic and scientific, then it makes no sense to blame any of the traditional religions of the world. Religion, on the whole, acted to check that materialism, to question human arrogance, and to hold in fearful suspicion the dangerous powers of greed. Religion, including Christianity, stood firm against a reductive, mechanistic view of the world. It pointed to a subordinate and restrained role for humans in the cosmos. And, most importantly for the sake of the biosphere, it taught people that there are higher purposes in life than consumption.[49]

A review of the history of the church, its teachings, and its practices leads to a definitive answer to Van Houtan's question, "Does the tradition regard conservation?" The Christian tradition does indeed regard it, and has understood and practiced it, at its best, as the service and protection of God's creation. That tradition must be recovered, but it does not have to be re-invented. The resources of God's revelation that speak to the human relationship to the Earth have been available in every age. And whenever they have been faithfully used, the effect has been transformative. The Church today has an ongoing duty to develop, interpret, and apply these resources. It can draw directly from them to develop clear, effective, and redemptive models of creation care in the modern world.

Hope in conservation is not an "unnecessary distraction." To work to preserve the Earth in the present, people must believe that they and the Earth have a meaningful future. Hope is a necessary condition for conservation to possess *purpose*. Purpose is a necessary condition for *meaning*, which Christian philosopher Dallas Willard elegantly defined as "a transcendence of whatever state we are in toward that which completes it."[50] Meaning is the prerequisite of *motive*. Environmental science can provide knowledge. Only faith can provide hope, and only hope can give conservation its necessary trinity of purpose, meaning, and motive. This is one appropriate reward that can come from repairing the rickety bridge between the conservation community and public perception and between the conservation community and the church. It is time to make that repair, the increasing cooperative engagement of the Christian and conservation communities in serving and protecting the Earth, one of the priorities of the coming years in conservation action and Christian life.

NOTES

1. Wendell Berry, "Why I Am Not Going to Buy a Computer." In *What Are People For: Essays by Wendell Berry* (New York: North Point Press, 1990), pp. 176–177.

2. Aldo Leopold, "The Round River." In *A Sand County Almanac, With Essays on Conservation from Round River* (New York: Ballantine), pp. 188–202, 197.

3. Ibid.

4. David Orr, "Retrospect and Prospect: the Unbearable Lightness of Conservation," *Conservation Biology* 23 (2009): pp. 1349–1351, 1350.

5. Ibid.

6. Ibid.

7. Oliver R. Pergams, Brian Czech, J. Christopher Haney, and Dennis Nyberg, "Linkage of conservation activity to trends in the U.S. economy," *Conservation Biology* 18 (2004): pp. 1617–1623.

8. Ibid., p. 1617.

9. Luke 21:1–4.

10. Luke 21:4.

11. Mark Sagoff, *The Economy of the Earth: Philosophy, Law, and the Environment* (Cambridge, U.K.: Cambridge University Press, 2008), p. 204.

12. Ibid., pp. 204–205.

13. Orr, p. 1350.

14. Sagoff, p. 207.

15. Francis Schaeffer, *Pollution and the Death of Man: The Christian View of Ecology* (Wheaton, IL: Tyndale, 1970), p. 58.

16. Evan Mortenson, "Green Plea Reactions," *The Classic* (Fall 2009), p. 3.

17. Chapter 3.

18. Psalm 19:1, NASB.

19. Romans 1:20, NASB.

20. Matthew 6:26, NASB.

21. David Kinnaman and Gabe Lyons, *unChristian: What a New Generation Thinks About Christianity and Why It Matters* (Grand Rapids, MI: Baker Books, 2007).

22. Ibid., p. 79.

23. Dallas Willard, *The Divine Conspiracy* (San Francisco: HarperSanFrancisco, 1998), pp. 283–284.

24. Chapter 7.

25. Chapter 4.

26. For a brief but useful summary of all three heresies and their effects on the Christian church, particularly the Evangelical church in the West in contemporary society, see Mark Noll, *The Scandal of the Evangelical Mind* (Grand Rapids, MI: Eerdmans, 1994), pp. 52–55.

27. Bill McKibben, *Deep Economy: The Wealth of Communities and the Durable Future* (New York: Time Books, 2007).

28. Reed F. Noss, "The Heavy Burden of Conservation," *Conservation Biology* 23 (2009): pp. 1354–1355, 1355.

29. Ibid., p. 1355.

30. Ibid., p. 1354.

31. Michael E. Soulé and Bruce A. Wilcox, eds., *Conservation Biology: An Evolutionary-Ecology Approach* (Sunderland, MA: Sinauer, 1980), p. 1.

32. Bryan G. Norton, "What is a Conservation Biologist?" *Conservation Biology* 2 (1988): pp. 237–238.

33. Dennis Murphy, "Conservation Biology and the Scientific Method," *Conservation Biology* 4 (1990): pp. 203–204, 203.

34. Dwight Barry and Max Oelschlaeger, "A Science for Survival: Values and Conservation Biology," *Conservation Biology* 10 (1996): pp. 905–911, 905.

35. Kyle Van Houtan, "Conservation as Virtue: a Scientific and Social Process for Conservation Ethics," *Conservation Biology* 20(2006): pp. 1367–1372, 1367.

36. Ibid., pp. 1370–1371.

37. E. O. Wilson, *The Creation: An Appeal to Save Life on Earth* (New York: Norton, 2006), p. 168.

38. C. S. Lewis, "First and Second Things." In *God in the Dock: Essays on Theology and Ethics* (Grand Rapids, MI: Eerdmans, 1970), pp. 278–281, 280.

39. David Orr, "Armageddon Versus Extinction," *Conservation Biology* 19 (2005): pp. 290–292, 291.

40. Rick Flood, "Speak Truth to Power: Thoughts on a Bold Strategy for Conservation Biologists," *Conservation Biology* 19 (2005): p. 293.

41. John B. Cobb, Jr., "The Responsibility of Progressive Protestants," *Conservation Biology* 19 (2005): p. 294.

42. The responses, collectively contributed by 33 authors, including some of the world's most respected conservation biologists, from five continents, included David Henderson, "Evangelicals are Conservationists," *Conservation Biology* 19 (2005): pp. 1687–1688; David M. Johns, "Orr and Armageddon: Building a Coalition," *Conservation Biology* 19 (2005): pp. 1685–1686; Simon N. Stuart and others, "Conservation Theology for Conservation Biologists— a Reply to David Orr," *Conservation Biology* 19 (2005): pp. 1689–1692; and Fred Van Dyke, "Between Heaven and Earth—Evangelical Engagement in Conservation," *Conservation Biology* 19 (2005): pp. 1693–1696.

43. In the Orthodox tradition, Christ was not born in a stable but in a cave, which served as a shelter for animals outside the inn in Bethlehem where his earthly parents, Mary and Joseph, were refused lodging on the night of his birth. The hymn and the work of Bartholomew I and the floating seminars are summarized in Martin Palmer with Victoria Finlay, *Faith in Conservation: New Approaches to Religions and the Environment* (Washington, DC: The World Bank, 2003), pp. 54–55.

44. Carl Pope, "Reaching Beyond Ourselves: It's Time to Recognize Our Allies in the Faith Community," *Sierra Magazine* 83 (1998): pp. 14–15 (November/December), 14.

45. Peter Harris, *Kingfisher's Fire* (Oxford, UK: Monarch Books, 2008), p. 29.

46. Ibid., p. 78.

47. I base this summary of the A Rocha USA strategy on personal communication with Tom Rowley.

48. Kyle Van Houtan, "Conservation as Virtue: a Scientific and Social Process for Conservation Ethics," *Conservation Biology* 20 (2006): pp. 1367–1372, 1371.

49. Donald Worster, *The Wealth of Nature: Environmental History and the Ecological Imagination* (New York: Oxford University Press, 1993), p. 218.

50. Willard, p. 386.

Index

Note: Biblical references are indicated in **bold**.

About the Author

FRED VAN DYKE is Professor of Biology at Wheaton College and the author of *Conservation Biology: Foundations, Concepts, Applications*; *A Workbook in Conservation Biology: Solving Practical Problems in Conservation*; and *Redeeming Creation: The Biblical Basis for Environmental Stewardship*, among other works. He has published widely on the topics of environmental ethics, conservation, religion and the environment, and related areas.